More praise for *Hope Against Hope*

"It's work like this that makes journalism truly matter, that makes clear that reportage is not merely about fact and argument and theory, but about human lives in the balance. In *Hope Against Hope*, Sarah Carr has taken an open mind and a careful eye to the delicate, complicated issue of public education and the fading American commitment to equality of opportunity. She does so not by embracing ideological cant or political banter, but by following people through the schools of New Orleans, a city that is trying desperately to reconstitute and better itself after a near-death experience. Don't embarrass yourself by speaking further on American education without first reading this."

—**David Simon, creator of** *The Wire* **and** *Treme*

"With grace and profound intimacy, Sarah Carr immerses us in the lives of a group of students, teachers, and administrators in New Orleans, ground zero for the debate over school reform, and lays bare all that we face as we try to strengthen our schools. Riveting. Empathic. Incisive. *Hope Against Hope* is storytelling at its absolute finest."

—**Alex Kotlowitz, author of** *The Other Side of the River* **and** *There Are No Children Here*

"New Orleans is a city like no other, and Carr demonstrates how its unique character has both helped and hindered its educational recovery."

—*Library Journal*

"[W]ith journalistic precision and a remarkably unflinching objectivity . . . Carr clearly delineates the strengths and weaknesses of both sides, admirably delving into the complex racial, political and social ethos underpinning each, and melding historical context and hard statistical data along the way . . . [W]hat makes the book special is its focus on the experiences of the teachers, students and administrators that form the true core, the heart, of *Hope Against Hope*." —*Philadelphia City Paper*

"[A] nuanced, concrete picture focused on individuals seeking to make the reform regime work for the children in their schools. The book is a tremendous achievement, and should be required reading on all sides of these debates." —*Bookforum*

"[Carr's] protagonists' perspectives capture subtleties rarely probed in a national debate more preoccupied with test scores, corporatization, and teachers' unions." **—*Publishers Weekly***

"As the nation looks to New Orleans as the model for education reform, we would do well to read this book closely. Sarah Carr's portrait of these changes, at once analytical and compassionate, reveals the human tolls and triumphs of this movement. Whether you support or oppose education reform, *Hope Against Hope* is necessary reading."

—Lolis Eric Elie, co-director of the
documentary *Faubourg Tremé*

Hope Against Hope

Hope Against Hope

Three Schools, One City, and the
Struggle to Educate America's Children

SARAH CARR

BLOOMSBURY PRESS
New York • London • New Delhi • Sydney

Bloomsbury Press
An imprint of Bloomsbury Publishing Plc

1385 Broadway	50 Bedford Square
New York	London
NY 10018	WC1B 3DP
USA	UK

www.bloomsbury.com

BLOOMSBURY and the Diana logo are trademarks of Bloomsbury Publishing Plc

First published 2013
This paperback edition published 2014

ISBN: HB: 978-1-60819-490-2
         PB: 978-1-60819-513-8
     ePub: 978-1-60819-495-7

LIBRARY OF CONGRESS CATALOGING-IN-PUBLICATION DATA

Carr, Sarah.
Hope against hope : three schools, one city, and the struggle to educate
America's children / Sarah Carr.—1st U.S. ed. p. cm.
Includes bibliographical references and index.
ISBN 978-1-60819-490-2 (hardback)
1. Children with social disabilities—Education—Louisiana—New Orleans—
Case studies. 2. Charter schools—Louisiana—New Orleans—Case studies.
3. Educational change—Louisiana—New Orleans—Case studies. I. Title.
LC4093.N49.C37 2013
371.9309763'35—dc23
2012027728

4 6 8 10 9 7 5 3

Typeset by Westchester Book Group
Printed and bound in the U.S.A. by Thomson-Shore Inc., Dexter, Michigan

For my parents,
Elliott and Susan Carr,
and for the many families whose grace made this possible

Contents

O. PERRY WALKER HIGH SCHOOL is operated by the Algiers Charter Schools Association, which formed late in 2005 and oversaw several of the first public schools in the city to reopen after Hurricane Katrina. Mary Laurie, a veteran New Orleans educator, has served as principal of Walker since the winter of 2005. Prior to the flood, she led Carter G. Woodson Middle School and William J. Guste Elementary School, both of which were part of the New Orleans Public Schools system.

SCI ACADEMY is a new charter school that opened in 2008 with only freshmen, and ambitions to grow into a full high school over the course of three years. Sci and several other schools were "incubated" by New Schools for New Orleans, a nonprofit formed after Katrina to support the growth of charter schools in the city. Aidan Kelly, a young Harvard graduate from New York, joined the staff of Sci Academy in 2010 at the start of his third year of teaching.

7th Ward

Treme

French Quarter

KIPP Believe

Mississippi River

Uptown

KIPP RENAISSANCE HIGH SCHOOL
is a new charter school that opened in 2010 as part of the Knowledge Is Power Program's (KIPP) network in New Orleans. KIPP, which originated in Houston, now runs some of the highest-performing charter schools across the country. Geraldlynn Stewart attended middle school at KIPP Believe when it opened after Katrina in 2006. She continued on to Renaissance four years later as a member of the school's inaugural class.

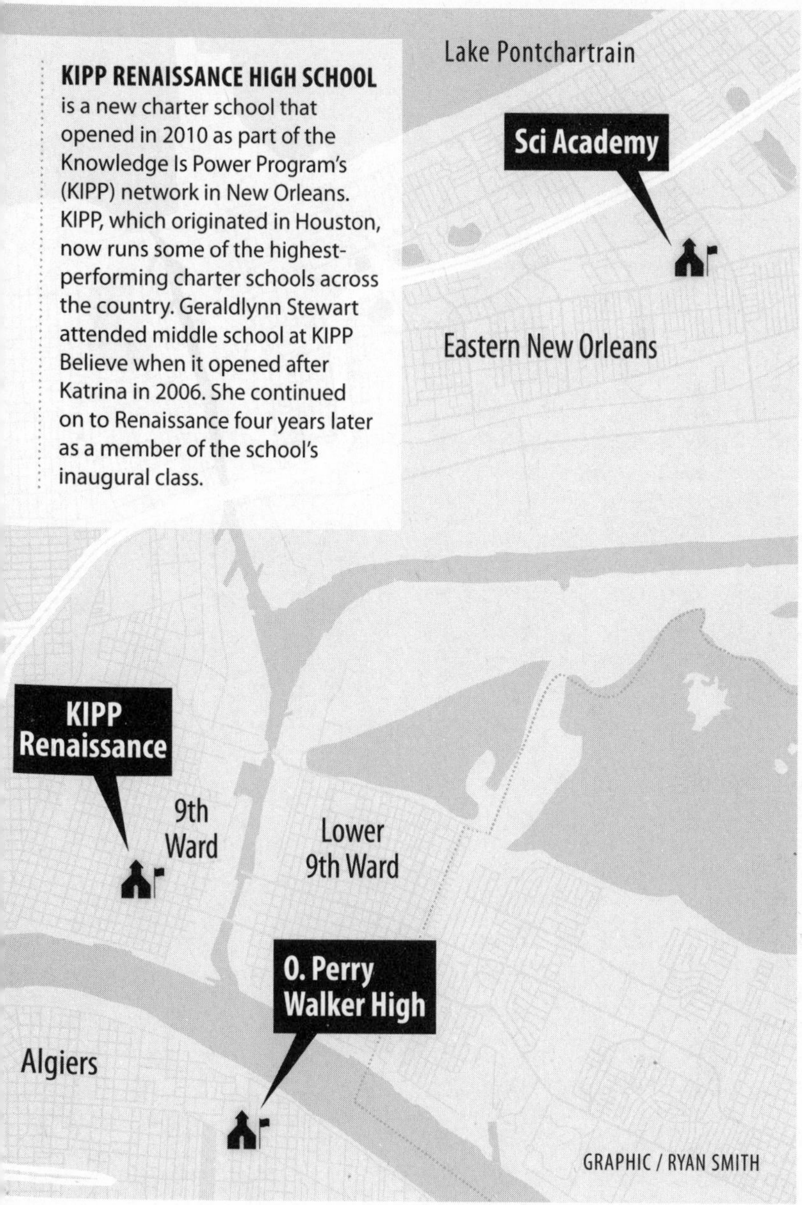

Lake Pontchartrain

Sci Academy

Eastern New Orleans

KIPP Renaissance

9th Ward

Lower 9th Ward

O. Perry Walker High

Algiers

GRAPHIC / RYAN SMITH

Author's Note

I have changed the first names of some children to protect their privacy, but no other facts. I witnessed more than half of the scenes. In order to re-create the others, I interviewed at least one person who was present at the time; whenever possible, I tried to interview multiple sources about the same scene or event.

The families and educators featured in the book have all shown remarkable courage in sharing their thoughts and experiences, particularly Mary Laurie, Aidan Kelly, Geraldlynn Stewart, and Raquel Dillon. They have each taught me important lessons not only about education but about the role of race, class, gender, and religion in twenty-first-century America.

I did not select the main characters or school sites to hold them forth as exemplars for critique or emulation. In none of their individual stories can be found a conclusive answer to the challenges facing our cities and their schools, or a tidy prescription for fixing them. I chose the principal, teacher, and family for their singular passion and contrasting backgrounds and convictions in the hope that, considered together, they might defy stereotypes and challenge the simplistic ideology of the day.

Their life stories and experiences in the schools did not always conform to the "script" I had subconsciously expected and planned, however. In that sense, they have already challenged me.

Prologue

(March 2010)

They met in the most neutral site that could be found: a New Orleans funeral home. There, just feet from caskets, urns, and rosaries, two competing visions for the future of America's poor and dispossessed collided.

The issue at hand, a proposal to turn Joseph A. Craig Elementary School into a charter school, drew dozens of parents, children, teachers, and community leaders from the surrounding neighborhood called Treme. At first, the gathering in March 2010 seemed routine and parochial. Teachers came concerned about their jobs. Parents needed to know if Craig would stay open. Neighborhood residents wanted to ensure the school's name remained the same.

The conversation that night quickly devolved into a public battle between two African-American men who, on the surface, had much in common. Both were lifelong New Orleanians who grew up attending the city's public schools. Both stood over six feet tall. Both were community luminaries well-known for their devotion to educating the city's thousands of schoolchildren. And both Jerome Smith and Tony Recasner brought the best of intentions to the meeting at the funeral home that night.

Tony Recasner had the look and bearing of a professor: tall, thin, and bespectacled, with a neatly trimmed mustache and a soft, friendly voice. As children squirmed and Craig's existing teachers looked on skeptically, he described the proposal to turn Craig into a charter school. Craig had been failing Treme's children for decades. It failed to meet minimum standards for academic performance when the Orleans Parish School Board ran it before Hurricane Katrina. And state intervention after the flood did little to change that pattern. FirstLine, the organization Recasner helped create, posted superior results at the two charter schools it already ran in New Orleans.

Recasner, a trained school psychologist, cofounded the city's first charter school in 1998; he hoped the increased flexibility afforded charters would allow him to better serve children. Some criticized him for leaving only one foot in the black community as he allied himself with many white business and political leaders in his efforts to change the education system. Now, four and a half years after Katrina, the movement Recasner had helped start prevailed: A coalition of local power brokers, backed by several of the nation's wealthiest foundations and top politicians, moved quickly to charter the city's schools.

At heart, many of the reformers were technocrats. They believed unelected experts, not politicians, should run the schools, and that decisions should be based on science and data, not relationships or tradition. But some of their language was anything but technocratic. They considered their cause the civil rights movement of the twenty-first century and often described themselves as part of "the Movement."

The meeting about Craig's future took place in the Charbonnet-Labat-Glapion Funeral Home, one of the country's oldest black-run parlors. Throughout the 1960s, civil rights leaders met secretly in African-American funeral homes to coordinate their efforts and find common cause. But rapprochement proved elusive that March night a half century later.

With ample knowledge of how quickly New Orleans public gatherings can turn into raucous shouting matches, Recasner tried to keep this one calm and focused on the issues at hand as he fielded questions about class size, teacher hiring, and whether a new Craig would accept children with severe emotional and academic needs. He kept his responses polite but brief. When one woman delivered a lengthy tirade about the quality of special education programs for disabled children at some charter schools, Recasner responded: "At the schools we operate, that would not be your experience."

Jerome Smith took a very different view and approach. Whereas Recasner had a psychologist's conciliatory, gentle-mannered air, Smith brought a preacher's fiery passion. He had been an activist since childhood, risking his life to ride public buses into the Deep South as a Freedom Rider in the early 1960s. During one ride, mobs of white bigots in McComb, Mississippi, used brass knuckles to beat him bloody and near unconscious. He believed in confrontation, tribe, and tradition as devoutly as Recasner favored compromise and pragmatism.

In recent years Smith had devoted himself to protecting modest corners of the Treme, walling them off from interference by the city's white elites or business leaders. In these forgotten pockets, he worked to teach children about the city's black culture. He ran the Treme Community Center, where neighborhood youngsters learned, among other things, about the Mardi Gras Indians: For a century and a half at least, self-described "gangs" of black men in New Orleans toil for months each year sewing elaborate suits of feathers and beads, an homage to the Native Americans who, according to their lore, assisted African-Americans during slavery. The gangs don their suits for a few annual events, including Mardi Gras, where they compete to see whose suit is "prettiest." Smith liked to point out that the men choose to emulate the Native Americans partly because the Indians refused to bow down.

Smith wore his trademark jeans, plaid shirt, and crocheted prayer cap to the funeral home that night. He stood in front of Recasner as he spoke, alternating his comments between general concerns and personal attacks. He decried Recasner's collaboration with white politicians and businessmen, recalling that his own mother would not even let the white insurance collector through her front door. After declaring, "My strength comes from growing up here," Smith, who attended Craig as a child, told Recasner the charter school founder had become a foreigner on the streets of his hometown.

During the meeting about Craig, Smith echoed many of the usual criticisms lobbied against New Orleans charter schools: They don't educate the most challenging students. "Businessmen," "corporations," and "outsiders" run them. Their backers disregard the will and input of the communities they serve. "I am not against charter—it's just a word," he said. "But . . . we have to control our own destiny."

Recasner looked Smith in the eye throughout the tirade. He tilted his head slightly every so often as if to acknowledge, yet not agree, with the words leveled at him. Those present sensed Smith's deepest ire was reserved for Paul Vallas, the white school superintendent who had asked FirstLine to take over Craig but did not show up at the meeting. In Vallas's absence, Recasner received the verbal assault.

In the end, many proponents of charter schools felt more convinced than before that opponents like Smith were rabble-rousers who cared more about tradition and control than the quality of schools. In their view, Smith failed to realize their effort was the next stage in the push for racial equality the old Freedom Rider had once led.

Smith's perspective hardened as well. In subsequent conversations he continued to refer to charter leaders as businessmen. But he added a darker implication as well. The "external management organizations" that run charter schools "are being given access to [school] buildings like it's cargo, like it's a slave ship," he said.

It was an inauspicious way to start, or end, a dialogue: Some viewed turning Craig elementary into a charter school as a victory for the civil rights movement; others likened the prospect to modern-day slavery. The very terms of the conversation incited mistrust.

My thoughts returned again and again to that night in the funeral home as I immersed myself in New Orleans classrooms during the months that followed. The issues the meeting raised became questions I asked throughout my reporting and writing: why people with the best of intentions can fight so bitterly; what principles and beliefs divide them; and how language can push them further apart. The debate over Craig helped frame my understanding of the conflict over urban education in New Orleans and across the country.

Partly because of that evening, I came to view the conflict as less about entrenched partisan politics than competing visions for how to combat racial inequality in America. Those visions, framed initially in the decades after Reconstruction by Booker T. Washington and W. E. B. Du Bois, have evolved and shifted over time with the changing context, and it would be facile to argue that a complete personification of either man's arguments exists today. Yet they continue to shape the debate over most of modern America's most pressing social issues, including education, housing policy, affirmative action, welfare, and race relations. According to one vision, which many leaders of the modern education reform movement accept, poor minorities will rise out of poverty and thrive only if they find a way to fit into the country's capitalistic traditions and outlook. This vision, championed initially by Washington, is pragmatic in its approach and puts more emphasis on blacks finding a home in the nation's economic structures than political ones. It prioritizes collaboration with whites, and finding solutions that are acceptable to both races.

The other vision is, like Jerome Smith, more confrontational in its approach. Its adherents do not believe that blacks should try to fit themselves into an agenda defined by white elites. Instead they should set their

own agenda, using their own rules, on their own turf. This vision prioritizes political over economic capital, and has helped foster the black power
and nationalism movements. It disregards compromise and appeasement
under the tenet that what the white power structure deems acceptable—in
this case, charter schools—will usually be bad for blacks.

I saw these contrasting ideals reverberate in the hopes and experiences of the people whose lives I chronicled in the schools: Mary Laurie,
a veteran principal; Aidan Kelly, a young teacher; and fourteen-year-old
Geraldlynn Stewart and her family. Each of them grappled at times
with the same tensions over racial autonomy versus collaboration, self-
determination versus appeasement, and tradition versus change that
formed the basis for the dispute over Craig. But inside the schools, the
war over education no longer seems so stark and clearly defined. Edges
blur, shades of gray abound, and simple solutions prove elusive.

Unlike most literature about New Orleans, this book focuses on what
makes the city ordinary rather than extraordinary.

A majority of the events that have prompted an enduring dialogue on
race have transcended a single place and date. They have been epic in
scope and sweep: the travails of Reconstruction, the mid-twentieth-
century migration of black citizens from the rural South to the urban
North, the civil rights movement of the 1960s, the crack cocaine epidemic
of the 1980s.

The aftermath of Hurricane Katrina, even though it was confined to a
specific place and time, briefly seemed as if it too might lead Americans
of all colors to see and examine race and poverty in new ways. But like
the floodwaters, the nation's attention receded, leaving behind people
more conscious than ever of their own fragility, yet uncertain how to feel
whole again.

After a time, the fleeting sense that what happened in New Orleans
was emblematic of something more universal largely disappeared. If the
rest of the country thought about New Orleans at all, it tended to view
the city as a physical anachronism at worst, doomed in an era of global
warming, receding shorelines, and government budget woes; or, at best,
as a treasured cultural outpost deserving of special attention and protection. With so much focus on the city's unique geography and traditions,
the country lost sight of how the city's near destruction might carry broader
lessons. It lost sight of New Orleans not as an exceptional American city,

but as one whose decayed infrastructure, overwhelmed social services, long-simmering racial tensions, and gross inequities make it perversely American.

And just as the disaster exemplified our government's widespread failure to protect its most vulnerable, the stumbling recovery of New Orleans can be read as a parable for what happens when well-intentioned, deeply divided people try to make things right. Some of the divide is political. But what separates the staunchest supporters of charter schools from their staunchest critics is often less about contrasting politics than about how our race, class, and differing life experiences shape our beliefs and understanding. It's harder to talk about these divides because we must venture out of political realms and into more personal ones, and the risk of offense rises. Too often we aren't even speaking the same language from the start.

FirstLine's leaders ultimately demurred from doing battle over Craig, saying they would not pursue the school without broad community support. Over the next year, similar scenes and tensions played out repeatedly in the debate over the future of urban schools, both in New Orleans and across the country.

The charter school leaders who followed Recasner in New Orleans— many of them, unlike him, white transplants to the city—encountered the vestiges of a public school system that had remarkably and tragically failed the community for decades in the city's undereducated children. Faced with sixteen-year-olds who could not read or do math at even the most basic elementary level, faced with thousands of students doomed to bottom-rung, minimum-wage jobs or worse, who can blame them for supporting the annihilation of the old system? Who can blame them for seeking a clean slate and a fresh start?

But Jerome Smith and other skeptics had watched time and again as progress for the city's elites and white community led to pain in the black community. They saw a city whose economic survival depended on tourism in a state where many small towns relied on prison jobs. Failing New Orleans public schools supplied a steady stream of low-wage workers and prisoners. For decades they had already wondered: Were the schools set up to fail? And why, if they looked to history as a guide, would this latest push for progress be any different?

Many of the most powerful people in the country have a plan for the future of education in America, one focused on more charter schools, technocratic governance, weakened teachers' unions, and the relentless use of data to measure student and teacher progress. New Orleans offers a test case, on an unprecedented scale, of how this vision plays out—of what works, what does not work, and for whom. The debate over urban education in America, crystallized in New Orleans, speaks to broad, deeply rooted tensions in our country over what the civil rights movement should look like in the twenty-first century and who should lead it. It speaks to fundamental disagreements over how the push for racial equality should proceed, at a time when the end goal remains as elusive as ever. And it speaks to a nationwide loss of trust—in our public institutions, each other, and ourselves. At its heart, this is the story of one community's painful struggle—in the wake of one of the most tragic disasters in our history—to rebuild that trust.

PART I

"The Christmas of school days."

(August 2010)

THE FAMILY

Try as she might, Geraldlynn Stewart could not get her KIPP Renaissance uniform to fit. She experimented with safety pins, bobby pins, and tape. She rolled it up at the waist, ran it through the dryer, and eventually just stared at it—willing the skirt to shrink. Geraldlynn went to bed early on the eve of her first day of high school. When her cell phone alarm beeped at six A.M., the house was eerily silent. Her mother had left an hour earlier for the French Quarter hotel where she worked as a housekeeper. Everyone else still slept. The white-and-blue plaid skirt loomed as large as ever.

The ill-fitting uniform seemed to reflect Geraldlynn's misgivings about KIPP Renaissance. In theory, everything the charter school promised sounded great: a warm, supportive atmosphere and an education that would prepare students for college. In reality, however, that meant preppy uniforms, crazy rules, and nights and weekends full of schoolwork. All that to earn four more years of studying? Geraldlynn felt ambivalent. No one in her immediate family had attended college, and despite her good grades in middle school, she remained deeply insecure about her "book smarts." Just weeks earlier, an ACT prep book had arrived in the mail for her older sister, Jasmine. Geraldlynn opened the package and scanned the math problems on one page.

Within seconds she threw the book on the floor, where it landed with a loud thud.

"I was scared," she said. "I thought, I'm not ever going to be able to solve these."

But Geraldlynn had no choice in the matter—at least when it came to KIPP Renaissance. Her mother had made that clear. "I think she's in love with KIPP schools. She probably will send me to a KIPP college," the fourteen-year-old said. "I been doing KIPP all my life. I might as well just finish with it."

At school later that morning, the students bantered quietly and compared schedules while their principal droned on about KIPP Renaissance's expectations for student behavior:

"If someone says hello or good morning to you, say hello or good morning back . . ."

"I want to go to sleep—or home."

". . . If you do something you shouldn't have done, then apologize . . ."

"We can't go home. We're stuck here for five years."

". . . If someone gives you something you need or ask for, say thank you . . ."

"What's this class on my schedule called CR?"

". . . About forty percent of KIPP Renaissance students said 'thank you' going through the cafeteria line—four out of ten is not a percentage we can be proud of . . ."

"I think that means college readiness."

Everywhere she looked, Geraldlynn saw physical reminders of KIPP Renaissance's overarching goal. College banners draped from the ceiling of the cafeteria. College flags lined the hallway walls. College diplomas hung in the classrooms. Her first day of high school concluded with the mysterious college readiness course, whose teacher, Mr. Saltmarsh, said it would "help us realize our big goal here at Renaissance: one thousand first-generation college graduates by 2022."

Geraldlynn listened closely as Mr. Saltmarsh described Louisiana's college scholarship program. It offered full tuition at any of the state's public universities for students who earned a 2.5 grade point average in high school and scored above the state average on the ACT. Geraldlynn had always wondered how she could afford college. The money her mother made cleaning hotel rooms and busing tables barely covered the bills. Mr. Saltmarsh's speech offered a flicker of hope. In eighth grade she had earned mostly As and Bs—well above a 2.5.

But when Mr. Saltmarsh told the class, "If you think you can earn a 2.5 and score a 20 on the ACT, please let me know by snapping [the KIPP Renaissance sign of approval]!" Geraldlynn kept her hands still.

THE TEACHER

One by one, each student rotated before Aidan Kelly's watchful eyes. He checked for the requisite khaki pants, black Sci Academy polo shirt, black shoes, and belt. He instructed them to take off wristbands, colored hair ties, and necklaces. Then he sent the students on their way. Another teacher escorted to the office the few whose uniforms failed to pass muster, where they secured the missing items. The rest continued on their way to breakfast. To get there they had to walk between two lines of black tape laid out on the outdoor walkway. Sci Academy teachers greeted the students at every turn, scrutinizing the children's comportment. One roll of the eye, muttered complaint, or step outside of the black lines and a staff member descended. The teachers did not want students to see a peer recognized for bad behavior, so they made a point of reprimanding and redirecting the students as subtly as possible. As one teacher put it: "We don't acknowledge things that don't lead us to college."

Aidan's first day teaching at Sci Academy moved with the precision of a military operation. The teachers had devoted several hours of professional development to rehearsing the day's maneuvers again and again. By the time Sci's freshmen arrived for a weeklong orientation, the staff members were able to move wordlessly between their predesignated stations, leaving the stunned students feeling as if they had stepped into an alternate universe, not a high school. After the uniform check, breakfast, and morning assembly, the students learned how to SPARK (S for sit or stand up straight; P for pen to paper and place your hands on desk; A for ask and answer questions with a straight Sci Academy elbow; R for respect at all times; K for keep tracking the speaker). Each letter was the subject of its own ten-minute mini-lesson.

Even on the first day of school, Sci's teachers tried to connect just about every lesson to college: Scholars should sit in SPARK so blood flows to their brains more easily, speeding up their thoughts and facilitating their path to college. Scholars should be able to transition from "silly" to "serious" with the snap of a finger or the clap of a hand because they do not have a second to waste on their path to college. Scholars should wash their hands before leaving the restroom because otherwise they might get germs, which might make them sick, which might cause them to miss school, which would interrupt their path to college.

Aidan, twenty-four, felt at home at Sci, with its clearly defined rules and aspirations. His first day at his previous teaching job at Martyn Alternative School in a New Orleans suburb could not have been more different. He had floundered through the opening days on his own. There had been no school-wide plan, no practice sessions, no guiding philosophy.

Aidan grew up attending rigorous Catholic schools in the New York City area. He gravitated to intense structure. If there was any place he felt he could thrive as a teacher, it was Sci Academy.

His mother taught kindergarten in a Catholic school and his father, an immigrant from Ireland, never attended high school or college. They had always stressed to Aidan the value of an education. He lived up to their hopes as well as his own, graduating from Harvard University, where he thrived amid the veneration for everything academic. Harvard became a proud part of Aidan's identity. Returning to his alma mater brought a unique joy he hoped his students would someday feel. Most of them, however, viewed the Ivy League as a foreign land—out of mind, out of reach, or both—hardly a target of their aspirations. At Sci Academy, Aidan planned to show them just how much was possible.

THE PRINCIPAL

All day long people brought their children to Mary Laurie.

An O. Perry Walker alum arrived with his daughter in tow. The family had just moved back to New Orleans, and he had heard good things about the soft-spoken principal who ran the school with an iron fist.

A teacher from one of the city's alternative schools showed up with a sullen-looking girl who wore her baseball cap backwards and a T-shirt that read, I LOVE MY RUDE SHAKER BARBIE BRE. He knew Laurie would take in the wayward student just as she had done with so many others.

A nineteen-year-old who looked like a student himself brought his younger brother. He had assumed the role of father after their parents passed away and wanted his brother to attend a school that treated him like family.

On this day, Laurie accepted all the children on faith. More often than not, they lived up to that trust. The proof was all around her.

In the cafeteria she spotted a confident-looking junior wearing the white shirt and orange and navy tie of a student athlete. Just eighteen months earlier, his mother had arrived at Walker sobbing. Her son had recently been arrested for attempted murder and she doubted any school would admit him. "*What am I supposed to do now?*" she had cried.

Laurie heard the story, saw the electronic ankle bracelet, and agreed to give it a try. Over time the teen thrived at Walker, defying his own stunted ambitions for himself. "He didn't know how good a person he was," Laurie says. "But he could have gone the other way."

Not every story has a happy ending. Laurie knew that all too well. But she pushed such thoughts from her mind today. Even in her late fifties, Laurie still viewed back-to-school season with the hope and excitement of a child.

During the morning, Laurie's pace was relaxed, her exchanges playful. She teased, cajoled, reprimanded, or praised nearly every student she passed as she walked around the worn-down campus. The students called out for her to join in when she arrived in the makeshift dance studio. But Laurie demurred: "I only got one move, one move, baby," she said. "And it was old when I was young."

In the afternoon, however, Laurie's tone grew more urgent and her steps quickened. With just a couple hours before dismissal, several students still awaited schedules or the final paperwork they needed to enroll. They sat in the cafeteria and main office, growing anxious and bored. Laurie wanted them all in class—any class—ASAP. "We're taking too long, get this young man a schedule!" she barked at an administrator. "Come on, baby, let's put you in band for now.

"We've got to move them through, move them through, so they can start their regular classes tomorrow!"

After more than three decades working in schools, Laurie knew that most days would not be like this one. On other mornings, the crowd of devoted parents, grandparents, and older brothers would be gone. So, too, would be much of the energy, the excitement, the sense of possibility and new beginnings. She needed to capitalize on that energy. She had to get the children through the door and into classes while they wanted to be there. Once inside, she hoped they would connect with a teacher, a class-mate, the feel of a horn in their hand, or the rush of a football practice—before they sought their thrills elsewhere. There wasn't a second to lose.

Some students she might not be able to keep for all the time she wanted. But hundreds of families had brought her their children on what she described as "the Christmas of school days." And Laurie intended to hold on to them for as long as she could.

PART II

Rebirth

(Summer 2005–Summer 2010)

THE FAMILY
"Don't be like me. Be a little better."

Geraldlynn's mother, Raquel Dillon, likes to recall the early-summer afternoon in 2006 when good fortune knocked on her door. Neighbors struggled to surmise the purpose of the lanky white stranger who approached Raquel's shotgun house on Columbus Street. He looked to be in his late twenties and had a ruddy complexion and light hair that curled despite the close crop. Clad in khakis and a T-shirt and carrying a black laptop bag, he did not have the look of a cop. Best anyone could guess, he came to sell flood insurance, or point residents in the direction of nearby mobile food vans. It seemed implausible that anyone too important would make a personal visit to the home of a hotel housekeeper and short-order cook at a time when even the city's most powerful residents jockeyed for attention from officialdom. Nine months after Hurricane Katrina struck, the area's black population slowly trickled home. Raquel's neighborhood in the city's 7th Ward hadn't started to gentrify like some other areas, so it seemed unlikely the visitor lived nearby.

Adam Meinig, the lanky stranger, viewed his mission as finding those families most neglected by the city's leaders and institutions. That winter and spring, the Colorado native met with newly returned families in motel parking lots and on the floors of gutted homes, pitching a new middle school he planned to open that August. It wasn't a hard sell, even though Meinig brought only his word and a clip from an Oprah episode touting his program, part of a national chain of charter schools called KIPP (Knowledge Is Power Program). Meinig would be principal of one of the first two KIPP schools to open in the city.

As the steamy afternoon turned into evening, Raquel sat on the brick steps in front of the green door leading into her house, talking with Meinig and her two daughters. On first glance, the whole family could have passed for schoolchildren. The girls had inherited their mother's petite stature and features. Raquel, who was in her early thirties, stood just under five feet tall and weighed about one hundred pounds. Sometimes strangers and acquaintances underestimated her as a result. But her small stature and surface timidity belied an exceptional strength of character and capacity for spirited resistance.

Geraldlynn, ten years old at the time and the target of Meinig's visit, could tell he was a stranger to the 7th Ward, and probably New Orleans, based on his accent. He caught her off guard when he started grilling her with questions.

"What do you want to do when you grow up?"

"What kind of education will you need?"

"What year will you go to college?"

"Do some math and answer with conviction, like you know it's true: WHAT YEAR WILL YOU GO TO COLLEGE?"

Geraldlynn spent much of the conversation fretting about her hair—a hot mess after hours of playing in the humid streets. She liked Meinig's slow cadence, though, and his tendency to repeat himself, since distractions like a screeching car alarm punctuated the conversation. Geraldlynn perked up when Meinig described annual school trips to cities like New York. But he lost her interest when he mentioned the school hours: seven thirty A.M. to five P.M., plus Saturday school.

Her mother appreciated Meinig's detailed plans, including the longer school day and the thorough description of classes. It sounded better than the school Geraldlynn had attended since the family returned from Houston just months after Katrina. At James M. Singleton Charter School, Raquel overheard young students cursing out the teachers when she visited, and Geraldlynn never once brought home homework. Meinig's questions evoked an ambition Raquel had rarely heard voiced by her own teachers in the 1980s and early 1990s, or her two daughters' teachers in the years leading up to Katrina. Moreover, no one else had knocked on her door asking permission to teach Geraldlynn. Compared to the hell of evacuating a flooded city, the heartache of missing home, and the frustrations of restarting her family's life there, saying yes to Meinig seemed so easy. So when he asked mother and daughter to sign their commitments to the KIPP regimen—of which Raquel had a good first impression but fuzzy understanding—she unhesitatingly agreed.

"Sometimes," she recalls, "you have to give a person a little bit of trust."

Unbeknownst to Raquel and thousands of other public school families, officials took a series of actions in the wake of the flood that would fundamentally alter nearly every aspect of the city's education land-scape. Critics called the changes disaster capitalism at its most flagrant. Supporters called it the flood's only silver lining. The story that unfolded complicated both assertions.

In September 2005, just days after the flood, the school board placed its thousands of employees on unpaid leave. Three months later it effectively voted to fire them, a controversial step that provoked years of tense litigation and helped lead, over time, to a significant expansion in the number of educators recruited from out of town. In November, the state legislature removed most of the city's public schools from the control of the locally elected school board and placed them in the Recovery School District. The state never planned to run schools in the long term, however. Instead, key officials intended to turn them over to charter operators.

Those actions effectively stripped both the locally elected school board and the teachers' union of their authority, paving the way for an unpre-cedented remaking of an urban school system.

The principles of the New Orleans school overhaul do not differ sig-nificantly from those guiding school reformers across the country. Most of them sought and still seek to reduce the power and influence of elected school boards and teachers' unions through the proliferation of charter schools (which have their own boards and tend to hire nonunion teach-ers), mayoral control or state takeovers (which often strip the elected boards of any real power), and efforts to make teaching more akin to a private-sector profession (where employers have increased control over whom they hire and fire and employees are more accountable to a bot-tom line, in this case, test scores).[1]

But in New Orleans, the changes happened virtually overnight.

Most poor residents like Raquel and her family heard nothing when the state legislature approved the measure that seized nearly all of the city's public schools from the elected school board. They never received word of the school board's vote to fire its teachers. They knew little of the charter schools that sprouted across the city, or what would distinguish them from the schools of their youth. New Orleans grew into a mecca for supporters of a parent's right to choose from an array of schools. But ironically, the new landscape originated in a series of actions more characteristic of a despot.

It is a testament to Raquel's calm temperament, and to her disenfranchisement, that she never expected to be consulted, or even notified, of the changes that would alter the course of her daughters' education. She and her husband, Langdon, noted quite pragmatically that it would have been difficult to gather all the public school parents together in one space in the months after Katrina, much less get the word out about a meeting. They felt grateful Meinig had stopped by that summer day.

The officials who sought a complete overhaul of the New Orleans education system in the flood's wake marshaled plenty of evidence to support their case: the failure of nearly two thirds of the schools to meet the state's minimum criteria for academic performance; the school district's impending financial ruin; nearly $70 million in federal money not accounted for properly; the FBI investigators who moved into the school system offices to probe financial irregularities; crumbling facilities where hallways smelled of urine; the near complete abandonment of the public schools by the city's middle and upper classes and the shocking disinvestment of those with power and money that ensued; the frustration and anger of many of those left behind; and the undervalued children who, taking stock of it all, not infrequently gave up.

Over time, two opposing narratives explained the schools' failures. One held that the traditional school system was inherently flawed, its structures—a centralized bureaucracy, democratically elected school board, and empowered teachers' union—outdated and its foundations rotten. Others countered that the system had been set up to fail: Politicians and the public had starved the schools of the support and money needed to thrive after the city's white families decamped for private and suburban schools. But, they argued, the system's foundations remained solid.[2]

Diagnosing the problems proved simpler than explaining the causes, however. Politicians and citizens grandstanded about white racism, the breakdown of black families, the selfish oblivion of the business community, or the intransigence of the teachers' union. More thoughtful observers hesitated to parse the causes of the troubles in New Orleans schools too neatly. Those who sought the education overhaul loved to tell the story of the pre-Katrina high school valedictorian who could not pass the state exit exam after multiple tries. But had the system failed her because of low expectations? A racist school accountability structure? Burnt-out teachers? Decades of damaging underfunding? Or some combination of them all?

For most of Raquel's life, and all of her daughters', the United States has been confronted with diminishing economic mobility and worsening inequality. She grew up in a change-averse city marred by these trends well before Katrina's devastation. Since the late 1970s, income inequality rose across the country. In the twenty-five years before Katrina struck New Orleans, more than 80 percent of the total increase in income fell in the hands of the richest 1 percent of Americans. A 2008 report by the United Nations found that New Orleans and a handful of other American cities suffer from the same level of inequality as African cities.

Meanwhile, Louisiana has never been known for liberal social services or for its ministrations to the poor. Since Raquel's first daughter, Jasmine, was born in 1995, the welfare rolls fell by 61 percent nationally. In Louisiana, they dropped by more than 86 percent. Comparatively speaking, New Orleans families like Raquel's have not relied on government aid for both practical and philosophical reasons. If unemployed, Raquel could receive a maximum of $284 a month in cash assistance from the state for herself and her daughters, one of the lowest rates in the country and hardly enough to pay the bills. Instead poor New Orleans families have gotten by—or not—by working low-paying, nonunionized jobs in the city's large service industry: myriad hotels, bars, restaurants, and a casino. Particularly before Katrina scattered much of the city's population, they also benefited from strong ties to community, neighborhood, and family that provided an alternative safety net of sorts. After the hurricane, countless grandmas, grandpas, sisters, brothers, uncles, aunties, and cousins never moved back to New Orleans. That meant those who did return had fewer relatives and friends to turn to if they needed emergency child care, could not pay rent for a couple months, or lost their homes and possessions in a fire.

In the last quarter century, America has invested in single-pronged, isolated strategies to curb poverty, such as school and welfare reform. Critics have described them as so-called silver bullets that overlook poverty's many dimensions and manifestations, while defenders have called them politically pragmatic and shrewd. In the 1990s, the government tried to overhaul welfare by placing women in job-training programs and helping them to find work, but undertook few other reforms to assist them. By contrast, the British government under Tony Blair unleashed a series of changes aimed at reducing child poverty. The changes, modest by European standards, not only focused on pushing welfare recipients into jobs. They also instituted the first national minimum wage (at a higher level than the minimum wage in America), provided generous new tax credits for working families, expanded free preschool programs, and extended paid maternity leave.

The effort to reinvent New Orleans after Katrina offered no exception to America's targeted, one-dimensional approach to poverty. Raquel and Langdon saw no significant change in their working conditions, pay, or access to health care and social services in the months and years that followed their return to the city. They had not expected anything better, though, and returned because, as Raquel put it, "when you're used to home, you're used to home." But any changes were for the worse, like the cuts to holiday pay rates at the hotel where Raquel worked; the closure of Charity Hospital, which ministered to the poor; or the steep hike in the city's average rental costs, which priced the family out of most houses and, for a time, the city itself.

Katrina struck the Gulf Coast at a time when the digital age had simultaneously eroded traditional lines of authority and, some argued, laid bare the shortcomings of American institutions across the country. Since its inception, the American public education system has struggled to educate the poor—at times scarcely attempting it. But that was never so evident as after the turn of the millennium, when No Child Left Behind required the public release of data showing just how well (or not) the nation's public schools did by poor students, rich students, white students, black students, Hispanic students, Asian students, disabled students, rural students, urban students, and suburban students—at least on the single matrix of an annual standardized test. Of course the government did not try to reduce to a single number or grade the quality of a child's health care, diet, home environment, peers, community resources, recreational options, or parents. So in some eyes the blame for the dismal results posted by many poor minority students fell largely on the schools.

At the same time, the Internet collapsed long-established hierarchies relating to the media and where to turn for information and expertise. For better or for worse, the structures and institutions that had come to define America no longer seemed so sacrosanct. The state officials who pushed through the changes in New Orleans tended to justify their actions with specific outrages: the FBI investigations of school district finances, for instance, or that endlessly repeated story of the high school valedictorian who couldn't pass the state's exit exam. But they operated in the broader context of a country whose citizens felt newly emboldened to question what had been taken for granted—particularly when it came to the fundamentals of the nation's largest public institution. The reinvention of New Orleans schools was an extreme example of the growing and controversial conviction that a changed educational structure on its own could be used to combat poverty in America. Under this line of thinking, "fixing" the schools will best alleviate poverty, not a more expensive and complicated blend of welfare reform, housing reform, health care reform, criminal justice reform, higher taxes, and increased government spending.

Unlike most of those who publicly debated the radical changes, Raquel did not view what transpired through the prism of ideology or politics or public good. She viewed it—at times approvingly, at times more critically—through the lens of personal need.

Raquel and Langdon, Geraldlynn's stepfather, had few fond memories of their own time in the New Orleans public schools. By the end of the 1970s, when they started kindergarten, white and middle-class flight were well under way. When they left high school, most of the city's more than one hundred public schools enrolled low-income, black student populations. The schools suffered from gross neglect when it came to resources and facilities, a neglect many attributed to the race and poverty of their students.

Langdon, smart and intense, loves to hold forth about the value of an education—using his own miseducation and subsequent struggles as testament. He often tells his children and stepchildren that his alma mater, James Derham Junior High School, was "the baddest school they had for little kids" in the city and Booker T. Washington, his high school, "the baddest school they had for big kids."

"We had dudes bringing guns and knives to school every day. Every day," he says, recalling his experience at Booker T. Washington in the late 1980s. The school drew many of its students from nearby housing projects. But weapons and violence did not make the school bad on their own, according to Langdon. He also cites a dangerous neighborhood, lack of parental support, negative public perception, and teacher apathy.

Langdon never knew his own father. And he did not know what to believe from the myriad accounts he heard of why the state took him from his mother. He lived with one foster mother until the age of eight, a woman who "treated me like a normal child." But when she died, the state sent him to a series of group homes that left him with a never-ending supply of Oliver Twist–style tales for his children and stepchildren: birthdays and Christmases with no presents, a home life spent sitting in a locked bedroom with three other foster boys, the time a group-home staff member punished a boy by putting a pair of pliers around his genitals and threatening to cut them off if he misbehaved again. When Langdon held forth, no one knew quite where fact ended and fiction began. But they understood his message: Growing up on your own, without parents who cared about you, wasn't anything pretty.

When Langdon was twelve his oldest brother, Tyrone, pulled him out of the group homes. Tyrone was a solid role model, but he grew so frustrated with his little brother's disobedience after a year that he sent Langdon to live with another brother, Levett, in the St. Thomas housing projects. Levett did not set a good example. While living with him, Langdon started to sell drugs, commit robberies, and avoid school. By the end of his sophomore year, he had dropped out.

Langdon sometimes wonders if more involved teachers could have filled at least part of the parental void. The teachers "didn't care if you did the work as long as you sat there and kept quiet. They didn't care unless you aggravated them," he said.

Raquel knew teachers weren't solely to blame for a school's troubles. When she attended New Orleans' Cohen High School, a lone student or small group disrupted many classes. By the time the teacher calmed those students down, or kicked them out, the class had ended. She thought most of the teachers were overwhelmed. Raquel still remembers a few who took time out and treated her like a daughter (as an adult she spent hours searching for one of them online to offer thanks). But others, defeated and resigned, wrote the material on the chalkboard before class started and then spent the rest of the period behind their desks. "They'd be like, 'Do this and call me when you are done.' Sometimes I'd look up and they be sleeping, so I'd go to sleep, too."

Raquel graduated from Cohen in 1992 and headed straight into a series of low-paying jobs: preparing sandwiches at Subway, working in the food court at Tulane University, cleaning hotel rooms at the Sheraton. She tried working for a temp agency but did not know what she was supposed to do at half of the assignments. Raquel received government assistance and food stamps for a brief period when her daughters were young. At one point the public assistance office assigned her to a job in a check-cashing storefront as a condition of receiving money. Another time they referred her to an unemployment agency that then dispatched her to a strip club in the French Quarter. Raquel had had enough. "I was so mad. Here I am thinking it was a real job," she said. "I was like, 'Uh-uh, I can find my own job.'"

She found work cleaning rooms at a French Quarter hotel instead, a job that has provided most of her income over the last decade. At the hotel, Raquel sees all sides of humanity: guests who tip well and bring gifts to the staff each time they visit, and ones who, trying to dodge the bill, swipe a stick of red lipstick across the sheets and then blame it on the maid.

For the first decade of her life, it seemed as if Geraldlynn would receive a similar education as her parents—although with more encouragement from home than her stepfather received. Her schooling got off to a rocky start at McDonogh 42 Elementary School in the Treme, where she attended kindergarten through fourth grade. She hung with a group of girls who liked to squabble more than study. She often told teachers she had to go to the bathroom, then cut class. If caught, she tried to skip out on detention. Her report cards were full of Cs and Ds. Geraldlynn never caused serious trouble, however; she drew the line at certain kinds of mischief, like pulling the fire alarm over and over again.

Geraldlynn knew from her first day of fifth grade that Adam Meinig's school, KIPP Believe College Prep, would be different. The school's rules made her dizzy: no talking in the hallway, no going to the bathroom between classes, walk on this side of the hall, snap your fingers to show agreement or approval, "track" the teacher or student speaker at all times. In math class that first morning, a teacher fussed at Geraldlynn because she had not participated enough and fell asleep in class. Skipping class, much less detention, clearly wasn't going to be an option.

Geraldlynn quickly learned about the Bench, the bane of every KIPP student's existence. Students who seriously violated one of the school's six values—responsibility, perseverance, integrity, empathy, courage, and community—found themselves isolated from their peers in classrooms and at lunch. They also had to cover the KIPP name on their uniforms with a piece of tape or a jersey, a symbol of their temporary estrangement from the school community. The humiliation underlying that controversial approach dismayed many parents, particularly middle- and upper-class ones. But it resembled Raquel's own discipline strategy. She often told Geraldlynn and her older sister, Jasmine: "I send you to school to do what you need to do and get out of there. If you cut up, you're embarrassing me, and that means I'm going to embarrass you right back."

"My mama take after my grandma's kind," says Geraldlynn. "She don't play. She'll knock me to the next century if she has to."

Every so often Geraldlynn found herself benched, usually for failing to do her homework or talking back to a teacher. Geraldlynn did not agree with her mother as to the Bench's merits, but she did appreciate her teachers' hard work and the extra effort they seemed to take with students. KIPP Believe teachers gave each student their cell phone number and called parents often. (Raquel always knew someone from KIPP was calling when a strange area code appeared on her cell phone.) One of Geraldlynn's favorite teachers, Ms. Drake, invited a small group of girls over to her house to bake cookies and took Geraldlynn out to lunch. Raquel viewed the small fleet of earnest teachers as college kids imported from across the country to help New Orleans schoolchildren after Katrina. It was only a slight misperception, as most of Geraldlynn's teachers weren't long out of school, and many were not from New Orleans.

Geraldlynn's grades improved each year at KIPP Believe, to mostly As and Bs in seventh grade. It helped that she stopped hanging that school year with two girls who always seemed to be in trouble. One had to repeat a year, and the school expelled the second (or "put her out") for repeated fighting. Without their distractions, Geraldlynn could focus on her work.

Her honor-roll grades held steady during her final year at KIPP Believe. Eighth grade culminated in the excursion Meinig had touted that afternoon on her front steps four years earlier: a class trip to New York City. "New York, oh, New York was very, very fast," Geraldlynn says. "They told us, 'Now don't go to New York walking like you walk in New Orleans, all slow like, because you will get hit.'"

Many of Geraldlynn's most vivid memories from KIPP Believe come from the annual class trips. The nearly all-expenses-paid forays into mainstream, American middle-class life included watching *The Phantom of the Opera* and a Mets game on the last trip, rock climbing in North Carolina, and visiting Selma, Alabama, where some of the most famous civil rights marches of the 1960s began. Raquel went along on a KIPP-sponsored trip to Washington, D.C., her first visit to the nation's capital. The other parent chaperones laughed when Raquel sat in a circle with the students during a lesson in a grassy corner of the National Mall. When Raquel kept piping up with questions, one of the KIPP staff members told her the lesson was designed for students, not adults. But Raquel brushed him off. She figured she was there to learn, too.

"I've just never seen anything like it," she says. "They take them from world to world, you know."

Raquel and Langdon never imagined defying the economic trends that defined America during their lifetimes. But like many parents, they held higher ambitions for their children. And in the years that followed Katrina, they adopted the ambitions of the young educators who descended on the city as their own, believing the city's remade schools might lead their children to a different, gentler fate.

Geraldlynn felt more ambivalent. By the time eighth grade rolled around, she did not consider applying for a spot at a magnet school or a scholarship at a private school. She passed the LEAP test, the state's high-stakes exam required to advance to high school. But she scored "basic" in all subjects, not the "mastery" and "advanced" designations characteristic of many students at the city magnet high schools with competitive admissions, like Ben Franklin. Nevertheless, for months the LEAP results remained taped to the wall of the tiny bedroom she shares with her sister, Jasmine.

"To me, I had low self-esteem," Geraldlynn says. "I didn't want to apply to Ben Franklin because I knew I wouldn't make it."

Like many of her classmates, Geraldlynn had a love-hate relationship with KIPP. She grew fond of some teachers and took pride in her academic growth. She could tell how much it meant to her teachers and parents. And she had fun on the end-of-year trips.

But at KIPP Believe, Geraldlynn complained, she and other students sometimes "felt controlled, like we were caged in," particularly when the staff ordered the students to walk in straight lines and told them exactly where to stand and sit. She resented having someone else dictate her every move. At its best, KIPP Believe felt like a special club with its funny slogans, chants, and focus on building academic self-esteem; at its worst, it felt like a preteen prison with long days, barked orders, and humiliating punishments. While the schools of her parents' youth might have lacked a sense of urgency, Geraldlynn sometimes felt that KIPP had *too* much. In her mind, even if not her parents', the jury on KIPP was still out.

Geraldlynn was her mother's daughter, physically and temperamentally. Because of her small size and soft voice, people often overlooked her in a crowd. At first glance, she came off as cheerful and obedient. But those who got to know her discovered a canny sense of humor, intense curiosity, and a mischievous streak. KIPP's New Orleans teachers—with their endless reliance on personality tests, theories of multiple intelligence, and "character" building—described Geraldlynn as having "social intelligence." She communicated easily with people of diverse ages and backgrounds, was acutely conscious of others' feelings, and possessed a shrewdness that allowed her to see through all manner of pretense. Geraldlynn did not miss much.

Alison Drake, Geraldlynn's favorite teacher from middle school, said the teen's greatest challenge in college will probably be self-advocacy. "It's important for our kids who go off to an environment where they don't have a lot of experience to be able to advocate for themselves," her teacher says. Alison, an Ohio native, taught in Gaston, North Carolina, through Teach For America and then joined KIPP in New Orleans in 2007. "Geraldlynn works really hard, but she's never been the kid with the highest skills. She doesn't have the ability to breeze through schoolwork and if, in a college class, she doesn't know what a professor is saying she's going to have to have the confidence to raise her hand or go see them later."

KIPP schools have always emphasized character. But in recent years, its leaders have focused more explicitly on teaching character traits after realizing that college success often hinges just as much on strengths like optimism and tenacity as middle- and secondary-school academic performance. As a result, many KIPP students receive not only traditional grades but also feedback on such characteristics as curiosity, grit, and zest. Although the term "self-advocacy" regularly comes up in conversations between KIPP staff and parents, Geraldlynn little fathomed what it meant. She, in turn, knew a whole vocabulary whose meaning eluded her teachers, like the word *teety* for aunt. Despite good intentions on both sides, KIPP's staff and families sometimes speak in different languages.

Geraldlynn wanted something new, and more "normal," for high school, a break from KIPP's relentless focus on discipline and routine. But her mother had other ideas. Raquel took comfort in KIPP's plans to open its first high school in New Orleans—one of the first fifteen KIPP high schools to open across the country—just in time for Geraldlynn's freshman year. KIPP Renaissance High School would start with just incoming ninth graders in the fall of 2010 and add a new grade each year after that. It promised families a continuation of the KIPP Way, straight up to college's door.

In the weeks leading up to the start of high school, Geraldlynn goaded Raquel and Langdon during conversations in the family's cramped apartment, trying to convince them that KIPP Believe was far worse than they thought.

"People are always thinking KIPP is such a great school, but deep down we have problems," Geraldlynn told them.

"Well, that's life, Scootah," replied her mother, using the family's nickname for Geraldlynn, Scooter, with the *r* usually dropped. Geraldlynn's aunt gave her the name as a baby because she zipped around the floor so quickly, pushing off with her hands as if on a scooter.

On and on Geraldlynn went, telling her parents about the time a student brought a knife in his backpack. Or the time one student tried to get everyone else to swallow unidentifiable tiny pills, pretending they were candy.

Raquel and Langdon listened, but they couldn't help wondering why Geraldlynn had waited over a year to tell them if KIPP Believe had been so frightening.

Langdon told her KIPP Believe's problems paled in comparison to those at Booker T. Washington. "You never hear people saying kids have guns at KIPP. You never hear people talking about KIPP students fighting," he told her. "It's like KIPP is just solid. At my school there was always some kind of trouble. Every day was a bad day."

Geraldlynn's hesitancy about KIPP ran deeper than typical teenage contrariness. Sometimes the snipes at KIPP Believe masked her more complicated fear that she was not college material.

As KIPP took control of a historic building in the city's 9th Ward named after Frederick Douglass, its thirty-one-year-old principal, Brian Dassler, filled every crook and crevice of the building with college paraphernalia. Beneath the college flags lining the corridors, index cards even listed the number of KIPP alumni nationally who have gone on to attend different colleges: Vanderbilt, 4. The University of Miami, 1. Texas A&M, 7.

The college banners and slogans belied the difficulty KIPP had already experienced keeping its graduates in college. One study showed that 33 percent of the first cohort of graduates from KIPP's two oldest middle schools had completed a four-year college ten years later. That represented an improvement over the national rate of 8 percent for students from low-income, minority communities, but fell far short of KIPP's goal of 75 percent. Almost as if to convince himself that KIPP Renaissance could defy those statistics, Brian Dassler recited KIPP Renaissance's mantra over and over: "One thousand first-generation college graduates by 2022."

Over time he said it so often it started to sound like a prayer.

Raquel and Langdon challenged Geraldlynn, trying to convince her that college remained within her reach. But with no firsthand knowledge on the subject, they, too, spoke mostly on faith.

One afternoon, just days after Geraldlynn started KIPP Renaissance, the family sat in their windowless living room. Two years earlier, a fire had forced them from their 7th Ward shotgun house. Langdon found a new apartment in a neglected, crime-ridden corner of a suburb called River Ridge. Wealthier residents of River Ridge, which includes miles of quiet cul-de-sacs snaking alongside the Mississippi River, deny the area lies within their town, even though the apartment building is clearly inside River Ridge's boundaries. The neighborhood—including a playground across the street—had been the scene of several recent shootings. In one of the most infamous, a stray bullet fired from a car pierced apartment walls, killing a seven-year-old girl while she slept in a complex less than a half mile from where Geraldlynn lives. Newspaper accounts of the shooting said it took place near "a neighborhood known for drug dealing called 'The Dump.'"

Raquel and Langdon did not view the neighborhood as unsafe, at least not compared to certain blocks in the city. They heard gunshots more frequently in parts of the 7th Ward. But having spent her whole life in

New Orleans (with the exception of her Katrina evacuation in Texas) Raquel found the area somewhat foreign. It bothered her that Jasmine and Geraldlynn navigated River Ridge's streets and shortcuts more easily than she did. Raquel liked to know exactly where her daughters were, whom they were with, and the fastest route to them.

The family kept the small apartment immaculate. During the holidays, their door was the only one in the building festooned with ribbons, Santa cutouts, and lights. The double bed the girls share was always neatly made; the table set with clean dishes as if company was on its way.

Seated on rented plush chairs and a couch that filled most of the small room, Geraldlynn and her parents engaged in what had become a familiar debate.

"How I goin' to go to college if we don't have any money?" Geraldlynn dove in.

Geraldlynn knew how hard her mother worked just to pay the bills. Raquel worked two jobs "since my girls were this high," she often said, holding her hand a couple feet above the floor. Neither busing tables at a moderately priced French Quarter restaurant nor cleaning rooms at a nearby hotel provided much opportunity for advancement in position or pay—much less the flexibility of starting a college savings account. After working at the hotel for more than a decade, Raquel earned just above ten dollars an hour, not an unusual wage in a city where few hotels have unionized workers.

But Langdon had heard word of scholarships for students with high grade point averages and test scores.

"Listen, listen!" he told Geraldlynn. "Y'all do good enough in high school, then high school will pay for you to go through college. They will give you scholarships. For people who want to go to college and can make it in college, but don't have the money, they got ways to get y'all in there. It ain't about money. I keep telling y'all, Do not settle for less.

"I want y'all to have a good life," he continued, on a roll now. "I don't want y'all working for no McDonald's or any of them places working minimum wage. Y'all don't have to live like that. I want y'all to live better."

"Can I say something?" Geraldlynn interrupted.

"Say what you want, Scootah," Langdon replied.

"I'm going to start making decisions when I'm seventeen," she said. "Now I'm not going to worry about it."

"No, you need to start planning what you're going to do with your life," Langdon replied. He knew firsthand how tough breaks and bad decisions early on could alter a person's path forever. Frustration over his own lost education had turned him into a zealot on the importance of school for his children and stepchildren. He stopped selling drugs in his late teens, and credits his first baby's mama with setting him on a straight path, convincing him to take a job at an A&P grocery store. He met Raquel when her girls were little and married her in 2004.

"You got to start planning now what you need to do to reach those goals," Langdon told Geraldlynn. "Don't wait until you're seventeen because seventeen might be too late for you to say, 'Well, what do I want to do now?'"

"I do know," Geraldlynn protested.

"Okay, what are you going to do?"

"I'm going to cosmetology school."

Hairstyle is the most striking physical distinction between Geraldlynn and her mother. Raquel almost always wears hers short and slicked down over her scalp, a simple and time-efficient style. But Geraldlynn styles hers in corkscrew curls, adds tracks, or painstakingly straightens and fluffs it out, depending on her mood.

"That's not college," Langdon responds.

"That's a trade," Raquel interjected.

"You could do that without going to college," said Langdon. "That's all right to do that, but what else are you going to do besides fixing hair?"

"Work."

"Work. What kind of work?"

"Nursing in the military. Or I could go to college to be a doctor."

"Well, don't sit back and be like, 'I got time.' Time waits for no one, Scootah."

"I know," Geraldlynn acceded.

"Before you know it, time going to have snuck up on you so quick," Langdon said, quickly snapping his fingers, "and you going to be lost. Because the way they making the jobs and technology now, there ain't going to be anything for you if you ain't smart enough or certified enough . . . Even if you look at the smallest jobs or the lowest jobs—the lowest jobs you can get would be working in a McDonald's, being a garbage man, cleaning up—"

Langdon paused for a few seconds, contemplating the economic prospects for a poor black undereducated American. He often discouraged his children from pursuing jobs in the fast-food industry, asking them,

Raquel Dillon embraces her daughter, Geraldlynn, who wears a KIPP Renaissance uniform. Geraldlynn began attending KIPP schools at the start of her fifth-grade year in 2006. Renaissance, the city's first KIPP high school, opened in fall 2010 when Geraldlynn started ninth grade. Photo by Susan Poag.

"Why they going to pay you a lot to cook something that's already cooked?" But now he wondered if those jobs would exist at all.

"Man, just think about it," he said. "Now you in the downtown area, who do you see in that area cleaning up?"

"Colored folks," volunteered Raquel.

"Black folk," Langdon continued. "Now they are starting to get machines, machines that's sweeping up, sweeping up. Even the garbage cans. They don't need people to pick up the garbage cans no more. Just one person to control the little switch," he concluded, shaking his head and turning to Raquel and Geraldlynn. "I'm just trying to show y'all the little differences. Them was the lowest jobs that a person who don't know how to read, write, or compute could get and they making it hard for you to get even those jobs."

"Like I don't see it, I don't get—" Geraldlynn stammered.

"Like at McDonald's, everything is going to be computerized. The manager going to be able to run McDonald's by themselves. They ain't going to need no food servers because the buttons tell you everything."

He addressed Raquel, a veteran of jobs in fast-food restaurants, food courts, and hotels. "You probably remember this from when you used to work at McDonald's. Remember the old cash register where you used to ring everything up? You used to have to count to figure out how much change to give the customer back? Go to McDonald's now, give a twenty-dollar bill, they don't have to know how to count. Just give a twenty-dollar bill, press the button, hang on a minute. They going to tell you how much change to give back. So what they need you there for?"

"So basically you saying that the jobs are running out?" Geraldlynn asked.

"No," her stepfather replied. "You going to have to have some kind of college up under your belt to get a job. You're going to have to have something up under your belt. You're not just going to be able to walk into jobs and get 'em as easy. But hey, you all are going to make your own choices. All I can do is just back you up whatever choice you all make. But y'all going to have the choice to whatever way your life turn out."

"Oprah went to college?" Geraldlynn asked.

"I just don't want her to make a wrong choice or let her peers give her the wrong goal," Raquel burst forth. She often sits quietly during conversations for several minutes, and then speaks quickly, like a balloon letting out air. "You know, like a dumb decision."

Compared to some others she knew, Raquel did not have it so bad. She did honest work and had held the same two jobs for more than a decade, retaining both even after Katrina; Langdon and her twin sister, Roxanne, did what they could to help with the bills and the girls; and Raquel adored her two sweet daughters. In many respects, she considered herself blessed. Still, like Langdon, she did not want Geraldlynn forced to live from paycheck to paycheck. She did not want her daughters consigned to eighty-hour work weeks cleaning up after strangers' messes. She did not want them ever to feel her only real regret: the sorrow of dozens of Christmases and first days of school spent working, away from family.

"I'm really willing to help her move up as much as possible. I didn't attend college. I never did plan to attend myself, to be honest. I finished high school. I wasn't no bad person. But I'm wanting [my girls] to attend college."

Turning to Geraldlynn, she added: "Don't be like me. Be a little better."

THE TEACHER
"Teaching is a series of things you do in response to the data you get."

Aidan Kelly never dreamed of becoming a teacher.

He agreed to meet with a recruiter from Teach For America during his senior year at Harvard University as a favor to a friend. Arriving at a Cambridge bubble-tea café for the informational interview one afternoon, Aidan felt the kind of ease that comes when little is at stake. His friend worked as a campus campaign coordinator for the domestic Peace Corps–style program, whose slick marketing campaigns enticed about one in ten Ivy League seniors to apply. When they asked Aidan to at least consider Teach For America, he did not want to say no. Senior year had just begun, and he had not yet decided what he wanted to do after Harvard. Graduate school in history and management consulting sat on the top of his list. But as Aidan walked into the tea shop that September afternoon in 2007, he felt open to anything.

Josh Biber sat camped out with his laptop, meeting with potential applicants for brief sessions. Josh, a graduate of Brown University just a few years older than Aidan, completed his two-year Teach For America stint at an elementary school in the Phoenix area and then took a job recruiting for the organization. Josh used the meetings as a chance to tout the organization to the ambivalent and undecided. Aidan told Josh he found Teach For America's work interesting and came from a family of teachers (many of his female relatives, including his mother, were lifelong educators). But he acknowledged his uncertainty up front.

Josh's presentation hit all the right notes. Aidan liked his strength of conviction. "The TFA approach was: You can't ignore this problem. And we're going to speak from a position of authority about it," Aidan says. The "problem," as Teach For America saw it, was the "achievement gap" between low-income minority students and their wealthier peers. Aidan liked Josh's dedication as he described spending evenings tutoring a student at McDonald's to bring him up to grade level. He also liked the letter Josh shared with him from a former student in Phoenix, proof that he stayed in touch even after the two-year Teach For America commitment ended. And Josh's description of a "classroom economy" he had created for his students stuck with Aidan. The "economy" was a variation on a strategy employed at many charters, including Geraldlynn's middle school alma mater, KIPP Believe. Josh's economy was based on "Mr. Biber bucks" that students could earn and then use to make mandatory rent payments on their desks. They received the pretend money for any manner of good classroom behavior: helping a fellow student, working hard on an assignment, improved grades. Most of the students grew deeply invested in the fake economy, Josh told Aidan. When one student ran low on classroom currency, he sold candy to his classmates in exchange for Mr. Biber bucks to make rent.

The idea of the classroom economy captivated Aidan, who found "incentive design" fascinating. In Aidan's view, Mr. Biber successfully tricked the children into valuing their space in his classroom over something with real cash value. "The student thought he was gaming the system when really he had bought in more than he could ever realize," Aidan said.

He left the brief meeting far more interested in teaching. "I sort of felt like the scales fell from my eyes," he said. From that point on, Aidan pursued a position with Teach For America aggressively. The more he learned about the organization, the more he identified with its mission and strategies. Before Harvard, he had attended Regis High School in New York, a Catholic all-boys school run by Jesuits. Regis emphasized the importance of community service and giving back. And Teach For America, too, had a missionary aspect to it, promising applicants they would help make the country a better place by teaching poor children how to read and do math. The Jesuits had also instilled in Aidan an absolutism of sorts, a trust in moral rules and a belief that there is one "right way to live," Aidan says. Teach For America had a similar absolutism about it, proffering a set of principles that guided the work: a commitment to closing the achievement gap, faith in the power of "high expectations," certainty that "effective teaching" could trump all—poverty, limited resources—in the battle to educate impoverished students. Aidan learned their code words quickly.

There was one problem he tried his best to ignore. Aidan had stuttered throughout his childhood and adolescence. In his late teens, when the problem peaked, he blocked a word or two in most sentences, with varying degrees of intensity. When he had to speak in class at Regis, he sometimes became completely out of breath and clenched his teeth so hard his head hurt. His stuttering decreased at Harvard, but it still flared up.

Aidan had long ago determined he would not let his stutter get in the way of living life, however. Whenever he felt a flicker of doubt related to his speech impediment, he forged ahead. He had signed up for Harvard committees and led campus tours partly to prove to himself that the stutter wasn't holding him back. He would not let it stop him from trying to teach.

The next step in the process was a phone interview with a TFA alum. He sat on a large red leather chair in a wood-paneled room of the *Harvard Crimson* office, where he had been co-chair of the newspaper's *Fifteen Minutes* magazine. The questions weren't hard ones for those who had done any reading about TFA. But Aidan grew animated as the interviewer asked about whether parents of low-income students care about education and the most important variables in determining a student's success. Aidan stood up from the chair and started walking through the room, gesturing in the air as he spoke. He could tell that he was giving the answers the interviewer wanted (low-income parents *do* care, and teachers play a crucial role in determining student success). Not too long afterward, he found himself at the final step in the interview process: an all-day series of in-person presentations at the headquarters of Monitor Consulting in Cambridge.

Early in the day, Aidan taught a sample lesson on a topic of his own choosing. Having rehearsed dozens of times, he scarcely stumbled as he taught the other applicants (as well as the two judges, the executive director of Teach For America's Connecticut office, and a TFA alum

attending Harvard Law School) how to scan a poem for meter. He began
with Shakespeare's eighteenth sonnet, "Shall I compare thee to a summer's day," which followed traditional poetic form, and concluded with
Edgar Allan Poe's "The Raven," featuring more irregular meter.

In an interview, he answered questions designed to see if applicants had
a good grasp on the difference between correlation and causation when it
comes to student achievement. *One school with bad attendance also has
drab gray walls. Is that important? Another with good attendance has a
morning assembly every morning. Is that important?*

That afternoon, Aidan presented solutions to a sample challenge
posed earlier in the day: You are a teacher and your students need to take
books out from the library to complete a research paper. No one has Internet at home and there is no public library in town. What do you do?
During a break, Aidan jotted down a plan for creating an in-house library. He would issue library cards, teach the kids how to check out books,
and put in place a library computer system. Arriving at his presentation,
he whipped the prepared notes from his blazer pocket. The interviewers
smiled at the earnest twenty-one-year-old with the curly red hair.

As part of his application, Aidan had to rank the cities where he most
wanted to teach. New York, his hometown, went first. He put New Orleans, a city he had never visited, as his second choice. One of his best
friends from Regis High School attended New Orleans' Loyola University when Katrina struck. Bob Payne finished out the year at Harvard
before returning to Loyola. Throughout college, Aidan stayed in touch
with Bob about the rebuilding efforts in New Orleans. His friend's love
for the city piqued Aidan's curiosity and gave him a personal connection
to the place. Teach For America talked about New Orleans so much in its
efforts to steer its recruits to the city (the only city in America, it touted,
where Teach For America teachers or alums taught at least one in four
public school children) that Aidan began to equate New Orleans schools
with the program. Aidan thought teaching in the city would offer an
"incredible chance to do a lot of good and get data on what works and
what doesn't."

In late October he was studying at a carrel in Harvard's Lamont Library when an e-mail popped up with a subject line about his TFA application status. For a second, he wondered if the formal tone meant
rejection awaited him. But the e-mail confirmed his gut feeling at the
start of the final interview session. Teach For America wanted him to
teach middle school math in the New Orleans region. (That year, about

half of the 160 Harvard seniors who applied to TFA joined the organization.) Aidan's mind had been made up for a while. He turned down a second-round interview for a consulting position at McKinsey & Company, dropped plans to apply to graduate school, and eventually hung a map of New Orleans on his dorm-room wall.

It wasn't until seven months later, a few days after his graduation from Harvard, that Aidan felt a short-lived surge of terror. He left campus the day after the ceremony. After stopping in New York, he embarked on the twenty-hour drive to New Orleans. He had never before traveled south of Philadelphia.

Aidan arrived at a welcome event just in time to hear Kira Orange Jones, Teach For America's executive director in New Orleans, welcome the new teachers in an opening ceremony. She asked how many of the group assembled were from New Orleans. Only a few hands went up. A few others had attended college in New Orleans. But dozens of the young twenty-somethings had never visited the city before—not even as tourists. Their conceptions of New Orleans were shaped almost entirely by Teach For America's background materials on the city and the internationally broadcast images of Katrina's devastation, which had hit as most of them started their sophomore year of college. In just a few days, they would leave for five weeks of intense training in Phoenix. And then it would be back to New Orleans and into their own classrooms. Many of them, including Aidan, would not receive their school assignments until weeks—or days—before the school year started. Sitting in a strange new city, the prospect of teaching children he knew so little about suddenly loomed before him. Aidan's thoughts returned to his stutter; his mind flooded with reasons becoming a teacher in New Orleans was a terrible, terrible idea. He broke into a cold sweat. What if he couldn't teach? Or speak to his students at all?

Teach For America had been placing corps members in New Orleans for nearly two decades by the time Aidan applied. But in 2007 its presence exploded as Paul Vallas, the new superintendent of the state-run Recovery School District, helped bring hundreds of young educators to the region. Vallas arrived in New Orleans in 2007 after a decade spent leading the Chicago and Philadelphia schools. He served as Chicago mayor Richard Daley's budget director until Daley tapped him as school CEO in 1995. In 2001, Vallas resigned to run for Illinois governor, narrowly losing to Rod Blagojevich in the 2002 Democratic primary. He then de-camped for Philadelphia. During his comparatively long stays in those two cities (the average big-city school superintendent serves less than four years), he attracted a healthy supply of both fans and critics for his willingness—at times, desire—to contract with a plethora of private groups to run alternative schools and provide any manner of educational support services. In Philadelphia, Vallas presided over one of the coun-try's largest experiments with school privatization. He arrived shortly after school leaders handed over the management of a few dozen schools to for-profit and nonprofit operators.

Vallas brought the mind-set of a frenetic businessman to the New Orleans superintendency: He hired all manner of consultants, many of whom he knew from his years in Chicago and Philadelphia, often paying them $2,000 a day for their services. He contracted with companies for curriculum, technology, even to run the alternative schools. And he al-ways remained focused on maximizing "profit" for the schools—in the form of foundation grants, FEMA settlements, and other funds. Vallas once referred to his broad goal in New Orleans as "buying momentum." He thrived and delighted in start-up mode, but not always in the day-to-day business of running a school district, as attested by the lackluster results at many of the schools he ran directly.[3]

Vallas helped triple the number of Teach For America recruits work-ing in the New Orleans region between 2007 and 2010, and the number of schools hiring teachers from the program more than doubled. Several area schools struggled at the time to find enough teachers since many fired veterans had not returned, could not get rehired, or switched pro-fessions. Lawyers representing the fired employees also argued that school officials made little, if any, effort to reach out to Katrina-displaced veterans in an attempt to recruit them back. Some critics of the Recovery School District claimed officials had fired the teachers to bring in cheaper employees. But average teacher salaries in the city actually went up 16 percent between 2005 and 2008, partly because of increased competition for teachers. Some charter schools spent far less on benefits, however, since they did not have to participate in the state's teacher-retirement program and could choose their own health insurance plans.

The Recovery District, which absorbed most of the city's public schools after Katrina, included both charter and traditional schools. Vallas hoped to turn nearly all of the schools into charters as quickly as possible. In 2006, when the first large wave of Recovery District schools reopened after Katrina, the number of teachers across the public schools had dropped from about four thousand pre-flood to eleven hundred. But the proportion of black teachers across the schools stayed constant, at about 73 percent. Starting in 2007, however, the city became a destination for young, aspiring, and ambitious charter school leaders from across the country who were far less likely to hire veteran teachers. Many of the new school leaders were brought to town by the nonprofit New Schools for New Orleans, which served as an "incubator" for new charter schools, providing them with access to experts, money for marketing, advice on teacher hiring, and political capital. Then the expanded Teach For America presence in the region—as well as the creation of another alternative teacher-training program called teachNOLA—glutted the job market with predominantly young educators from out of town. Starting in 2007, the percentage of black teachers began to drop steadily each year, to 63 percent during the 2007–2008 school year, and 57 percent the next year. Between those two school years the number of black teachers in the public schools fell by about one hundred while the number of white teachers rose by a similar number.

Teach For America routinely encounters resistance from unions and the education establishment. But in New Orleans the debate was especially fraught, since thousands of veteran educators had lost their jobs in Katrina's wake and now watched as the Recovery School District aggressively wooed young college graduates with little teaching experience, even promising relocation bonuses at one point. Vallas publicly championed the program. He provoked controversy when he told the *Times-Picayune* newspaper in 2009 that, when it comes to teaching, "experience can be overrated."

Teach For America's recruiting techniques closely resemble those of top management consulting firms like McKinsey & Company, which has attracted top graduates of the nation's most elite colleges with promises that, at the age of twenty-two, they can learn how to run the world. A 1999 *New Yorker* article dissected the growing popularity of the consulting companies among the Ivy League set. They "have figured out how to win over the hearts and minds of perfect twenty-one-year-olds, and how to use a big, ambitiously conceived, heavily government-supported national university system as a hiring hall for themselves," the article stated.

A few years after that piece appeared, Teach For America had become the popular new postcollege destination for "perfect twenty-one-year-olds." Like McKinsey, it hired recruiters to drum up interest at specific college campuses. And like McKinsey, it told college seniors that even a two-year commitment would make them better academics, lawyers, politicians, or entrepreneurs, and promised—even encouraged at times—recruits not to view being a business analyst or a teacher of low-income children as a lifelong career choice. Both used selectivity and elitism as a main draw: At Harvard more than a quarter of every senior class, or about 450 people, applied for about ten entry-level spots at the Boston Consulting Group in the late 1990s. In recent years, more than 10 percent of Harvard seniors have applied to Teach For America. The organization's acceptance rate hovered around 30 percent in the late 1990s, but has stayed in the teens for most of the last decade.

It's understandable that consulting companies and an ambitious non-profit like TFA might adopt the same hiring strategies: saturate the potential applicant pool with information and build allure by convincing them that only the chosen few get in. But the similarities between rookie consultants and Teach For America corps members persist even after they have started working. Corporate principles, goals, and language infuse America's public schools more than ever, particularly an unrelenting focus on "results," "outputs," "value added," or "what works." For the majority of America's history, educators and education policy have focused much more on inputs (the degree of training required of teachers, the level of public funding) than outputs (the percentage of students proficient in reading and math, the number of a teacher's students who can pass state tests). Many of today's leading school reformers, like McKinsey consultants, believe the results of almost everything, from a child's success to the impact of a given social policy, can be quantified and boiled down to a set of numbers in a PowerPoint presentation. Louisiana school superintendent Paul Pastorek even helped recruit McKinsey in 2008 to create a plan to improve the state's teaching corps, formalizing the mingling of the two professions.

Two of the school reformers' bibles—the business book *Good to Great* and the education book *Teach Like a Champion: 49 Techniques That Put Students on the Path to College*—highlight the striking new parallels between management consulting and teaching. The two books sit prominently in the offices of many charter school principals, top the reading lists for new teacher professional-development sessions, and inform even casual conversations between staff members at a growing breed of schools.

At Akili Academy, a New Orleans charter school, the principal handed each of the first-year teachers (all of them TFA corps members) a copy of *Good to Great* to peruse during their scant free time at TFA's five-week summer training in 2010, known as Institute. He advised them not to be intimidated by the fact that it's "a business book." *Good to Great* is the only book he required the novice teachers to read from cover to cover.

One section of *Good to Great* that gets cited particularly often details "the Hedgehog Concept," the idea that to thrive, businesses should, like hedgehogs, "do one thing and do it well" rather than undertake several different pursuits at the same time. The hedgehog reference comes from Isaiah Berlin's essay "The Hedgehog and the Fox," in which the hedgehog employs only one strategy against the fox—rolling up into a protected ball—yet always wins. Hedgehogs "simplify a complex world into a single organizing idea, a basic principle or concept that unifies and guides everything," the book states. "It doesn't matter how complex the world, a hedgehog reduces all challenges and dilemmas to simple—indeed almost simplistic—hedgehog ideas. For a hedgehog, anything that does not somehow relate to the hedgehog idea holds no relevance."

At Akili, principal Sean Gallagher used the concept to remind his novice teachers of what he felt should be their single-minded focus on student academic achievement. If the school tried to do too much—provide health care services or parenting classes, for example—it risked failure on its core mission, he argued, in the same way that the fox's myriad plots are no match for the hedgehog's obsession with a single strategy. "We have to be very deliberate about what we are and aren't," he told teachers during their orientation sessions. "Akili is not ever going to be a school that spends money educating parents."

The Hedgehog Concept is emblematic of a mind-set that has traditionally been more associated with economists than educators, one in which complex phenomena can be reduced to a single concept or a data point. The drive to quantify and label the performance of teachers, students, and schools has its origins in several trends, particularly the incorporation of business-world practices by the public schools. But it also stems from the American obsession with the clearly defined, measurable outcomes of sports, as well as the growing popularity of books, including *Freakonomics* and *The Tipping Point,* which put forward neat theories that purportedly explain what had been considered unfathomable or more complicated. Such theories make an overwhelming world seem knowable, governable. Persistent problems no longer appear intractable. And failure or success no longer depends on fate, luck, or a constellation of forces that can't be replicated.

For better or worse or both, the reformers brought this mind-set to the schools. Good teaching no longer seemed to be a mysterious, undecipherable act, the result of natural charisma or traditional training at schools of education. Instead they considered it the result of a series of actions that could be learned and perfected by those who are "mission aligned" and possess "a growth mind-set."

The second reformer guidebook, charter school founder Doug Lemov's *Teach Like a Champion*, is also filled with cleverly titled principles and theorems. It was published in 2010 and codified many of the teaching strategies and philosophies school reformers have embraced in recent years. "The 100 percent technique," for instance, holds that "champion teachers" get 100 percent of students to do what they want 100 percent of the time. In order to accomplish this feat, Lemov advises teachers to use "the least invasive form of intervention" to redirect students (a hand gesture, for instance, that does not interrupt the flow of the class), and to keep "corrections private" whenever possible, perhaps by telling off-task students, "You know who you are." The approach to improving teachers advocated by Lemov and his disciples is similar to the training McKinsey provides to its new business analysts: "You get videotaped role-playing with mock clients, and then you watch yourself while a coach gives you tips: Keep your hands on the tabletop. Make and maintain eye contact. Don't be confrontational. Don't raise your voice. Keep to the point. Get yourself unobtrusively in control of the rhythm of the encounter."

The reformers approach students they perceive as disadvantaged in much the same way they do struggling teachers. Just as young instructors need to be taught, explicitly and step-by-step, how to be good teachers, low-income children must be taught, explicitly and step-by-step, how to be good students. Staff at a growing number of "no-excuses" charter schools—which are highly structured and emphasize college matriculation—are prescriptive about where new students look (they must "track" the speaker with their eyes), how they sit (upright, with both feet planted on the ground, hands folded in front of them), how they walk (silently and in a straight line, which is sometimes marked out for them by tape on the floor), how they express agreement (usually through snaps or "silent clapping" because it's less disruptive to the flow of the class), and, most important, what they aspire to (college, college, college). This conditioning (or "calibration," or "acculturation," as it is sometimes referred to inside no-excuses schools) starts with the youngest of students. In one kindergarten class at Akili Academy, which embraces the no-excuses model, the teacher momentarily stopped the nine youngsters seated in front of her from spelling out words like *meat* and *sack* to tell them: "We have a lot to do this year—a lot if we want to go to the first grade. The first graders already have read this book and moved on to other books. I know all of you want to go to the first grade because all of you want to go to college. But you need to show discipline over your bodies to do that. Your eyes should be burning holes when you are looking at me."

The young teachers arriving in today's no-excuses schools find themselves in jobs that more closely resemble those of McKinsey business analysts than traditional civil service positions. Their goal, however, is not to help a company to maximize profits, but to integrate predominantly poor minority children into America's economic mainstream. The end they have in sight for those schoolchildren—college and a middle-class life— is very much the same that most of them would wish for their own children. But the educational means to that end are often very different.

Not long before the start of the 2008–2009 school year Aidan learned, with a twinge of disappointment, that he would not be teaching in New Orleans. Teach For America had secured him a job at John Martyn Alternative School in Jefferson Parish, just to the southwest of New Orleans. Since Katrina, suburban Jefferson Parish's population had surpassed that of New Orleans by nearly ninety thousand. Both parishes had their fair share of struggles with crime, education, public infrastructure, and race relations. (Teach For America, after all, had promised a challenge.) But state officials had left the school system in Jefferson Parish relatively intact. The parish had few charter schools, an elected school board still called the shots, and the teachers' union never lost the right to bargain collectively for the system's employees (who had not all been fired after the hurricane). Granted, the Jefferson district was not in financial arrears when Katrina struck and it did not post academic results as abysmal as New Orleans: 15 percent of schools were failing under state standards, as opposed to 62 percent in the city. But critics of the state takeover in New Orleans wondered if race and politics had played a role. In Republican-dominated Jefferson Parish, white residents outnumbered blacks by more than two to one, and whites led both the school board and the teachers' union. Not long after Aidan's time teaching in Jefferson Parish, an investigation uncovered disturbing irregularities in the application process for coveted spots at the parish's magnet schools. A community group alleged that at least one school had turned down qualified black applicants in favor of unqualified white ones. Across the board, the process lacked consistency, paperwork, and oversight. Once Aidan had spent a few months in the parish's schools, such stories did not surprise him.

Theoretically, Martyn Alternative School existed to serve students who wanted to prepare for the General Educational Development (or GED) test and bypass the traditional college-prep track. But in practice, as Aidan quickly learned, some Jefferson Parish middle school teachers and administrators used it as a dumping ground for students they did not want to teach or felt they could not teach. Not infrequently, students arriving at Martyn told him their guidance counselor had insisted the alternative school would be a "better fit" and coaxed them into enrolling, promising they would easily pass the GED. African-Americans comprised about half of the school population but only about a quarter of the parish's population overall. Because of tight space, Aidan shared a classroom with another Teach For America instructor. The school assigned him to teach middle school math to high school–age students.

On his first day that August, Aidan wore a tie and a navy-blue blazer that sagged in the shoulders, his default attire the few times he had to dress up in college. Aidan stood more than six feet tall, but because he had a skinny frame, oversize clothes gave him the look of a kid dressed up like an adult. He spent more than an hour reviewing a long list of rules and procedures he had culled and fine-tuned (some from Teach For America materials): Don't talk while the teacher is talking; always raise your hand. The rules were his attempt to lay down the law and let the kids know "this is the way it's going to be." But the kids looked dead.

He attempted a pep talk, reminding the kids that wherever they went and whatever they did, knowing math would come in handy. They could be anything they wanted, he told them.

A student named Alexander interrupted at some point. He stood below average height, about five foot seven, but despite his small stature, he looked tough. Alexander had a light mustache on his upper lip and wore his pants slung well below his hips.

"I can't become a judge," Alexander said. "I am going to prove it to you."

He then lifted up his pant leg, exposing an ankle bracelet Aidan knew was there for monitoring, not decoration.

Aidan could think of no quick, motivational comeback. After pausing he mumbled something like, "I'm sure that wouldn't stop you."

Aidan's biggest challenge would not be getting the words out. He had stuttered during his practice teaching at Bernard Black Elementary School in Phoenix that summer, but not as much as he had feared. A classroom had so much going on at any given moment, he realized, that he had no time to think about the speech impediment. A bigger challenge would be finding the words to say.

For the next few months Aidan struggled with many aspects of his job. He had hoped to spend a day reviewing each of the four arithmetic steps—addition, subtraction, multiplication, division—and move on to more complicated material from the middle school curriculum. But it took nearly two weeks to get through the basics; in hindsight, he wished he had spent even more time on them. Aidan had understood long division for as long as he could remember. He wrestled with how to explain it. He also had little idea how to motivate his students—much less convince them to sell candy in exchange for a seat in the classroom, as Mr. Biber had done. When the students stopped misbehaving, it felt as if they had granted Aidan control over the classroom, not that he had earned it. At Martyn, Aidan encountered students like Lee, a quick-witted teenager who made it clear he had no use for his teachers' rules through curse-filled rants: *Fuck this school. This ain't no real school. Fuck the teachers. They ain't no real teachers. I could be out on the street selling rock. I don't need this fucking school . . .*

(Two years after Aidan attended Institute, TFA shifted the training site for New Orleans corps members from Phoenix to Atlanta. Some TFA corps members believed it was because of their persistent complaints that the students in Phoenix-area schools did not prepare them for the children in New Orleans, who were generally more vocal in their anger, and specifically much more likely to stand up and tell their teachers to fuck off. A TFA spokeswoman said training sites move for a variety of different reasons.)

Partly because Teach For America had impressed upon him the need for constant reflection, Aidan tried to analyze during the car ride home each day why a given lesson did not go as planned. He gave himself until the first major turn onto Jefferson Highway to feel generally sorry and despondent, and then the self-critique began: How could he have handled a troublesome student differently? What did he need to do to make his lesson more interesting tomorrow?

"It depressed me to obsess over my failures every night," he said. He did not always know where else to turn for advice. Martyn's principal only visited Aidan's classroom for occasional required observations and left the school at the end of Aidan's first year. Aidan liked the advisor (or program director) Teach For America had assigned him. But once the advisor realized that Aidan was unlikely to quit his job or TFA, she spent more time on corps members who were flight risks. Alternatives like Martyn had reputations as dumping grounds for teachers other school leaders did not want. Noting Aidan's persistence in wearing ties to school every day, one colleague informed him that he, too, had worn ties every day "until I lost the will to teach."

At the very least, Aidan enjoyed living in New Orleans. He liked the lushness of the city, which made New York and Boston seem drab by comparison. He liked the worn, decaying look of the houses and streets and sent a friend a T-shirt from a local store's "The Beauty of Entropy" line. He liked most of the city's signature draws, including brass bands, po'boy sandwiches, and sazeracs, a New Orleans twist on the old-fashioned. Returning to the Northeast in November for the Harvard-Yale football game, Aidan took a little comfort in the fact that many of his friends also seemed to be stumbling into their postcollegiate lives with little idea of what they wanted to do in the long term. For the most part, however, Aidan spent the fall thinking he was a terrible teacher.

At some point in the winter, things stopped getting worse. Aidan's confidence increased; he knew his students a little better, and the nightly self critiques helped. He had long ago ascertained the students' skill levels in math fell all over the map. And he tried to learn something about their interests and backgrounds. Alexander liked the rappers Yung Joc and Young Jeezy, so Aidan used their music as an entrée. He had discovered the fifteen-year-old wore the ankle bracelet because he was on court-ordered monitoring after various drug and assault offenses. Alexander had spent time at Jefferson Parish's juvenile detention center. Sometimes he displayed his old jail-issued shoes. The cheap slip-ons brought a certain kind of stature, proof that he had done time in juvie and managed to sneak out a piece of state-owned property.

Only two of Aidan's students passed the GED that year. The class disruptions continued. But Aidan made it through the school year without any huge disasters and only one classroom fight, which he broke up before it came to blows.

Before the start of his second year, Aidan planned out everything, including the way his classroom should look, sound, and feel. Keeping in mind Teach For America's constant focus on results (the very phrase "focus on results" has become a mantra at many no-excuses charter schools), he zeroed in on specific desired outcomes—fewer student interruptions, more of his class passing the GED. Then he "backward planned" from the result he wanted through the steps he thought it would take to get there. He assumed, for instance, that students acted out partly because they did not realize the importance of earning a GED. So he delivered lessons on wage statistics for high school dropouts compared to those who had earned a GED. He also made a point of contacting students' parents to learn more about their home lives. And he continued to make an effort to assign projects that actually interested the students, like allowing the boys to study statistics by analyzing results from their favorite sports. It helped that in the 2009–2010 school year Martyn started grouping students by skill level and assigned Aidan those with the higher skills. When far more of his students passed the GED, it was impossible to tell if the bump stemmed from more advanced students, better teaching and student-motivation strategies, or, most likely, some combination of the two.

Alexander had returned to the juvenile detention center in the middle of that second school year. Lee never abandoned his filthy talk. But he grew into one of Aidan's most advanced students. Lee's teachers agreed he was ready to take the GED in the middle of the 2009–2010 school year. To take the test, however, students need a state identification card. And to get a card, a parent or legal guardian needs to sign a form. Lee lived with his grandmother; neither knew his mother's immediate whereabouts. So unless he dropped out of school without a GED or diploma, he had to bide his time at Martyn until he turned eighteen and could get a card on his own.

The state finally allowed him to take the exam in the summer of 2010.

"Man, Mr. Kelly, keep teaching," Lee told his teacher upon hearing he had earned his GED. "This fucking shit is *your* fucking shit."

Aidan wasn't always so sure. For much of his time at Martyn, he assumed that when his two-year commitment ended he would be finished
with teaching. He thought he might like to work for TFA; most of their
recruiters and program directors were recent alums, teaching "veterans"
in their universe. But in November of his second year, Aidan started
considering job openings at several young New Orleans charter schools.
They did not sound anything like Martyn, where, Aidan thought, the
system had burned out and jaded some teachers. These newer schools
made education sound like a great crusade. They promised teachers they
could "close the achievement gap" and "rebuild New Orleans" in a work
environment where "all the barriers and frustrations you feel in a traditional school are removed by the phenomenal leadership." Aidan decided
to apply to three charter schools, including the New Orleans Charter
Science and Math Academy, known as "Sci," which opened in 2008.
A no-excuses school with a large number of Teach For America alums
on staff, Sci was ambitious, idealistic, and growing fast. Both Aidan and
his program director agreed it sounded like a good fit.

Sci touts its numbers. In its first two years, the school posted among the
highest test scores of any open-enrollment high school in the city (in
New Orleans "open-enrollment" schools are supposed to take all comers
or hold a lottery if oversubscribed; by contrast, "selective-admission
schools" have requirements such as minimum test scores or grades).
About 90 percent of Sci's students qualify for free or reduced lunch, and
about 15 percent receive special education services. In the school's early
years, roughly a third of Sci freshmen arrived reading at or below the
fourth-grade level, according to a diagnostic exam the school used.[4]
Whether high test scores translate into high college graduation rates
will remain the core question at the heart of Sci's existence for years to
come, since even its inaugural class will not complete college until 2016.
The same question looms over the entire New Orleans school experiment. Overall, test scores have risen substantially: In 2004, only 30
percent of the city's public schoolchildren attended schools that met
the state's quality standards, compared to 60 percent in the year before
Aidan started at Sci. But it will take many more years to determine
whether the improvements are sustainable and if they lead to better
life outcomes for kids.

A typical Sci teacher attended an Ivy League university or other elite college; is white and childless; is in his or her twenties; is not from Louisiana; has a couple years' teaching experience, most of it through TFA; and, while expressing a general commitment to education, feels more ambivalent about staying a classroom teacher for the long term. A Sci teacher might consider a business-analyst position at McKinsey comparatively relaxing and devoid of feedback: First-year Sci teachers often work about eighty hours a week. Their official school day begins at seven fifty A.M. (most arrive on campus earlier) with a staff meeting during which they form in a circle, make a drum beat by slapping their thighs, praise their colleagues for hard work, persistence, or any other manner of successes or virtues, and then chant those colleagues' names in unison. Administrators and mentors stop in each teacher's classroom at least twice a week, but often daily, providing feedback on topics including their lesson plan, student behavior, strength of voice, choice of words, desk arrangement, gestures, or economy of movement. Teachers can clock out completely only after nine thirty P.M., when they no longer have to take phone calls from students who need homework help or want to talk. But many of them never turn off their phones or stop responding to texts or e-mails, even when teaching.

Sci's principal, Ben Marcovitz, was twenty-eight when he opened the school. Ben, an intense and self-assured Yale graduate, was accepted by Teach For America his senior year. But he "chickened out" because even a two-year commitment felt like too much at the time. "I wasn't ready to commit to anything for more than one year. That was the one thing I knew about myself." He ended up taking a teaching job in New Orleans after graduating, but not through Teach For America. Before founding Sci, he taught for a few years in New Orleans and Boston and earned a master's in education at Harvard. He briefly served as assistant director at the (similarly named) New Orleans Charter Science and Math High School before launching his own school. Above all else, he believes in the power of change, explaining that he founded Sci on the principle that "high school is not a lost cause; and any human being, regardless of where they are, can effect radical change in their trajectory."

Indeed, change sometimes seems to be the only constant at Sci: change of class schedules, teacher duties, school rules, and learning strategies. The changes come in response to ever-evolving data culled from each class every day, including what percent of students mastered the daily goal and how many are on pace to pass the state tests. Many of the no-excuses charters in New Orleans focus heavily on data, but Sci sometimes takes that preoccupation to new levels.

Working at Sci can be all-consuming, particularly for new teachers. If a first-year teacher puts in an average of eighty hours a week, that works out to about $12.75 an hour in pay during the school year and about $14.40 if you incorporate a summer vacation (assuming a teacher salary of about $53,000). A few teachers have departed or been fired over Sci's three-year history. One became pregnant and moved back to her hometown to be closer to family. A second told Marcovitz she did not think she would ever meet eligible men in New Orleans. A third expressed dismay that the more she improved, the more the school demanded. "Some teachers are stroked by the idea that they work in a terrible school and are the best teacher there," he says. "They grieve over the loss of that stature. Teachers like that will never be happy at Sci."

After applying, Aidan heard more and more about Sci through his TFA networks. "Everyone said that it was rigorous and tough to work at, but that things got done," he said. In February, Ben came to Martyn to observe one of Aidan's classes on irony. His feedback lasted for forty-five minutes and covered everything from Aidan's tone of voice to his posture. Ben introduced Aidan to the concept of "Key Three," which he said can move a class from good to great. The Key Three, as the name implies, includes three steps: Give students a task. Tell them how they will be assessed. Then assess them and share the results. Ben was less concerned with the quality of Aidan's first lesson than seeing if Aidan incorporated his advice during a follow-up visit to the classroom. When making hiring decisions, Ben believes that a "capacity for growth" and "philosophical convergence" matter more than the quality of teaching he sees. For the second observation, Aidan tried to incorporate Ben's feedback into his lesson on *The Merchant of Venice*. He was teaching a different group of students, however. And Ben did not feel as if he had a strong enough read on Aidan's teaching or the adjustments he had made in response to his first critique. So Aidan taught a third lesson—on sequencing—this time at Sci.

In the spring of 2010, Aidan received job offers from three New Orleans charter schools, including Sci. All three seemed like places where he could grow as a teacher. But so much about Sci fit with his worldview: its relentless focus on academic achievement and self-improvement. Its obsession with data. The missionary zeal with which it approached the work. A sense of sureness and absolutism around its goals. An optimism that good teaching, like anything else, can itself be taught. "Teaching is a series of things you do in response to the data you get," Aidan says. There wasn't any more exciting place to be for a young educator in 2010 than a New Orleans charter school. And there wasn't a more exciting charter school in New Orleans than Sci Academy. Completely unfettered by bureaucracy or tradition, teaching at Sci felt like a chance to show the world what was possible.

THE PRINCIPAL
"We are going to get this thing called education right."

A rainbow of colors filled the courtyard at O. Perry Walker High School on December 14, 2005, the first day that several public schools reopened in New Orleans. Many of the students, newly returned from Houston, Atlanta, Baton Rouge, and countless other cities and towns across the country, wore uniforms from the high schools they attended before Katrina upended their lives. Former Landry students came in blue and gold, Fortier students in blue and silver, Walker students in khaki and orange. Others dressed in their street clothes. Only public schools on the city's West Bank, which had not flooded in the storm, reopened that week. The assemblage at Walker included some students who had never before crossed the Mississippi River to visit the city's less iconic West Bank neighborhoods. Walker was one of only two public high schools in the city open; many students had no choice but to enroll there. Homesick for their old schools and distrustful of yet another change, some viewed attending Walker as just the latest in a series of already demoralizing events.

Students who recognized friends or former classmates clustered together in the courtyard, a sunny space sandwiched between the school's cafeteria and classroom buildings. Most wore world-weary, somber expressions; those who chatted did so in hushed tones. With temperatures rising up into the sixties, it felt more like spring than mid-December. The National Guard unit stationed at Walker after Katrina repainted parts of the building and scrubbed clean the concrete walkways in the courtyard. Despite the campus's damaged sections, the courtyard had a

Mary L. H. Laurie, the principal of O. Perry Walker High School, extends her arm to signal for quiet during a morning gathering at the school. Susan Poag/New Orleans Times-Picayune.

fresh look and scent. The teenagers shuffled with quiet excitement as they waited for the first "morning gathering"—a time when the entire school would come together for a mixture of celebration, lecture, logistics, and uplift. They all needed a little uplift after months spent in strange cities and schools, long trips home, and new lives that for many began in government-issued trailers.

Morning gathering opened with a prayer. Then Mary Laurie stood before the three hundred teenagers and raised her hand, telling the students that this would now be the symbol for silence—even though this morning, at least, quiet seemed to be the natural state. Until she introduced herself as principal, a few students mistook Laurie for someone's mother or grandmother: in her early fifties; her stature not tall or short, skinny or fat; her words a reliable mixture of prodding and praise. Everyone had warned her not to attempt a morning gathering with hundreds of unknown teenagers. Brian Riedlinger, the head of the newly formed charter school association that ran Walker, conceded Laurie had used the ritual to good effect at the elementary and middle schools where she served as principal before Katrina. But he cautioned that high school was different. The students might find the tradition babyish and act out. He was nervous about how the whole day would go. No one knew how many students would show up and from where. Riedlinger feared that teenagers from different parts of town—thrown together at school for the first time—might clash. During the months before

Katrina, neighborhood and school-based rivalries had grown particularly intense.

Laurie believed that above all else she needed to make it clear to teachers, staff, and students that public education in New Orleans would be different; the expectations would be higher but the support deeper. In the end, Laurie decided she had only one chance to set a new tone. She would go ahead with her plan. "We're a family now, and this," Laurie gestured toward the assembled teenagers and staff, "is how we conduct family business."

Laurie wore a dark dress, black belt, and bright orange shawl. Her black hair puffed softly around her face. Standing before the students, Laurie acknowledged the differences of school, neighborhood, ward, culture, and language that divided them in a city famous for its hyperlocal habits and tastes. "The schools you attended before will always be a part *of*," she told them. (She often ends statements with an emphasized preposition—a rhetorical device that helps hold the listener's attention.) "Your love for where you came from doesn't disappear," she continued. "It will always live in your heart. But we are now a family. You are now a Charger. We don't have this ward and that ward, this school and that school. We are all united here as Chargers."

Cornelle Carney, one of Walker's new students, half listened at first. The generally mild-mannered sophomore had spent the first few minutes of the day taking note of everything he disliked about the school: the metal detectors at the entrance and the staff who dug through bags looking for contraband; the first long walk down a narrow corridor surrounded by unfamiliar faces; the obvious lack of diversity—Cornelle did not see a single white face among Walker's students—a stark contrast to his old school. At Chalmette High School in nearby St. Bernard Parish, he was one of only a small number of black students. Adjacent to New Orleans, St. Bernard's population swelled in the 1960s and '70s as working and middle-class white families fled the newly integrated schools of the city. Katrina's eye devastated the eastern part of St. Bernard, and the subsequent flooding left more than five feet of standing water in nearly every building in the parish. Cornelle's family did not have the money to rebuild, so they resettled on New Orleans' West Bank, not far from Walker.

Dozens of students, missing their old schools, shared Cornelle's initial mistrust. It didn't help that a school shooting in March of 2005, witnessed by Cornelle's older sister, defined public perception of Walker in the months leading up to Katrina. Cornelle could not imagine himself ever wanting to wear Walker's orange-and-khaki uniform. In his eyes, the school uniforms many of the city kids wore seemed to be preparing them for lives spent in prison or low-class jobs. He viewed Walker as too ghetto for his style and ambitions.

Despite his determination to hate everything about Walker, however, Cornelle found himself starting to warm to Ms. Laurie the longer she talked, apologizing for the failures of the New Orleans public schools.

"I am sorry," Laurie said. The students were stunned to hear an adult—an authority figure at that—apologizing to them. "I am sorry we didn't get this right for you all before. I am sorry we haven't gotten it right yet. We are the adults in this city and I commit that we are going to get this thing called education right for you. We are going to be here for you, but you need to be here for yourself. We might seem hard and strict at times, but we are doing it because you all deserve the best."

They might have doubted her capacity for strictness that morning, but not for long. Her round face, probing eyes, and circular glasses gave her the appearance of an owl. She had the sharp eyes of one, too. Ms. Laurie walked and spoke softly most of the time. But that only meant you didn't see her coming. And when Ms. Laurie came down on you, she came down hard.

"We don't play here at Walker," Laurie drove the point home. "But we are doing it because we love you. I love you."

Cornelle had never heard a teacher or principal open school with a declaration of love and personal responsibility. Like many of the students who stood in the courtyard, he had little reason to trust officials in a city where far more black men spent time in the correctional system than graduated from college.[5] He had no other options at the moment, however. So Cornelle took a little comfort from his gut instinct that when Ms. Laurie said "I love you," she meant it.

In the 1960s, Laurie's mother, Luerean Hunter, often looked over at her only daughter and declared: "You are going to be a teacher." Next she would turn to Mary Laurie's twin brother, Joseph, and proclaim: "And you are going to be a minister." Never mind that Laurie, who loved math, wanted to be a mathematician. If her mother decreed something, well, that was that. "That was her way of saying, 'You are going to go to college. You are going to be somebody.' Teachers were held in such high esteem," Laurie recalls. Luerean Hunter was determined to see her children rise to positions of respectability. After the birth of her four children in the Mississippi Delta, her path turned into a version of the American Dream where each step moved her children forward.

In 1954, the twenty-four-year-old mother left the Delta for better opportunities in New Orleans, where a sister had already settled. In the Delta everything seemed static. Babies were born, grew up, and died in the same spots as their grandparents, with little chance at a different life. Hunter brought three of her four children to New Orleans, including the two-year-old twins. She separated from her husband and raised the children as a single mother.

The grand department stores, bustling saloons, and colorful traditions of New Orleans contrasted with the simpler pleasures of Mississippi: moon pies and fresh cheese and porches full of familiar faces who called you cousin. In New Orleans, Hunter found work as a domestic. She settled in a neighborhood known as the Hoffman Triangle, located in the city's Central City region. Her three children attended segregated elementary and middle schools they could walk to in the neighborhood. As a young child, Mary Laurie never realized her family was poor. She had seen little of the world outside of the fifty or so blocks bordered by Claiborne and Washington avenues, Martin Luther King Jr. Boulevard, and Broad Street in the heart of New Orleans, or the hardscrabble lives of farmers in the Delta. Neither environment offered more than a fleeting glimpse at the lives of wealthy New Orleanians or whites. Besides, Laurie and her brothers never suffered from hunger or homelessness. Not even Hurricane Betsy in 1965 disrupted Laurie's sense of safety. The family stayed put in the second-floor apartment of the fourplex where they lived. As Laurie, in seventh grade at the time, crouched with her brother and mother in the bathroom, she listened to the wind rage and feared the walls might crash down around them. But the house still stood when the storm ended, albeit at a permanent tilt.

When Laurie and her brother started high school in the late 1960s, two major changes thrust them into far greater contact with the white world. First, her family moved into a newly integrated housing project called the Iberville, located in the Treme neighborhood not far from the French Quarter. The Iberville apartment, with its two stories and separate bedrooms, felt luxurious to Laurie. Second, the high schools desegregated. Laurie and her brother suddenly found themselves bound not for Booker T. Washington High School, where black students from their neighborhood historically attended, but Warren Easton, where they would be among the first black students at the school.

At Warren Easton, Laurie sometimes felt subtle and not-so-subtle discrimination from her white teachers and peers. The staff members did not nurture and encourage her in the way many teachers at her segregated elementary and middle schools had. She tried to join the female equivalent of the Key Club, convinced her grades and record met the criteria for admission. But the club's advisor rejected Laurie's application, never providing a real explanation; she simply said, "A lot of people apply and don't get chosen." Yet Laurie benefited from several strong teachers and credits her time at Warren Easton with proving she could compete successfully with students of different races and socioeconomic backgrounds. "I had the chance to be exposed to lots of different folk," she says. "And you never know that you can walk in any arena and be part of the conversation if you've never walked in those arenas and had those conversations."

Laurie's success helped give her the confidence to ignore the judgment cast her way when she became pregnant her junior year. The summer before her last year at Easton, she married the baby's father and transferred to a school for pregnant girls in the city's 9th Ward called Margaret Haughery. At the time, expectant teenage mothers weren't allowed to remain in traditional high schools. Laurie's young husband, Roy, dropped out of high school to support his wife and baby. But Laurie did not give up, drop out, or put her college plans on hold as many, including the guidance counselor at Warren Easton, expected. She gave birth to a baby boy in November and reenrolled at Warren Easton for her last semester of high school. That spring of 1971, Laurie graduated sixth in her class. She took comfort in the clear, irrefutable evidence of her success at Easton as defined by her grades, test scores, and class rank. Some might have viewed her as a poor black teen mother destined to a life of poverty. But the numbers did not discriminate.

Over the next decade, Laurie worked her way through college with the help of myriad social service programs that arose out of the civil rights and antipoverty movements of the 1960s. She gave birth to three more sons and separated from her husband, all the while studying for her degree in education at the University of New Orleans. Her start at college coincided with the debut of what is now known as the federal Pell

Grant program, which paid for most of her tuition. She started working at a community center called Kingsley House through a work-study program. The position very quickly became a full-time job that Laurie balanced with school and caring for her young sons. After a few years, she moved in with her mother, who helped out with child care. Kingsley, the first settlement house in the South, opened in 1896. By the 1970s it provided various programs for all ages, many of them financed through initiatives that grew out of President Lyndon Johnson's War on Poverty. Laurie worked with preschoolers in the Head Start classroom, a federal program aimed at getting low-income children an early exposure to school and health care. She liked the fact that Kingsley House attempted to address poverty across multiple dimensions: The center featured not only Head Start but after-school programs for teens, swimming classes for children in the housing projects, recreational opportunities for the elderly, and much more.

At long last Mary Laurie earned her education degree in 1986—her oldest children already teenagers. She took a job teaching sixth grade at Lusher Elementary School. Located Uptown, Lusher featured one of the city's most diverse student bodies. Poorer children from the neighborhood mingled with the sons and daughters of Tulane University professors. As middle-class and white families streamed out of the public schools, only Lusher and a couple of other programs retained them. The school's Uptown location and emphasis on the arts undoubtedly helped, but so did its selective admissions policies, which started in the 1990s and meant students who did not live in the attendance district had to test and meet other criteria to gain admission. That shut out weaker students who did not meet the at-times complicated entrance requirements, or disenfranchised families who did not even know to try. By the turn of the millennium, policies of exclusion tainted the success at the city's few high-performing, racially diverse schools. (Lusher, like many of the city's schools, was named after a decidedly unheroic historical figure. Robert Lusher, the state superintendent of schools in the late 1870s, was a "rabid Confederate and outspoken racist," according to *Crescent City Schools*, a history of public education in New Orleans from 1841 to 1991.)

Laurie fulfilled her mother's dream to see her daughter a teacher. But she didn't stop there. After five years, she left Lusher for a series of administrative positions in central office, including local director of safe and drug-free schools and leading a parent-involvement program known as HIPPY. In 1996 she applied for principal positions, having earned her master's degree in educational administration by taking night classes. The superintendent chose her for Guste Elementary, a school very demographically different from Lusher. While Lusher sat in one of the wealthier parts of the city, Guste was in the heart of Central City, an impoverished section of New Orleans with few middle-class families. Many of Lusher's families could afford private schools but chose to remain in the public system. Guste had no white or middle-class students. Its families usually had no other options.

The state introduced its new school accountability system in the late 1990s while Laurie led Guste. The new program mandated high-stakes standardized testing in the public schools with the results published annually for the world to see. When Laurie and the Guste staff received the school's pilot scores in 1999 they were devastated. In the fourth grade, only 18 percent of the students passed the new state language-arts test and only 13 percent passed in math. The staff came together and pledged, "'We will *not* be defined like this, we will *not* be defined as a school that's not achieving,'" Laurie said, banging her hand on her desk at the memory. Testing mandates exploded across the country a few years later under No Child Left Behind. The increased testing divided educators and the public: Many considered it crucial for identifying the abysmal quality of some schools, particularly those serving poor children; others argued it stripped the curriculum of breadth and stigmatized teachers working in the toughest schools, as well as children who could not pass.

Laurie had mixed feelings about testing mandates. She thought students, parents, and teachers deserved to know if children weren't learning at acceptable levels. She even appreciated the much-mocked slogan "No Child Left Behind": She agreed schools should not tolerate a single student failing a test of basic skills.

Laurie liked to repeat a favorite saying of Barbara Woods, a veteran Guste teacher the young principal looked to as a mentor. Woods often said: "Black people taught me to read."

"She came up during segregation, but in the midst of all that, she was taught," Laurie said. "How dare anybody in this time say you can't teach children? How dare you say they can't learn? How dare you say we can't teach them? In the face of all those obstacles [during segregation], the biggest obstacles, children were taught."

But when school principals like Laurie saw the annual rankings of schools by test score in the newspaper, they couldn't help but consider it unfair. Inevitably, Lusher would rank near the top and schools like Guste near the bottom. Many Lusher students had to score well on a test just to get in; they would pass the state tests regardless. Many Guste students, on the other hand, came in years behind, and some struggled to pass with the help of even the very best teachers.

Laurie felt the students at Guste deserved what had come to be known as "the Lusher Way" as much as their more privileged peers uptown. She introduced much of what she had learned at Lusher at Guste, and then again during her second principalship at Woodson Middle School in Central City, for which Guste served as the feeder. From Lusher she brought the morning gathering tradition, an emphasis on the arts, and a focus on collaborative decision making among staff. From her own experience she brought the belief that "school reform" is a series of small changes that add up, not a single, sweeping about-face. "Everybody in education is looking for the big answer," Laurie said. "But big answers come from little answers."[6]

In keeping with that philosophy, Laurie put herb gardens and a rabbit pen in the courtyard at Woodson, once the site of a nationally publicized shooting. She extended the school day and added after-school and weekend tutoring and mentoring. She tied back the doors to the classroom buildings, letting in the light so students would not feel as if they were learning in a dark dungeon. She partnered with local nonprofits and city agencies to bring in dental care, eye screenings, part-time social workers, mentors, and extra art classes.

During Laurie's years at Woodson and Guste, the public and politicians increasingly blamed teachers for the failings of urban schools. They devised policies calling for the replacement of most or even all of the teachers at the most low-performing schools. And they began clamoring for changes to teachers' union contracts that would make it easier to fire bad or ineffective teachers. Laurie took a different approach, keeping teaching staffs largely intact but working to support them better. "Prior to Ms. Laurie, no one ever listened to us," said Sybil Pierce, a veteran Woodson teacher. "They just came in, carved out their space, and started issuing orders. She treated us more like human beings than anyone ever has. We got together in the school's library and she asked, 'What do you need?'"

By the time Laurie left Guste in 2000 and Woodson five years later, test scores had risen significantly, even though they still fell short of the state's minimum standards. At Woodson, the school rose from a dismal 15.8 on a 200-point ranking system in 2001 to 46 in 2004. The media and school district hailed Woodson as one of the Orleans Parish Schools' greatest success stories: a sign of Laurie's achievements but also the tragic underperformance of the system, since a 46 remained so low.

Just as important as the test scores, Laurie turned both Guste and Woodson into safe, welcoming spaces in one of the city's most downtrodden neighborhoods. Before Laurie arrived at Woodson, the school traveled for all of its athletic games because the district did not believe students would be safe playing near the school, located across the street from the Magnolia Projects. People were terrified of visiting nearby A. L. Davis Park, site of Woodson's athletic fields. But Laurie told one of the district's athletic directors, Tarence Davis, "I want some home games." Davis acquiesced. The school grilled hot dogs, and residents from the projects set up folding chairs to watch. Over time the students ventured out into the community and the community ventured into the school.

Laurie grew into a neighborhood fixture known for her gentle demeanor and unique fashion sense. She would show up to school wearing accessories like a tiger-striped hat in a beehive shape, the stripes a nod to the school's mascot. One school volunteer lovingly described her fashion sense as "ghetto nerdy."

When public schools in New Orleans opened in mid-August 2005, Laurie was starting her fifth year at the helm of Woodson. Ever restless, she planned to expand Woodson into the high school grades within a year. The opening days of school were hectic ones filled with last-minute enrollees, staff changes, and scheduling glitches. So when Laurie heard on Friday, August 26, about a late-summer hurricane bearing down on the Gulf Coast, she hoped school would be canceled for at least a day or two to give her time to finish the master schedule and complete some paperwork. She spent the Saturday before the storm at Woodson, moving computers and covering equipment, making no plans to leave town herself.

Hunkered down at her home on the West Bank the next week with her mother, Laurie saw only a few downed trees in her neighborhood. Only by watching a battery operated television did she learn of the horrors unfolding just a few miles away across the Mississippi River. Laurie left town more than two days after most of the East Bank flooded, driving to Houston with her mother, an adult son, and other relatives. She left her husband, a police officer, behind in the city where he worked on flood rescue and recovery.

In Houston, Laurie lived in a residential hotel her husband's relatives found. Strangers offered words of support and opened their wallets. The diner across the street from the hotel gave her a discount. Sympathetic Texans regularly offered to buy her gas. Their compassion did not blunt the pain of the news from New Orleans in the coming weeks, however.

Laurie cannot remember where, or exactly how, she learned that she—and about seventy-five hundred other school district employees— had been placed on unpaid leave. At the time, New Orleans had one of the highest percentages of black teachers of any urban school district in the country, at about 75 percent.[7]

Sometimes Laurie thinks the news of the employees' dismissal might have come in a form e-mail, brief and tersely worded. Other times she recalls seeing a news conference on television, one that left her with the feeling the old public school employees were not welcome back in their hometown. What she remembers most of all is the action was "not kindly done." It felt to her as if the teachers became scapegoats for the schools' failings. While Laurie knew there were teachers who should not have been in the classroom, she believed the majority of New Orleans educators worked hard every day to serve the city's children.

"One day you had a job and the next day you had no job," she said. "Even Walmart was saying, 'Just go to your nearest Walmart. You are going to have a job.' We had nothing. Everybody got lumped into this barrel of horrible folk. So many people's hearts were broken."

That fall, Laurie also learned that the vast majority of public schools in the city would not reopen for at least a year—if they were to reopen at all. Guste and Woodson, the schools she had worked to revitalize for years, would likely cease to exist. The approach to school change in New Orleans might never again resemble her own incremental, organic style. It would feature radical, abrupt change and a complete departure from the past, not a collage of modest answers that added up to something bigger.

The first public schools in New Orleans opened in the 1840s after local leaders solicited the advice of Horace Mann, the Massachusetts educator and politician who advocated for universal education throughout the country. Many of the fledgling system's teachers were imported from the Northeast, and tensions over outsider educators quashing local culture have surfaced intermittently since then. Louisiana officials were so dead set against the state's black populace receiving an education that they made it a crime to teach slaves how to read and barred blacks—both free and enslaved—from attending the initial public schools that opened in New Orleans.

Yet by the end of the Civil War, nearly 40 percent of the adult black population in New Orleans was literate. An unknown (and probably small) number of light-skinned black children managed to "pass" as white and attend public schools. More significantly, the free black community, and later the Catholic church, sponsored private programs for African-American students during the first half of the nineteenth century. At first the classes were held in homes under a shroud of secrecy. But as the Catholic church's involvement increased, the broader community became more aware of the schools. In 1837, a free African woman named Marie Couvent left a bequest with the Catholic church to open a school for the children of black artisans, which finally opened in the late 1840s. Since the Couvent school also received a few public grants, it is considered the first example of a government-subsidized school for blacks in the South.

For a brief period after the Civil War, New Orleans became a national model for school desegregation, with several short-lived integrated schools. In the mid-1870s the political winds changed, however, ushering in a return to segregation and decades of underfunding of both white and black schools, which in turn led to a deterioration in quality across the system. The black schools suffered far more, particularly when school officials decided in 1900 to limit public education for African-Americans to grades one through five. By 1910, the city had sixty-eight schools for white students and only sixteen for black students, all of which were elementary schools.

Over the next four decades, black community leaders and activists fought battle after battle: for their first public high school, for evening programs to accommodate working students, for equitable salaries for black teachers, and for adequate school facilities. Each time a new school opened for black children, it prompted a backlash from whites. The authors of *Crescent City Schools* wrote of that period: "If the unusual persistence of its black leaders, which was a legacy left by the city's large and assertive antebellum free black population, set New Orleans apart from most other cities, so did the frequency and high degree of violence of white protest that surrounded the building of virtually every new black school. The violence was, in part, a reaction to the very persistence that characterized New Orleans' black leadership: exceptional black assertiveness engendered exceptionally strong white resistance."

The black community won several individual fights. But by the time *Brown v. Board* reached the U.S. Supreme Court in the early 1950s, New Orleans had eighty-seven schools for whites and thirty-four for blacks, even though as many black students attended public schools as whites. The first desegregation efforts in New Orleans were voluntary and extremely limited. More than one hundred black families applied to send their children to all-white schools, and ultimately four young black girls were selected to integrate William Frantz and McDonogh 19 schools on November 14, 1960. Despite the presence of federal marshals, mobs of angry white adults chanted, "Two, four, six, eight, we don't want to integrate!" at the schoolhouse doors.

The city witnessed one of the most rapid, wholesale instances of white flight in the nation's history. Frantz and McDonogh 19 enrolled about one thousand students in 1959. But within a few hours of the young black girls arriving that morning, all the white students at McDonogh 19 decamped for other schools, leaving just the black youngsters. At Frantz, only two white girls remained by the end of the first week. They were taught in a separate classroom from the school's lone black enrollee, Ruby Bridges. Six-year-old Ruby studied with one teacher in total isolation from other children for the entire year; she had no idea at the time whether other students even attended Frantz. Anti-integrationists so harassed the two white families who kept their children there that the families had to take shelter with friends, and move often, to avoid attacks. Hotels refused to admit them.

Despite that inauspicious beginning, desegregation continued steadily over the next decade. Teaching staffs followed, sped along by the merger of the white and black teachers' unions in 1972. By 1980, tens of thousands of white families had abandoned the city's public schools for suburban or private options. A public system that had enrolled equal numbers of black and white students at the advent of *Brown v. Board* now enrolled five times more black children. Over the next quarter century, right up until Katrina, the elected school board ran one of the most racially segregated urban school systems in the country. By 2004, 94 percent of the city's public schoolchildren were black, and just 3 percent were white. At 114 of the city's 129 public schools, more than 90 percent of the student population was black. Sixty-five schools, just over half, had no racial diversity whatsoever.

The schools' failures have become infamous locally and nationally, although the causes remain under dispute: Some blame forces outside of the system's control, like underfunding, racism, and poverty; others fault systemic problems, including school board corruption, institutional lethargy, and incompetence. Most everyone agreed something needed to change. They disagreed as to what and how.

The "recovery" in Recovery School District alludes to academic failure, not Katrina. The state created the district two years before the flood as a vehicle for turning around low-performing schools across Louisiana by chartering them or putting them under direct state supervision. The legislation creating the RSD in 2003 had to be approved both by state lawmakers and in a public vote, since it required a constitutional amendment. The move garnered statewide political support partly because many Louisiana citizens and politicians viewed the RSD as a barely disguised attempt to take over the reviled Orleans Parish school system—not as a threat to local control throughout the state.

The Orleans Parish schools burned through two regular and six interim superintendents between 1998 and 2005, many of whom complained they were micromanaged by a fractious local school board. The system suffered from countless accounting problems in addition to outright fraud. The district did not produce an accurate financial statement in the five years before Katrina. An FBI task force investigation into school district finances in 2004 led to the convictions of more than two dozen school district employees and vendors—for everything from payroll fraud to bribery and embezzlement.[8] In the months before Katrina, the city's public school system was declared effectively bankrupt. A private accounting company took over its finances.

Despite chaos at the top, the system made significant academic gains in the years before Katrina. But by the time the storm struck, a majority of the schools were still considered failing. The Recovery School District had absorbed only five of the city's more than one hundred schools since its creation, turning each over to a charter operator. In the wake of Katrina, a small, powerful group of state officials decided they needed to take more drastic action.

The coup would be led by two key players: state schools superintendent Cecil Picard and Leslie Jacobs, a member of the state board of secondary and elementary education. Picard, an unassuming but cunning Cajun politician, was dying from Lou Gehrig's disease when Katrina hit.

He resolved to focus on the New Orleans takeover until he could no longer speak or walk.

At first glance, Jacobs appeared to be an unlikely crusader for public education reform. A brusque insurance mogul, she lived in a mansion on St. Charles Avenue, the city's grandest tree-lined boulevard. But she had long been deeply invested in changing the city's education system. During her tenure on the Orleans Parish School Board during the 1990s, she had grown convinced the traditional education structure prized compliance over performance. She left the local board for a position on the state board, where she designed Louisiana's accountability and high-stakes testing system.

Driven by frustration with the Orleans Parish School Board, the two officials helped orchestrate a plan for the state to take over nearly all of the city's schools in Katrina's wake.

In November 2005, the state legislature approved a measure that did just that: It allowed the RSD to absorb any public school in New Orleans whose performance fell below the state average—not just schools beneath the "failing" threshold. The action shifted 114 New Orleans schools out of the hands of the Orleans Parish School Board and into the RSD. Only seventeen schools remained under the auspices of the elected local board, several of which converted to charters to gain more autonomy. The result is a bifurcated system in which both the RSD and Orleans Parish School Board run schools directly and oversee charters. But the RSD, composed mostly of charters, dwarfs the old board-administered system.

In December 2005, the Orleans Parish School Board voted to lay off its employees. The motivations for the firing would be hotly disputed in a lawsuit that dragged on for years. "It was a pragmatic choice," said Jimmy Fahrenholtz, a board member at the time. "We had no schools, no kids, and no money coming in." But the timing convinced many people the state had essentially forced the board's hand with the intention of installing a very different kind of school system in the coming years: one dominated by charters who employed nonunionized teachers. Although the Orleans Parish School Board technically fired the employees, it did so just days after the state seized control over the schools. "They took not only our buildings, but our ability to employ," said Torin Sanders, board president. He maintains the state takeover was the real reason for the mass firing.[9]

Over time, the state takeover and subsequent employee firing allowed for not only a rapid growth in charter schools but the importation of a new group of teachers, principals, and education leaders. Control of the city's schools passed from a predominantly black political class to a largely affluent and white corporate elite.

Mary Laurie does not belong among the city's new school reformers. She connects with her students without having to try too hard. She has lived their lives, growing up poor and black in one of America's poorest, most racially unequal cities, with an absentee father and a strong mother working tirelessly to keep the family afloat. She knows, like many of her female students, the challenges of caring for a baby while finishing your own education. She recognizes the same neighborhoods and faces they do. And she understands the torture of watching your hometown nearly drown.

Yet Laurie does not entirely belong among her students either. She came of age during the civil rights era, a time when the struggle for black rights empowered and inspired young people in a unique way. She moved into the projects before they became "the projects," synonymous with crushing poverty. For her, moving to the Iberville felt like a step up. She learned as a teenager that she could hold her own among all walks of people while most of her students, in their de facto segregated schools and neighborhoods, never get that chance. Moreover, she raised her babies and earned her college degree with an array of new government programs providing support, before teen mothers and welfare recipients became the subject of so much scorn in some circles, before the term "welfare queen" spread throughout the lexicon.

Poverty had a gentler face when Laurie came up. Neighborhoods might have been segregated by race, but they were more integrated by class. Poor blacks did not live in intense isolation from the rest of society. And blacks of all social classes were united in a fight for their equal rights as American citizens. Laurie's early obliviousness to her own poverty, to her own "station," was, in some respects, a source of strength. The perceptions of others and of society at large did not limit her imagination or lower her expectations. Many of her students are not so lucky. They grow up hyperaware of their alienation from mainstream America, including the black middle class. Stereotypes do not surprise them—but defying them does. For even in the most democratic societies, the idea of caste can wield a destructive power, one that invades the mind, and then destroys it.[10]

A month after Katrina, Laurie jumped immediately at the chance to run Walker. "I didn't even lose a breath before I said yes."

Laurie was one of fewer than a dozen public school principals with an immediate job prospect in her hometown, her pre-Katrina reputation having put her at the top of everyone's list. Walker marked a continuation of the career trajectory Laurie had started thirty years before, moving from an early childhood center to an elementary school to the middle level and, now, to a high school. She had always been curious about what happened to her students when they left her, what caused some of them to founder and fail. Now she would have more of an answer. It would haunt her for years to come, however, that of so many fired school employees, she was one of only a small number invited to keep a job.

Early in the fall, Laurie thought the Orleans Parish School Board would run Walker and the other four schools to open in Algiers. But no sooner had Laurie expressed interest in the job than the school board voted to reopen Algiers schools under the umbrella of the Algiers Charter Schools Association, partly so the schools could access millions in federal start-up dollars for charters. Laurie and Coach Gibson, the assistant principal, went online to find out everything they could about charters.

Although Walker, like most of the city's schools, became a charter after Katrina, it was not typical of the new charters founded by transplants to the city. It employed many veteran educators who had worked in the schools before the flood. And the Algiers Charter Schools Association functioned more like a traditional school district, with the chief executive officer playing the role of superintendent. Algiers once housed a thriving shipping industry and an active naval base. But by the time Katrina hit, the mostly residential neighborhood had a sleepier feel than other parts of the city. Ferries shuttle back and forth across the Mississippi River every thirty minutes, connecting New Orleans' east and west banks.

Unlike some who saw charter schools as a way of blowing up the old bureaucracy and diminishing the power of teachers' unions, Laurie did not much care whether she led a charter school or a traditional one. Sometimes she wished city leaders had dreamed even bigger and tried to address the conditions most of her students lived in outside of the classroom, or thought about ways to encourage more school integration.

In interviews with teacher applicants at Walker, Laurie grilled them to make sure they were ready for more work, higher expectations, and a changed Walker. Math teacher Nolan Grady was one of a few pre-Katrina Walker teachers hired back. Grady had taught at Walker for thirty-three years, starting there when the school was more than 95 percent white. The desegregation of teaching staffs began in 1966. But it did not take place at a significant degree until the early 1970s, when the school board made it more of a priority. In the fall of 1972, the central office sent a young Grady over to Walker to fill a teaching vacancy coded "black." When he arrived, however, the principal made it clear he had already met his quota of black teachers. So it wasn't until a black teacher left in the middle of the school year that Grady started at Walker. He watched over the next three decades as Walker's white students departed for magnet, suburban, and private schools.

About two months after Katrina, Grady, exiled in Dallas, heard Walker would be one of the first public schools to reopen. So he packed up his belongings and headed back to New Orleans along with his mother, hoping to secure his old job. Arriving in New Orleans, he learned the board had voted to convert Walker to a charter while he was en route. To make matters worse, it quickly became clear that the FEMA money to rebuild his house would be long in coming. He worried about supporting his mother with no income and no place to live. He pursued a job at Walker with all his heart. He took the new basic-skills test required of all teachers applying for openings at the Algiers charter schools (a similar test would later be used by the RSD). The exam included several math problems written at the sixth-grade level; applicants also had to write a paragraph. After the mass teacher dismissal, the test seemed to add insult to injury.

A friend asked him, "You have over thirty years of experience. Why are you going through this rigmarole?"

"But God worked it out," Grady said.

He passed with no problems. About 20 percent of his colleagues did not.[11] Their applications went in red folders in the human resources office, most of which would never be picked up again.

Grady recalls meeting Laurie in her office at Walker one morning just weeks before the school reopened. Laurie wasted little time on small talk or introductions.

"Grady, will you come along with me on this journey?"

"Journey?" he asked.

"We want to bring Walker back to its glory days," Laurie explained. "It's going to take hard work and people who are committed to the cause. The children have been done a disservice. Would you come along with me on this journey? Are you willing to put in hard work after thirty years? It's going to be bumpy."

"I'm going to put on my armor."

Grady smiles when he remembers that first meeting.

"Lord," he says, shaking his head. "I've been bumping ever since."

The media flocked to Walker that December morning in 2005, since it was one of the first schools to reopen after Katrina. For weeks Laurie's staff could not keep the different outlets straight as national television networks, National Public Radio, PBS, and the New Orleans *Times-Picayune* all descended on the school to report stories. With each passing year and hurricane anniversary, however, they started to notice the media increasingly went elsewhere: to organizations who boldly pronounced their break with the "old way" of running schools through names like New Schools for New Orleans, New Leaders for New Schools, the New Teacher Project, and ReNEW Schools. To schools and nonprofits whose supporters included some of the wealthiest men in the world: Bill Gates, Eli Broad, and the children of Walmart founder Sam Walton. Suddenly all sorts of powerful white folk seemed to care an awful lot about the education of poor black children in New Orleans.

The small band of homegrown charters on the city's West Bank, part of a shrinking minority of schools led by veteran New Orleans educators, seemed forgotten.

As the 2010–2011 school year began, journalists from throughout the world came to New Orleans to file stories commemorating the fifth anniversary of Katrina. They reported on the enduring devastation of the Lower 9th Ward, post-storm divorces, and the oil seeping through the Gulf waters. Searching for bright spots, several focused on the rebirth of the city's schools, sometimes offering up simplistic accounts of how charter schools had revitalized the New Orleans education landscape. But no one visited Walker.

It wasn't that Laurie craved newspaper articles or television segments. She craved what they seemed to bring and represent: Respect. Prestige. A future. "We've done what everybody said we should do, which is taking every kid, and they went every direction but here," Laurie said. "Five years later, and we are still fighting this perception of what was. We are still fighting the same fight about Walker's right to exist."

The school stood on a precipice, one where the line of danger kept encroaching inward. In 2010 Walker rose out of the academic failure zone for the first time since Katrina. But that same year, state officials voted to raise the standards. Once again, the school needed to achieve significant gains in a short time span or face closure. After considerable hustle and with a new eye to marketing, Walker drew about nine hundred students when school reopened on August 10, one of the largest student bodies in the city. But that same week, L. B. Landry High School reopened in a glistening $54 million new building just over a mile from Walker's campus. Walker's classrooms were alternately freezing cold or uncomfortably warm. Some of its ceiling tiles were missing. And the auditorium remained shuttered since the state had not yet allocated the money for repairs. Walker staff members quietly wondered whether families would remain loyal when their children could attend school in more lavish surroundings down the street. "I feel like they are trying to shut Walker down in a funny sort of way," Grady mused one afternoon.

For Laurie, Walker's survival meant more than a job or a stepping-stone to a better one. Approaching her late fifties now, she had entered the twilight of a long career. For her, the school's success would show that you could educate the city's students without turning into an explicit or de facto magnet school, where the strong results depended at least in part on the exclusion of less privileged students. Success at Walker would show that a charter school could thrive without the benefit of big money or national media attention. It would prove that classrooms full of poor students could learn without being, as Laurie put it, "lock-stepped" in the style that seemed to prevail at many of the city's new charter schools: told at all times when to move their lips, how to walk, whom to sit with at lunch, where to put their bodies, their hands, their eyes.

She worried, though, about Walker's competitive edge in an education landscape—in an America—where the rules had changed: where the language of the marketplace had invaded the public sphere; where institutional knowledge and history increasingly felt more like a liability than a blessing; where self-promotion and image meant more than ever; where some education leaders quietly wished they could have buried all of the city schools' past—not just nearly all of it—in the flood's wake.

Laurie cared about results. She wanted Walker's kids to go on to college and succeed there. But she could not, at a moment's notice, rattle off each of Walker's data points. She could, however, look at any number of her students and tell you about their mama or their auntie and the block they went home to at night. She could tell you about the one who started smoking pot to dull the pain after a brother's shooting. Or the one who kept skipping school because he had to watch two babies for his mother, who worked a double shift at Walmart and had graduated from Walker herself in the early 1990s. Laurie could tell you about the people who vouched for Walker's children, and the ones they had lost. She spoke in stories. And while some educators touted how far each student climbed on the step test, the iLeap test, or the ACT, Laurie told other tales.

"There are so many stories," she said one afternoon, sitting on a bench under Walker's breezeway. "I worry that they will get lost, that there's no one to tell them. My big fear is that all folks will remember is that when Katrina hit, people had to ride in on their white horses and save the children of New Orleans." She shuddered at the thought.

PART III

High Hopes

(Summer/Fall 2010)

THE TEACHER
"A broken window means a broken path to college."

Aidan's Sci Academy teaching career began with a ten-minute lesson on school bathroom policy. He rehearsed it several times, his fellow teachers pretending to be students. Over and over again he instructed them on how to fill out the bathroom log reporting the time they left class, showed them the campus signs that pointed to the bathroom, and physically took them to the site, where he provided a succinct overview on bathroom etiquette. By the time Sci Academy's new students arrived on August 9, Aidan and the other teachers had planned and rehearsed for every possible contingency, including students talking back, asking tough questions, stepping out of line, or disrupting the lesson. When the school year started in earnest, Aidan would teach three sophomore writing classes and a rhetoric course for juniors. But for one day at least, he was all about the bathroom.

Only freshmen came for the entire first week, which Sci devoted to outlining the school's rules and values. In the mornings, teachers rode on each of the buses to ensure that students were not messy or rude. They considered bus misbehavior "a big broken window" at the school. (The broken-windows theory posits that small signs of disorder can trigger much more serious criminal activity. Schools like Sci have embraced the theory and believe they must crack down on seemingly small issues

Ben Marcovitz, the principal and founder of Sci Academy, greets students as they arrive at the school's campus in eastern New Orleans. Photo by John McCusker/New Orleans Times-Picayune.

like dress-code violations or rowdiness on the bus to help prevent more serious infractions.) Ben Marcovitz, the school's principal, greeted each bus and sent the students off for their uniform checks; then they proceeded on down the straight line, marked by tape, to breakfast and assembly.

At the school-wide assembly, Marcovitz informed the students that henceforth they would be known as scholars. "This is a serious place," he told them. "We call you *scholar*, which means you are not only someone who comes here to learn, but someone who lives their life to learn." Over the course of the day, teachers taught mini-classes not only in bathroom protocol and the meaning of SPARK or SPARKing, but how to greet someone (shaking hands firmly while looking the other person in the eye), voice volumes considered appropriate at the school (level 0 = silence, level 1 = whisper, level 2 = quiet talk, level 3 = scholarly voice), and the importance of saying thank you (it shows respect and enthusiasm). A voice from the hallway signaled when teachers had one minute left in each of the ten-minute classes, which concluded with a cry of "Rotate!"

Teachers who were new to the school, like Aidan, taught the classes while the returning ones hovered in the background for support like a coterie of more seasoned consultants. To show solidarity, many of the teachers wore the freshmen uniform of polo shirt, khaki pants, belt, and black shoes. A few students protested with sullen glances or disobedient gestures. (One year, a student declared, "I'm not doing this," turned around, and left. A staff member followed him home and tried to convince him to return—without success.) But for the most part, the students were stunned into a quiet submission.

Several felt intimidated by the onslaught of rules. Particularly in Sci's first years, most of its incoming students and families had little idea what to expect. They chose the school because they saw one of its promotional signs or happened to meet the principal. Some even thought they were enrolling for the similarly named Sci High in Uptown New Orleans, and didn't realize the mix-up until after school started. "When you are coming out of junior high school, you are expecting a change," said Marquisha Williams, recalling her first day in the fall of 2008. "This was a different kind of change. It was like an academic boot camp where they said, 'These are the rules. They are not changing. Follow them.'" Her classmate Je'on Domingue added that it "really freaked me out that all the teachers knew our names on the first day. I didn't like all the rules and the fact that we always had to SPARK." Even worse to Je'on was NO-DAH, another acronym introduced to the students her freshman year. It stood for "no desk, arm, or hand," as in: Do not rest your head on your desk, arm, or hand during class. Je'on liked to cup her head in her palm when concentrating.

During Sci's opening week, the freshmen came just for half days and Aidan spent part of his afternoons calling parents of his advisees to introduce himself. Each Sci Academy teacher is assigned a group of ten to fifteen students to mentor and serve as liaison between family and school; in Aidan's case, his advisory consisted of freshmen boys. The advisories take the name of their teacher's college. Aidan's stutter was worst in unfamiliar situations and during telephone conversations with strangers. But after cold-calling his advisees' parents over and over again, his fear gradually dissipated and, once again, he sensed his stutter would not be the source of his biggest challenges. The school waited until the third day to explain the advisory concept to freshmen, which meant students were baffled during the first two days when their teachers referred to groups of them collectively as "Harvard" or "Chicago."

In Aidan's eyes, almost everything that opening week seemed flawless: lessons neatly delivered, transitions smooth, lines straight. At the end of each day the teachers gathered together in a circle where they praised each other for such accomplishments as noticing a uniform violation, which, in the words of one Sci teacher, "means a broken window which means a broken path to college." Aidan, who was starting his third year of teaching, was blown away by the precision. At Martyn, his old school, the teachers showed up just a few days before the students and were left to plan the school year on their own. In his view, one of the main purposes of Sci's freshman orientation was to introduce the school's "common language" and the idea of "scholar talk." The students are told, for instance, that scholars never give single-word answers and should always respond in complete sentences. The week ends with a trip to Tulane University, where the students are supposed to practice their newly acquired scholar language and habits in a different setting and receive firsthand exposure to the school's ultimate goal of college admission and success. Everything about the week seemed to align with Aidan's own philosophy, including his faith in higher education, his moral absolutism, and his fidelity, strengthened by his Jesuit education, to the idea that there is "one right way to live."

Some people think "freedom comes from not having to do anything," Aidan says. But the "only true freedom is complete obedience. It's when you submit to a code." In this case, the Sci Academy code.

Sci Academy is a technocrat's dream: run by graduates of the nation's most elite institutions, steeped in data, always seeking precision, divorced from the messiness—and checks and balances—of democracy. Sci is located in eastern New Orleans, a large, suburban-feeling section of the city unknown to most tourists. In the decades before Katrina, the East, as it's known, increasingly became home to the city's upwardly mobile black population, including many of its teachers. The thriving neighborhood came to symbolize the capacity of the teaching profession to lift families from the working poor to the middle class.

Five years after Katrina, eastern New Orleans still felt like a ghost town in parts. The area lacked many basic services for years after the flood; the hospital there never reopened, and very few food markets, coffee shops, or other businesses returned. Visitors to the school could easily miss Sci: It's located off a bumpy driveway amid a cluster of indistinguishable modular buildings, some of which house another school.

An appointed board of directors runs Sci but gives the principal considerable latitude. School leaders at New Orleans charters often make hiring decisions, set pay, decide what courses will be taught (within the confines of state requirements), fire employees they feel aren't doing their jobs, determine how the school's budget will be spent, organize student recruitment, and set the school's calendar and schedule. Under the centralized system that existed before Katrina, good principals sometimes felt stifled by an overabundance of bureaucracy. At the charter schools, principals find comparatively little bureaucracy to tangle with and exert unprecedented power, for good or for bad. In Marcovitz's case, most of the school's teachers consider it for good.[1]

Marcovitz considers hiring teachers the most important decision he makes. During the initial phone interview he stresses the potential drawbacks and frustrations of working at Sci to avoid attracting teachers who will be miserable at the school. He tells applicants, "We don't believe in long hours, but we believe in getting the job done," which for many first-year teachers takes eighty hours a week. He describes to them the emphasis on "constant flexibility." In practice that might mean that, if on a Friday students score lower than expected on an important practice test for a state exam, on Sunday the entire staff gathers for dinner and upends the schedule. And on Monday the instructors find themselves teaching different classes. Aidan experienced that flexibility as early as the end of the first week of school, when teachers had to pack up and move to a new campus. At both campuses the classes were taught in modular units constructed by the Recovery School District. Marcovitz says he prefers the modulars in some respects because they are so "fungible" and serve the school's goal of flexibility. During his initial conversation with applicants, Marcovitz also informs them that standardized tests are not the be-all and end-all of Sci's mission, but the school takes them very seriously and values "data-driven instruction." If the teacher finds the idea of standardized tests repugnant, he says, Sci might not be a great fit. After that preliminary conversation, he tells applicants to follow up at least a day later if they are still interested. Only about one in three does.

As with Aidan, Marcovitz then observes each candidate twice, holds a group interview in which other teachers have a chance to ask questions, and then calls between three and five references for conversations that last for about an hour each. About half of the teachers Marcovitz observes in person ultimately get hired. A "philosophical convergence" and "growth capacity" matter more to Marcovitz than the quality of teaching during the first sample lesson. Each teacher receives an individual one-year contract and can be fired at any time. Under a collective bargaining agreement, teachers share the same contract, which often protects more senior teachers in the event of layoffs, sets standard salary levels based largely on experience, and makes it more difficult to fire teachers (*how* difficult is a major point of contention in the debate over unions).

During its second year, Sci offered collective teacher bonuses based on overall student performance, a practice Marcovitz decided to stop. He had read a book called *Drive: The Surprising Truth About What Motivates Us*, which he says underscores "the folly of giving bonuses for things people are motivated to do already." He assumed his teachers were already motivated to help Sci's students achieve academically. Partly for this reason, he decided to offer bonuses only for specific tasks connected to Sci's "core mission" that teachers might consider drudge work. Starting in 2010, Sci awarded teachers bonuses if their advisees' average daily attendance stayed at 95 percent, if they talked with each of their advisees' parents once every two weeks (including holidays), if they got report cards out in person to parents, if their advisees showed up for detention, and if they submitted 100 percent of their lesson plans on time for review. Teachers receive $100 per quarter for each target met. In 2011, the school added more bonus opportunities, including whether teachers record on a Google spreadsheet their "daily goal mastery" (the percent of students who mastered the stated objective for each lesson).

Marcovitz often compares his vision of teaching to the medical profession. He bristles when asked about the sustainability of Sci's model given the inevitability that some, if not most, of its staff will someday want to work fewer hours and start their own families. "People need to see the high stakes of the teaching profession," he says, noting that few raise a hue and cry about medical residents putting in eighty-hour weeks. Although many of his teachers are alums of Teach For America's five-week training regimen, he fantasizes about a day when teachers are selected and trained much like doctors. He compares the state of traditional teacher training today to medical training more than a century ago, when professional standards fell all over the map and peers sometimes approved new doctors based on popularity, not merit.

In 1910 Abraham Flexner skewered American medical schools in a lengthy report commissioned by the Carnegie Foundation (Marcovitz handed a printout of the 330-page document to a visitor when asked about it). The report concluded that there were too many medical schools, most of which offered substandard training. Flexner wrote, "The organization of medical education in this country has hitherto been such as not only to commercialize the process of education itself, but also to obscure in the minds of the public any discrimination between the well trained physician and the physician who had had no adequate training whatsoever." The report singled out Johns Hopkins's medical school as an exemplar and instigated a series of changes that led to the standardization and strengthening of medical schools along the lines of Johns Hopkins. "I know my organization can't be the Flexner report and change all medical schools," says Marcovitz. "But I'd like to be like Johns Hopkins. If teachers were treated like doctors in society, imagine what an amazing thing that would be. People would brag about having a teacher for a spouse." That increased stature alone would keep many of his teachers in the profession for the long term even if their pay did not rise significantly, Marcovitz maintains.

"I want to be a place that's already thinking about the best way to do it, so when they do elevate [teaching] to the social pedestal it should be on, places can look to institutions like ours," he says.

It's tough to argue with Marcovitz's insistence on the vital importance of attracting high-caliber college students to teaching and improving their training. That said, the country needs about four times as many teachers as doctors, and educators' modest compensation levels are already under attack from some politicians. Studies show most teachers do not rate pay as high as other factors in determining a good work environment. But it's hard to imagine many doctors would endure the rigors of residency without the prospect of fewer hours and significantly better pay in the not-too-distant future—a payoff that does not exist for those who want to teach in intense urban schools in the long term.[2]

Marcovitz does not hire many first-year teachers, preferring those who, like Aidan, have at least two years' experience. But he is part of a movement whose hiring and training practices are, in some respects, just as antithetical to medicine's as those of traditional education schools. Medical schools, residency programs, hospitals, and clinics do not accept or hire people based on their growth mind-set or whether they are mission aligned; they hire those who bring a certain aptitude and proven record. And young doctors in training practice in actual laboratories on cadavers for years before they are left alone with real, live human patients. They do not practice in figurative laboratories with the nation's most vulnerable children as their test subjects.

Marcovitz acknowledges that Teach For America has not developed into an extensive training program of the caliber of a top medical school. But he argues TFA has helped push teacher recruitment and preparation in the right direction, citing the organization's focus on using data to drive practice, its emphasis on recruiting quick learners, and its efforts to raise the social cachet of teaching.

For the time being, the contemporary education reform movement's notion of teacher quality appears to rest on two principles: First, the teaching profession should become more elitist, even if that means increased turnover in the classroom and it lacks feasibility at a large scale. Second, teaching should be viewed as more of a science than an art, with a greater emphasis on data collection and accumulation of the kind of transferable strategies Lemov describes in his book *Teach Like a Champion*. This vision prioritizes technique over content: There's more focus on how lessons should be delivered than on what kids should know (at least in a broad sense that extends beyond standardized tests, discrete skills, and college aspirations). Learning for the sake of learning becomes a luxury. Knowledge becomes the means to an end.

Historically, most Americans have viewed schools as reflections of the communities they serve. Sci Academy and several of the other new charter schools in New Orleans represent a fundamental shift of this paradigm: Their leaders hope the families absorb the school's values. It's not unprecedented, or even unusual, for a school to instruct its students in a kind of social code, way of living, or set of aspirations. Aidan was the product of such a school himself. But it is uncommon to find such explicit instruction in a public school. Moreover, the cultural and social conditioning of young children at most Catholic schools, for instance, is the product of a mutual understanding between the school and the families that it serves. The school's mores are an extension of the parents' own—not so much a shaper of them. Many of Sci's parents value the school's overarching goal of college success and support the school's reliance on rules and structure. But Sci, unlike some private schools, does not reinforce and build on the values and habits most of the students bring with them to the school. Instead it aims to supplant them. "The first week of school is all about compliance," said Kaycee Eckhardt, one of the founding teachers. "It's about creating this feeling that everything is different."

The intense structure that defines no-excuses charter schools like Sci became popular in the 1980s and 1990s when many educators responded to high crime and murder rates by placing urban schools in "lockdown mode," says Andre Perry, an associate director at Loyola University's Institute for Quality and Equity in Education. In cities across America, schools instituted stricter uniform policies and cracked down on more minor offenses.

"We've never come out of [lockdown]," Perry says. Indeed, schools have taken the approach to new extremes in recent years—essentially turning into what he describes as "behavior modification programs." While Perry believes some kids work well in "constrained environments . . . we have some kids who work well in messy environments. When an entire system, or most of a system, follows a rigid notion of discipline, that's a problem for some kids." More broadly, Perry says he is troubled by the idea that children—and poor children of color most especially—need to be controlled. "There's an insidious mistrust of children reflected in having them walk on lines or making them stay silent."

Marcovitz said he has two major motivations for creating such an aggressively routinized environment at Sci. First, he hopes to achieve significant "time savings," since there will be fewer distractions during class and fewer confrontations in the hallway. He argues time is particularly critical when so many students come in years behind. "If you have one emotionally challenging or high-anxiety exchange in between classes, your ability to focus [during the next] class is reduced by ten or fifteen minutes," he said. Second, he hopes the structure will help create a safe atmosphere at Sci so the students can focus on learning. Many students arrive at high school expecting it to be a "physically and emotionally scary" place, he says. "We try to overturn that assumption very quickly by showing them the adults are extremely in charge." Marcovitz attended Maret, a private school in Washington, D.C., where his father worked as a teacher. While that school had comparatively little structure, he argues elite private schools could also benefit from more school-wide routines—including required uniforms—of the kind found at Sci.

"Kids are succeeding at fancy prep schools oftentimes despite the lack of structure," he says.

In a subtle way, Sci illustrates a broader shift in American education. Proponents of charter schools like Sci often argue that in order to improve public schools, communities must cede some control in exchange for quality. Underlying this belief is the notion that local control has not always produced good schools, and the federal government (or in this case, a band of well-educated outsiders) must step in to impose their expertise. But Americans have long been accustomed to local control when it comes to their public schools and, as a result, state lawmakers, local school boards, and individual teachers have exerted more influence on the day-to-day operations of schools than the federal government. That balance of power shifted with the passage of No Child Left Behind, and then again with Race to the Top, President Barack Obama's signature education initiative. Race to the Top gave states financial motivation to embrace charter schools, national standards, and tying teacher pay to performance.

Like most recent Democratic presidential candidates, Obama ran on a largely undefined education platform and with significant support from teachers' unions. Since the 1990s, the Democratic Party has been divided over charter schools and unions. One side supports locally elected school boards and teachers' unions and remains somewhat skeptical of charters and the motives of their big-money backers. Members of this coalition complain of a stealth agenda of privatization and union crushing (their worries are sometimes justified, although they too often ignore the other motivations behind charter backers) and view the charter mania as a convenient ploy to ignore the true causes of bad schools: poverty and insufficient funding. Many of those seeking an education overhaul, on the other hand, may not go as far as Republicans in embracing vouchers. But they view the teachers' unions and the debates over funding and poverty as outdated impediments and excuses. To one side, the New Orleans experiment is anathema; to the other side, it's a dream come true.

Barack Obama won election at a time when this split in his party had crystallized. Competing manifestos asked the nation's education leaders to attach their names to the ideals of one coalition. In the weeks before Obama announced his pick for secretary of education, insiders put both

Linda Darling-Hammond, a Stanford professor and vocal opponent of the reformers, and Jon Schnur, the founder of New Leaders for New Schools and a vocal proponent of the reformers, at the top of the list for a cabinet or undersecretary position. In selecting Chicago Schools CEO Arne Duncan, Obama appeared, at first, to bridge the new divide. Duncan was the only big-city superintendent to sign both manifestos. On the surface, at least, he seemed to represent a shrewd, pragmatic compromise from a president who loved both pragmatism and compromise.

But in practice, both in Chicago and since assuming the top education post, Duncan has proven himself a reformer through and through. He not only advocates for more charter schools and performance pay for teachers, but against elected school board control of large urban districts. Duncan's agenda fits well with his boss's moderate approach and technocratic bent. Although their support for charters and teacher performance pay has made it harder for Republicans to criticize the president on education, Obama and Duncan differ from conservatives in one fundamental respect: Obama views overhauling the nation's education system as a means to make government more effective, while his political opponents view it as a means to shrink government's role in running schools, or even eliminate it entirely.

Critics on both the right and the left (particularly the far right and the far left) pilloried Race to the Top for very different reasons. Part of their opposition to Race to the Top arose from the specific policies the program favored, not from perceived federal intrusion in and of itself. Conservatives have always been more resistant to common standards laid down by Washington. And some liberals have long been suspicious of market-based solutions for social issues, including charter schools. Race to the Top favored both national standards and charter schools. But some of the opposition had less to do with the *what* than the *how*. Conservatives, for instance, have no problem with trying to mandate curriculum and textbook priorities at the state or local level. And liberals tend to be more supportive of charter schools that emanate from grassroots groups than from those that are superimposed. Race to the Top struck many as an unwelcome imposition of values and priorities in a country accustomed to battling out its education agenda at town halls, school board meetings, statehouses, in principals' offices, and at teacher conferences.

Both Sci Academy and Race to the Top grew out of a skepticism with traditional forms of local control and out of mounting conviction, particularly among a coalition of moderate Democrats and moderate Republicans, that a technocracy might better serve the nation's urban public schoolchildren than a democracy.

In some respects, the young educators who lead, teach, and tutor in schools like Sci resemble the settlement house workers of a century ago. That long-abandoned movement brought hundreds of middle- and upper-class young adults (in the United States they were often women educated at elite colleges) into settlements in the ghettos to work with urban poor families, typically ethnic immigrants. The "settlers" aimed partly to educate immigrants in a set of American mores and ways of living. They bore a striking resemblance to today's charter school teachers and Teach For America corps members in terms of their missionary zeal, outsider status, ties to elite institutions, and limited length of stay. The median number of years spent in a settlement was three; about 56 percent of TFA teachers leave their initial placements in low-income schools after two years. The female settlement workers in particular "experienced their life choices in a manner that could be compared to a nuns' sensibility—they were dedicated to a great cause, and family obligations must not interfere," writes Linda Gordon in *Pitied but Not Entitled: Single Mothers and the History of Welfare*. The settlement movement also paralleled today's school change efforts in its ability to capture the imaginations of an eclectic group including wealthy philanthropists and idealistic college students, and its capacity to divide liberals who all claim to work on behalf of social justice and profess to have the best interests of the nation's poorest children at heart.

Just as the settlement workers usually came from different ethnic and class backgrounds than those they aimed to help, the staff at many (although by no means all) of New Orleans' new charter schools tend to come from different cultural and class backgrounds than their students. But in the latter case, a long history of racism and racial mistrust must also be overcome. When Aidan started, Sci's staff included sixteen whites, three African-Americans, three Asian-Americans, and one Hispanic.

Tensions over "outsiders" educating New Orleans schoolchildren have erupted at different points since the city's first public schools opened in the nineteenth century. After the United States acquired New Orleans as part of the Louisiana Purchase in 1803, the newly constituted territory's first governor, William Claiborne, tried to create a public school system headquartered in New Orleans and based largely on the New York model as part of the "Americanization of the polyglot population of Louisiana."

As reported in the book *Crescent City Schools*, Claiborne's "efforts floundered because a deep rivalry over power led to a paralyzing conflict about the goals of public education. The Creoles, as Louisiana's French-speaking natives were called, had their own ideas about the future of their society and the kind of education it required. The way they saw it, they were not immigrants coming into some new society in need of 'Americanization.' From their point of view, the Americans were the newcomers who should adapt to the well-rooted culture."

Similar sentiments echo in critiques of the post-Katrina education overhaul, particularly efforts spearheaded by young white educators who are new to the city. The transplants broach the subject of race in different ways, if they broach it at all.[3]

At NOLA College Prep charter school in Central City, the school's founder asked the teachers during professional development to discuss what it means to be a predominantly white staff trying to work in an overwhelmingly poor, black neighborhood. Vanessa Douyon, a first-year teacher at the school who is Haitian-American, was pleased the leaders tackled the subject of race head-on. But as the school year progressed, she came to understand how much more difficult—although not impossible—it is to build trust and rapport with families at a school where most staff members are white. "To be quite frank, when you have a lot of white teachers teaching black students, there's a lot of, 'You don't have my best interest in mind.' Sometimes the kids are hearing that at home from parents, which is why it's also important to have parents bought into systems. And not all of our parents are bought in."

At KIPP Renaissance, the principal asked his teachers during their first week what led them to want to teach low-income, minority students. Their answers ran the gamut. A white female teacher said she was drawn to New Orleans, not to teaching a certain type of student; she said she would have felt just as happy teaching Asian-American as African-American ones. (Black staff members privately expressed concerns afterward about her color-blind response.) A black female and black male teacher both said they made a conscious decision to teach African-American children because they wanted to be models for the students. A white male teacher said, "The world is highly inegalitarian and people need to work to create the conditions of equality." And a white female teacher recited the quote from Lilla Watson, an Aboriginal activist and artist: "If you have come here to help me, you are wasting your time. But if you have come because your liberation is bound up with mine, then let us work together."

White teachers who talked openly about race and class at staff meetings sometimes hesitated to raise the subject in the classroom—at least in more personal, and less academic, ways. Marcovitz said the topic comes up among Sci's teachers "quite a bit," but less so in public conversations between the school's staff and students. When the subject is broached, the discussion does not always get beyond a superficial level. At a lunch for honor-roll students, staff asked what the teens thought about the racial composition of their teachers. The students unilaterally replied that "it doesn't matter. What matters is how good of a teacher you are," Marcovitz recalled.

He wanted to attract a more diverse staff. Like many principals, he recruits within his own personal and professional networks. And he realized after Sci opened that "my network is not really diverse." Once the school gets a reputation for a certain staff profile, it "becomes a vicious cycle and it gets harder and harder to change it," he says. Marcovitz saw examples of the ways in which race seemed to affect different dynamics at his school. Parents sometimes felt more comfortable talking to African-American than white school leaders. Sci's few black teachers became popular among students more quickly than the white teachers; they could sometimes push students to take on challenging tasks more easily; and they broached subjects in class that Marcovitz knew many white teachers would shy away from.

But the dynamics were not something he could capture in a number. "I do tend to measure things quantitatively," said Marcovitz. "I have yet to have an experience indicating that [a teacher's race] has an impact on results. But anecdotally it's compelling."

Charter schools like Sci expect a certain degree of compliance—or mission alignment—from their teachers as well as their families. During student orientation, the teachers dress like the freshmen not only to model the uniform but also to show solidarity. And during part of professional development, the teachers adhere to many of the rules and procedures they expect their students to follow. They always walk on the right side of the hallway, for instance. And every morning they greet Marcovitz just as their students would, shaking his hand (firmly while looking him in the eye) and providing the only acceptable answers for the two questions asked of each arriving scholar:

Why are you here?
To learn.
What will it take?
Achievement, respect, responsibility, perseverance, teamwork, and enthusiasm.

Principals at the schools pump up their young teachers at the start of the school day and year, striving to show them the importance of their work. At Akili Academy, principal Sean Gallagher opened professional development in 2010 by telling his young teachers: "If this morning you woke up and are a kid in the United States who doesn't have a lot of money, there is a ninety-five percent chance you are going to a terrible school where the education is among the worst in the world." (He did not provide a source or explanation for the 95 percent figure.) He then recounted the recent rape and murder of a waitress in Philadelphia, arguing that the failure of the city's school system to educate her eighteen-year-old attacker led directly to the tragedy. "This is a really serious way to start things, folks," he concluded. "But what you do is the most important work in the world. It's the most urgent work in the world."

Gallagher's speech represented an extreme example of the rhetoric that pervades the charter school movement. But it also seemed intended, whether consciously or not, to elicit a kind of monastic intensity—and fear of what would happen if the young teachers chose not to do "the work."

Liz Rainey, one of Sci's former college counselors, says she was struck immediately by the single-minded devotion of Sci's staff to their mission: how they e-mailed all weekend, might call at nine A.M. on Sunday morning to review lesson plans, ended the work week each Friday with a Sci happy hour, sometimes socialized and dated among their own, and gave over all aspects of their lives to the cause. The school felt like an anachronism in an otherwise easygoing and at times lackadaisical city. "There's this sense of urgency there that you don't find in so much of the rest of New Orleans." When she told her father about the school, he said it sounded like a traditional Catholic school minus the religion, with the teachers playing the role of the nuns minus the celibacy and seclusion.

MATCH charter schools in Boston have taken that dynamic to another level. The schools hire about 120 full-time, live-in tutors to ease the workload on the teachers and personalize attention for kids. Many of the tutors (most recent college graduates) live three to a bunk room in a dormitory-style space above the high school. In exchange for working ten-hour days, they receive free housing, health insurance, and a monthly stipend of $625. Despite the meager salary, more than two thousand candidates from the nation's top colleges vie for the positions each year.

To make it at Sci, a teacher has to be not only dedicated but a true believer. The hours are too long, the work too all-consuming, the personal sacrifices too great, and the lifestyle too rigorous for equivocators to tolerate, the administration tries to make clear. As Rainey puts it, the message always remains: "What we are doing here is extraordinary. It takes extra effort. And there is no exception."

Aidan was a true believer.

He loved Sci's sense of mission and collective purpose, having missed his Catholic high school's emphasis on outreach during his time at Harvard. He dove right in, starting with a monthlong professional development session during which the teachers studied Doug Lemov's "taxonomy of effective teaching practices." They also read and discussed books like *Difficult Conversations*, a communication guide; role-played difficult moments in class; and rehearsed the first week's classes.

Once staff and student orientation ended and the school year started in earnest, Aidan's life followed a predictable pattern. Every weekday he woke up by six A.M. and arrived at school by six forty-five. He taught during four one-hour class periods, spent most of a period with his advisory, a sixth supervising his advisory during a study hall, and a seventh (two days a week) manning a table stationed in the hallway. That left him one or two blocks for prep time. Most students departed around five P.M., but Aidan stayed on campus for about two more hours to call parents, prepare materials, and make copies. He usually left Sci Academy around seven P.M., more than twelve hours after he had arrived. At home in the Treme house he shared with friends, Aidan worked for two more hours and took any calls for homework help from students. He went to bed around ten. On the weekends he spent much of Saturday grading student work and the first part of Sunday planning his lessons for the next week. All told, he worked more than eighty hours a week.

Aidan had worked hard at Martyn, too. But there he almost always left by three P.M. Once home, he planned the next day's lessons for about two hours, finishing in time to watch *Jeopardy!* He rarely worked through the entire weekend. Several factors accounted for the shift. Sci had a school day that was two hours longer. Aidan and the other teachers were responsible for far more phone calls than at traditional schools, both incoming ones from students and outgoing ones to their parents (they kept their advisees' families abreast of everything from academic progress to changes in the bus schedule). Lesson planning accounted for perhaps the single biggest increase in time, however. At the start of the school year, Aidan spent about an hour preparing for each of his classes, or about fifteen to twenty hours a week. At Martyn, administrators rarely reviewed his lesson plans, and then in a perfunctory way. But at Sci every lesson plan for the upcoming week was due at three P.M. on Sunday. In the early weeks of the school year Aidan often put off much of his planning until the last day and woke up early on Sunday morning to meet the deadline. By the time he recovered from the rush of finishing the lesson plans, it was nearly time to start teaching them.

One written lesson plan on thesis statements went on for five pages. It began, like all of Sci's lesson plans, with the SWBAT (Students Will Be Able To), which in this case was "explain what a thesis statement is and why it is important for an expository essay" and "craft a clear, compelling thesis statement." For each "lesson step" Aidan included a time estimate, teacher action, student action, and materials needed. The "Do Now," a student task that opened every class at Sci, lasted for five minutes. Then came the minute-long "Hook," for which Aidan wrote a lengthy description of the teacher action: "Yesterday, we talked about why writing is important, and how brainstorming is the first step in a writing process that you're going to master. Today, you'll work on the most important sentence in any essay, a skill that separates good writers from weak writers. If you master that skill, everything you write will be comprehensible and focused, and will be graded more highly on standardized tests. If you do not, you will not be able to create an essay that really influences people. This is the big chief. The head honcho in charge. This is . . . the *thesis statement!*" For the same one-minute time period, the desired student action was to "listen in SPARK. T (teacher) will visually check for tracking to ensure attention." Notes for the twelve-minute "Intro to New Material" and twenty-minute "Guided Practice" were even more extensive. In them Aidan included a "quick gimmick": "Hold up a copy of my senior thesis and point out the thesis statement; 'even a paper that is 100 pages long has a thesis statement. This skill will carry you all through college.'" The lesson plan also included sample thesis statements for the students to vet, specific moments when Aidan planned to circulate throughout the room or tell the students to track their guided notes, and a reminder to demand a redo if students failed to pass out papers in under twenty seconds on the first try. It closed with Aidan's passing out the "exit ticket"—another staple at Sci and similar charter schools across the country that often requires students to regurgitate or summarize key points from the lesson—and telling the students, "Complete these at a level 0 (silence); keep your attention on your paper; work your hardest to show me what you know."

Aidan's lesson plans were impeccable, but he sometimes struggled with delivery. An administrator or colleague observed him at least briefly several times a week. They stood or sat unobtrusively in his room and punched real-time feedback into an e-mail that would arrive in Aidan's iPhone while he was still teaching the lesson. Some teachers checked the e-mails midclass so they could implement the advice immediately. Most of the students also knew the drill. During the first few weeks of the school year, Aidan's feedback ran the gamut. One day his supervisors told him that some of the students were wearing hoodies over their school uniform and that he should check more carefully in the future; another time they reminded him that a teacher should have a different classroom presence when explaining concepts as opposed to giving directions. Often they told Aidan he was too verbose and moved around too much; his students, too, complained that he talked a lot. At one point he tried putting down small pieces of tape at different spots in the room and staying rooted to them. It didn't work. Other ideas were more successful. Marcovitz advised him to stop staring exclusively at the student answering a question because it gave the rest of the class a license to goof off. Marcovitz also taught him the "self-interrupt," a teaching technique included in Lemov's *Teach Like a Champion*, where a teacher abruptly halts speaking for a few seconds until he has the attention of the class. Then he resumes as if nothing ever happened.

Aidan spent his first adrenaline-fueled weeks at Sci in awe of the school's esprit de corps and relentless pursuit of perfection. But he learned quickly that just because Sci wasn't an alternative school like Martyn and had much more structure in place, that did not always translate into better student behavior. Sci teachers saw their share of cursing, students talking back and disobeying requests, and, occasionally, fighting. More of the Sci students arrived with strong academic skills (by definition the students at Martyn were those that other schools thought might not make it to college). But both schools had a high free and reduced lunch rate (about 90 percent at Sci, 80 percent at Martyn), and the student needs were just as intense at Sci.

When the adrenaline started to wear off, Aidan also had to confront the fact that he did not feel like a star teacher anymore. The extra efforts that he had undertaken at Martyn—calling parents regularly, spending hours planning lessons, constantly reflecting on what worked and what did not—weren't considered exceptional at Sci: They constituted the minimum expectation. Aidan's classes, particularly fourth period, sometimes descended into a state of low-level chaos where students talked over each other and their teacher. His best-planned lessons sometimes fell flat. When he visited the classrooms of fellow Sci teachers like Kaycee Eckhardt or Jerel Bryant, the students often sat rapt and even the most troublesome ones appeared more attentive. They weren't as likely to tell a classmate to shut up, refuse to sit in their seats, or nod off.

Marcovitz tried to build a strong team spirit among his staff so no teacher felt alone in his or her achievements or shortcomings. The teachers were there to learn from each other, not compete. In keeping with that philosophy, Aidan studied Kaycee's technique, paying close attention to the way in which she "infects passion into her classroom," and he analyzed Jerel's "economy of language and movement." Then he tried to apply what he had gleaned in his own classroom. Aidan believed almost any student misbehavior or problem "can be attacked in some way if you remind yourself that *you* are responsible for your students' outcomes." But with all the effort he put into planning and adjusting his teaching practice, and no matter how carefully he plotted the appropriate teacher and student actions he submitted with his lesson plans every Sunday afternoon, whenever Aidan entered his classroom he remained partly at the mercy of forces outside his control. The fear-inspired compliance began to wear off, and the student actions did not always conform to the script.

THE FAMILY
"We don't desire because we don't know what we are missing."

At the end of a steamy late-August work day, Raquel joined dozens of parents as they trekked up two flights of stairs to KIPP Renaissance's first parent meeting. The parents brought all their ambitions and fears for their children with them to the school's makeshift library that night.

Raquel, just off a hotel shift, wore her heavy, black, tunic-style uniform with white trim. Her work schedule often prevented her from attending school gatherings. But she did her best to make it whenever she could, and she did not want to miss this first one of the year. Other parents came in crisp white shirts with the McDonald's logo, the brown attire of a Harrah's casino worker, the bright scrubs of a home health care assistant, and T-shirts with KIPP's mantra COURAGE TO BE FIRST written on the back. Sitting in rows of desk chairs amid stacks of unpacked books, they listened to principal Brian Dassler describe his ambitious plans for the young school, which had opened just two weeks earlier.

Dassler wore his usual khakis, tie, and button-down shirt. He looked more nervous than usual standing in the front, as if he had invited a group of people to a party and was surprised they had shown up. After appealing to the parents to see themselves as allies in the push for better schools in New Orleans, Dassler described the many structural flaws of the approximately seventy-five-year-old building KIPP Renaissance inhabited. He told the parents he hoped to install air-conditioning in the once-magnificent, now-decayed auditorium; replace the plastic, broken windows with new ones; and fix the leaking roof. "We need you to be our advocates to FEMA and the Recovery School District," he said. "Great things are going to happen in this building. We're going to launch one thousand graduates to college, and they deserve to have a safe, well-lit, air-conditioned building." For decades the building's students had endured stifling classrooms, malfunctioning toilets, and windows painted black. Several KIPP Renaissance parents knew those indignities firsthand, having attended the school in its previous incarnation as Frederick Douglass High. But at this meeting they did not want to talk about the past. One parent asked Dassler when the name on the building would change from Douglass to KIPP Renaissance—noting the switch could not come soon enough. Others murmured quiet amens when he mentioned Douglass's closure the previous spring. (The school had been closed ahead of schedule, and its remaining students scattered, to make way for KIPP Renaissance. Those students included Geraldlynn's cousin, Lionel, who bounced from school to school after Katrina because of instability in the RSD.) Dassler relaxed as he sensed the parents' enthusiasm. Over the last year he had attended meetings with community members and Douglass alums who were irate about the pending change in name and leadership at a school with a rich, if tragic, history. Tonight he could focus on the future, not the past.

KIPP is famous—infamous in some eyes—for its discipline and structure. But for every rule Dassler proposed that night, the parents seemed to crave more. Many of their children had, like Geraldlynn, attended KIPP Believe. A smaller number graduated from McDonogh 15, a KIPP middle school in the French Quarter. Fewer than half of Renaissance's students had attended KIPP middle schools, although their parents were disproportionately represented at school meetings. For some parents, KIPP Renaissance could not be "KIPP" enough.

Dassler's description of Renaissance's "No Idling" policy—designed to prevent students from loitering in the halls, stairwells, or bathrooms—drew a cry of "I'm lovin' you already!" His announcement that the school's students would have to meet the "Renaissance requirement" of participating in at least one sport or club drew no protest. The parents only wanted to make sure the school would have a lacrosse team, a sport they associated with KIPP (not, like many Americans, with predominantly white private schools on the East Coast) since the organization had introduced lacrosse at some of its New Orleans middle schools two years earlier. When Dassler answered "absolutely" to lacrosse, a few parents broke into finger snaps.

In KIPP language, that meant amen.

After Dassler noted that the Renaissance staff had not been vigilant enough about preventing the students from rolling up the sleeves of their uniforms, a mother shouted, "Get even stricter, Mr. Dassler, do it!"

"You have to be hard and strict," added a second mother and Douglass alum. "You can't be soft because you *know* how these kids are."

"I'm always going to be honest with you," Dassler told them. "We've already suspended three students—"

"Do it!"

"Do it!"

"*Every chance you've got!*"

"Any student suspended is on a probationary contract," Dassler continued. "We're not going to let the misbehavior of one affect the destiny of all."

Several parents snapped.

"That means someday that one of you might be mad at me."

Some of his initial nervousness returned as Dassler scanned the parents' eager faces. He told them one of the suspensions stemmed from a student making a gang-related symbol.[4]

"Let them *know* you ain't playin'!"

"We're loving in a strict way, strict in a loving way," said Dassler.

"I'm lovin' it, too!"

Several of the parents fanned themselves in the now-crowded library with copies of KIPP Renaissance's discipline matrix.

"Zero tolerance!" someone cried out, referring to the practice of punishing students without regard to circumstances and usually used in the context of weapon- and drug-related school expulsions.

"That's right, zero tolerance, baby!"

Knowing that hotel, restaurant, and casino companies were hardly "tolerant" if an employee showed up late or talked back to a customer, one parent added: "If you mess up once at Harrah's [casino], you are going to be fired!"

Dassler paused for a moment before continuing. "Our message to our kids is: We love you and our expectations are high," he said. "With the demerits we try to address things early, so they don't become big problems." Renaissance gives out demerits for not turning in homework partly because high school "GPAs are the most important factor in predicting college success."

"That's right!"

"You have our cell phone numbers," Dassler concluded. "We do home visits. That's KIPP."

A chorus of satisfied snaps ensued.

Some parents looked to KIPP Renaissance to teach their children "the rules" they would need to learn if they wanted to make it through high school and college. In exchange for that knowledge, they were willing to embrace the school's oddities—like the snapping—and comply with its demands. Other families enrolled their children by accident, choosing KIPP solely because they still thought of the building as Frederick Douglass High School, a neighborhood institution despite its struggles. Still other students signed themselves up for KIPP Renaissance because they wanted a break with the past and had heard that KIPP was, if nothing else, *different*. Many of these families had few nice things to say about the pre-Katrina schools, although the reasons were complex.

The parents included Keyoka Taylor, a McDonald's franchise manager who took a chance four years earlier on KIPP Believe when it was an unknown school with a funny name and slogans. Taylor liked the fact that KIPP's teachers came from across the country and exposed her daughter, Kotsha, to different places and cultures. She also appreciated their attention to detail. She described KIPP using the expression: "They plan their work; they work their plan."

Taylor had just started at Delgado Community College in New Orleans when she became pregnant with Kotsha. After giving birth, "I went back to school, but the drive wasn't in me like before," she recalled. "So I dropped out and raised Kotsha how my mom raised me. She was a single mom and as a child I saw what she was going through, struggling to pay the bills. She always said, 'Go to school. Be someone.' But I got pregnant with Kotsha . . ." She was determined her daughter avoid that same fate.

Edward Wiltz, whose son, Tyrin, also graduated from KIPP Believe, was even more emphatic about the program's virtues. Part of his approbation stemmed from the political support and resources KIPP schools seemed to enjoy (particularly when compared to the pre-Katrina Orleans public schools). While sitting with his son at the family's truck-repair store one afternoon, Wiltz explained that before the flood, the New Orleans school system felt like a physical and intellectual anachronism. Tyrin attended Coghill Elementary School, his father's alma mater, in the years before Katrina. But to Wiltz it did not look like the building had been updated or improved since his own time there twenty years earlier. Tyrin brought home textbooks whose battered condition and long lists of past owners suggested they had not been replaced in decades.

Both father and son lamented that, before he started at KIPP, schools often valued Tyrin, who is tall and broad shouldered, for his athletic promise.

"Every school you went to, the first thing they said was, 'Are you going to play football, football, football?'" Edward Wiltz recalled.

"Just because my shoulders are big and I have height, it doesn't mean I want to play football," added Tyrin.

Like Jerome Smith, the Freedom Rider who protested the opening of a charter school in the Treme, Wiltz believes the public schools were kept down deliberately before Katrina to supply low-wage workers for an economy built on tourism. "We were allowed to be ignorant," he said. "New Orleanians have been softened to just sit back and take what's given." Unlike Smith, however, Wiltz sees charter schools like KIPP as a way out for his son. Wiltz never finished college and works at the truck-repair business with his own father. He wants his son to have other options. He loves that KIPP never mentions football to Tyrin (many of the schools do not have football teams). But "they have more drilling—five, six, seven, eight!—on college than I had all through high school," he says. Wiltz went along as a chaperone on several KIPP middle school trips, including Washington, D.C. "Living in New Orleans is like being locked in a box. It's like being on an island," he says. "I would never have brought my child to Columbia University on a field trip or Morehouse [College] or to the opera or whitewater rafting . . . We don't desire because we don't know what we are missing."

Echoing the sentiment of other parents, Wiltz said he sometimes wished KIPP Believe, his son's middle school, had found some way of kicking out a student everyone suspected was dealing drugs instead of giving him chance after chance. And when Tyrin complained about KIPP's many strictures that afternoon, his father took the school's side.

"I think they look for things sometimes to put you on Bench: the tiniest things, little petty things," Tyrin said. "I was benched once for not writing my last name. Is that really a big deal? Not putting my last name?"

"When you take the ACT you get . . . points just for writing your name," his father retorted. "So that *is* a big deal."

Edward Wiltz had his own KIPP-inspired ambitions. During a visit to Howard University in Washington, D.C., with his son's class, he had marveled at the small city within a city that drew together ambitious black students from across the country. Wiltz pledged that as soon as he could, he would go back to college himself.

"My dad worked on trucks," he said. "His dad worked on trucks. I want to break the cycle." He laughed quietly to himself before adding, "Really, I hate trucks."

Some of the parents wished KIPP and the other new charters employed more black teachers and looked skeptically on the schools as a result. But although they feared implicit or explicit racism from the white teachers, several also felt they had suffered from classism in the pre-Katrina schools.

Raquel said a few of her teachers did not seem to care whether their students received an education, making it clear that they would get paid no matter what. "To me, a lot of the teachers when I was coming up had the attitude: 'I have mine. You got to get yours.'"

The children were more reluctant KIPP converts. Many of them enjoyed the trips (those who violated KIPP's rules too many times were barred from the excursions, however), spoke enthusiastically about at least one or two of their teachers, and experienced some degree of academic growth after starting at KIPP. But they chafed under KIPP's rules and long hours, and all but a few had some story of an unfair benching or other punishment.

"Mr. Dassler says we won't have bench at his high school, which is a good thing," said fifteen-year-old Moira, just days before starting at KIPP Renaissance. "The kids call KIPP Kids in Prison Program because we don't get out of school until late," she added. "I joked to one friend, 'Next year I'm going to be there at KIPP Renaissance with a lot of convicts.'"

By the time Geraldlynn started KIPP Renaissance, two members of her extended family also attended KIPP schools. They had strikingly different experiences. Geraldlynn's younger cousin, Maurice, Roxanne's son, struggled to make it through KIPP Believe middle school. The work sometimes overwhelmed him. And once frustration hit, his mouth got him into trouble. Roxanne said the school held him back in the sixth grade because of his test scores and behavior issues. She was not a fan of high-stakes testing after seeing the effect it had on her son.

The twelve-year-old was intimately familiar with the Bench. On most any day in most any classroom in KIPP Believe, a "benched" student or two (usually boys) wore masking tape across the backs of their shirts with words like *community* or *responsibility* written on the tape to denote whichever value they had violated. They worked by the wall, ate lunch alone, and could not talk to their peers. Since the approach had such vehement detractors, a Recovery School District official charged in 2008 with spreading KIPP's strategies to non-KIPP schools did not venture to encourage the adoption of the Bench.[5]

Maurice usually found himself benched for speaking out of turn or making rude comments to teachers, a problem that stemmed from his not understanding the material, said his mother. If he's confused about schoolwork, he "feels like the world has turned on him," said Roxanne. Like her sister, Roxanne supported the Bench as a discipline tool for her son, describing it as "good for him." At the two schools Maurice attended before KIPP Believe, he received numerous out-of-school suspensions. Benching him sent a message, Roxanne felt, without requiring him to miss school. Maurice sometimes repeated KIPP's own mantras. "If I don't have consequences," he observed once, "then I won't learn from my mistakes."

Meanwhile, Geraldlynn's younger stepsister, Mary, excelled at KIPP Believe. Mary earned record-setting daily "paychecks" for good behavior that could be redeemed for pizza or buffalo wings in the cafeteria. While most students attended KIPP at their parents' request—or command— Mary, Langdon's daughter, had selected the school on her own. She went to a winter concert at KIPP Believe with Geraldlynn in 2007. Once there, she talked to Adam Meinig, the principal, about letting her finish fifth grade at the school. The amount of time Geraldlynn spent on homework intimidated her a little. But Mary decided it had to be better than continuing fifth grade at Wicker Elementary School, where the chaos in the hallways frightened her and she felt as if all but a few of the teachers had given up on the students, most of whom, come eighth grade, could not pass the state tests required to advance to high school.

"I felt like I was the only one trying to get the classroom organized," Mary recalled. Her experience mirrored students' at non-charter schools like Wicker that the Recovery School District continued to operate. As time passed, the more informed and motivated families avoided the so-called "RSD direct run" schools and decamped for the new charters. That left some of the most challenging students in a dwindling pool of schools run by RSD superintendent Paul Vallas, which posted the worst test scores, particularly the high schools. Only after the concert did Mary inform her mother that she would not be returning to Wicker Elementary after Christmas. Her mother asked that in the future, Mary let her know before finding herself a new school.

Not every student who chose KIPP voluntarily was as dutiful as Mary. Brice had already been put out of one school when Brian Dassler showed up at his middle school in the spring of 2010 to talk about KIPP Renaissance. Even though he was constantly in trouble, Brice liked Mr. Dassler's description of KIPP's disciplined approach. He sensed the school would cut no corners. He considered O. Perry Walker High School as well, but worried that he knew too many other teenagers bound for Walker. Brice, who lived with his mother in Hollygrove, could feel himself getting pulled into a scene of drugs, fast money, and guns. Hollygrove is a working-class black neighborhood perhaps best known outside of New Orleans as the childhood home of rapper Lil Wayne. Brice wanted to back away from the drug scene in his corner of the neighborhood and thought a clean break from some of his old friends might help. "I know how I am," he said. "I know I'm bad. You got to be really big and really on top of your game to make me do what you want." Brice hoped that KIPP, and Dassler in particular, might be "big" enough to keep him in check.

At first glance, Brice's assertion seemed absurd: Although he puffed his chest out and walked with a swagger, he stood about five foot six and weighed 105 pounds, smaller than many of the girls. But despite his small stature, Brice loomed large in the lives of just about everyone he met. Even teachers frustrated with his nonstop talking, curse-filled retorts, or mischievous pranks agreed that Brice was special. There was a quickness and generosity of spirit about him, a bluster that only thinly veiled his vulnerability and fear over his own future. "Brice's mouth is his weapon," explained Nathaniel Lang, the school disciplinarian. "But if you don't understand Brice, you would think his weapon is more than his mouth."

Brice desperately needed KIPP Renaissance to work. He could not envision any other escape route than through a school. And Renaissance was the one he had decided would give him the best odds.

For the first sixty years of its existence, the school building KIPP Renaissance inhabits went by the name of Francis Nicholls, after a Confederate general. The building was constructed in the 1930s for white students only. The school is located along St. Claude Avenue, a main thoroughfare that cuts all the way through New Orleans' 9th Ward. In the early to mid-1900s, working-class whites populated the neighborhood around the school, although the demographics began to shift in the middle part of the century, accelerated by the start of school desegregation in 1960. Whites moved in droves to St. Bernard Parish to the east of New Orleans, and growing numbers of blacks migrated into the neighborhood, also known as the Bywater. In the 1990s, whites (particularly artists) began to return to the Bywater. By the time KIPP Renaissance arrived, the area around the school was racially and economically diverse by New Orleans standards, with some blocks home to primarily low-income residents, and others more gentrified.

Nicholls desegregated in 1967 (around the same time Mary Laurie enrolled at Warren Easton as part of one of the first cohorts of black students there). Like Laurie, Nicholls's first black students said the experience of desegregating the school toughened them and inspired them to fight for their community. Gwendolyn Adams, a black student who transferred there in 1967, recalled six white teens from the neighborhood throwing her through the plate glass window of a grocery store across the street from the school. She survived relatively unscathed. In an ironic twist, flying glass injured some of her attackers.

Over the next decade, white students steadily left Nicholls as their families enrolled them in Catholic schools or moved to St. Bernard. By the late 1970s, Nicholls had become a community fixture and source of pride for black families in the neighborhood.

Nicholls's post-desegregation renaissance was brief. Like many New Orleans neighborhood high schools, Nicholls—eventually renamed Frederick Douglass after the self-educated and self-liberated slave—suffered during the 1980s and 1990s from a lack of resources, a chronic churn of principals and teachers as the district superintendency rapidly changed hands, increasing drug and gun violence in the surrounding neighborhood, and competition for stronger students posed by citywide magnet programs. In the years before Katrina, a small group of educators who ran a nationally recognized writing program called Students at the Center started working with other community groups to revitalize the flailing Douglass from the ground up. But after the storm, when the Recovery School District operated Douglass, it quickly became clear that Superintendent Paul Vallas intended to hand the building over to a charter school operator, most likely KIPP. During the 2009–2010 school year, the last before Douglass closed, the RSD treated the school's remaining students and staff with a callous disregard. After waffling all school year on whether Douglass would stay open and share the building with KIPP Renaissance's new crop of ninth graders, RSD officials decided to close Douglass completely. Some parents of students with intense special needs did not receive word of the decision until the summer and scrambled to find new schools at the last minute.

KIPP hardly suffered from a lack of political clout. For years the program's strong results had made it the darling of the charter school movement, adored by a group of influential funders, politicians, and journalists as well as some parents. Dave Levin and Mike Feinberg, two young Teach For America alums, founded KIPP in Houston in 1994. Initially, they modeled their teaching style on that of Harriett Ball, a veteran African-American educator who taught in the Houston school where the two young TFA corps members started out. Ball captivated her students with her constant movement and use of mnemonic chants to teach the rules of grammar and mathematics. Levin and Feinberg began with a single class of students in Houston, expanding quickly to two full schools, one in Houston and one in New York. In 2000 Don Fisher, founder of the Gap clothing chain, offered them money to expand beyond the two sites, and over the next eleven years KIPP slowly grew into a network of a hundred schools spanning twenty-one states and Washington, D.C. By 2011, KIPP schools, most of them focused on the middle grades, served twenty-seven thousand students, forming a moderately sized urban district linked not by geography but by philosophy and approach. KIPP started its first high school in 2004.

Even though KIPP enrolls only a fraction of the approximately two million charter school students nationally, it exemplifies a breed of relatively new schools, like Sci Academy, with which the charter movement is most closely associated in many cities. The schools tend to feature longer days and years, incentive structures with clear rewards (school paychecks) and punishments (time on the Bench), an unrelenting focus on college preparation, younger teachers who work longer hours as a matter of course and must take calls from students into the night, and well-defined structures and expectations, from mandatory Saturday-school sessions to pieces of tape down the hallway that students walk on.

The paternalism and intense structure of most KIPP schools remains controversial. Supporters point out that poor children often start school behind academically, come from single-parent households, and live in dangerous neighborhoods. For these reasons and others, they argue low-income children need increased structure, longer school days, and more guidance to set them on the "right path." Chester E. Finn Jr. and Marci Kanstoroom argue in a foreword to *Sweating the Small Stuff: Inner-City Schools and the New Paternalism* that "if the term 'paternalistic' didn't make people queasy, they would immediately recognize that schools and teachers, along with parents, are supposed to civilize, incentivize and nurture children. It's just that schools serving inner-city kids may need to do more of that and do it more intensively."

Others take offense at the notion that poor children require a more didactic and militaristic education—often at the hands of teachers who know little about their communities, culture, or home lives. "'Those children need it,' 'they' are not like 'my' or 'our' children. I had not as bluntly confronted this language since I began teaching in 1962 when I heard it from both left-wing and traditional conservative teachers," wrote long-time education activist Deborah Meier in 2010 after attending a course on charter schools. In a 2012 post for *Education Week,* she wrote that no-excuses charter schools like KIPP have "a code that rests on humiliating those less powerful than oneself and reinforcing a moral code that suggests there's a one-to-one connection between being good and not getting caught. It tries to create certainties in a field where it does not belong."

Two KIPP schools, KIPP Believe and McDonogh 15, opened in New Orleans within a year of Katrina. By the fall of 2010, the network ran a half dozen schools in the city, with plans to increase that number in the coming years. As in other cities, KIPP schools post relatively high test scores, draw more applicants per seat than most of the city's other open-enrollment charters (if schools are oversubscribed they are supposed to award seats through a lottery), and benefit from strong political connections and deep-pocketed supporters.

Nationally, and in New Orleans, most of the network's students come from minority households ranging from very poor to lower middle class. KIPP's website boasts that 95 percent of its students are African-American or Hispanic and over 87 percent qualify for free or reduced lunch. KIPP's critics argue the organization and other like-minded charter school operators have not done enough to integrate their schools. Frederick Hess, a scholar at the conservative American Enterprise Institute, supports charters and KIPP. But in one essay, he critiqued their single-minded focus on educating a certain demographic of student: "Today, school reformers, state and local education officials, exemplary charter-school operators, and managers of philanthropic foundations make it very clear that they are primarily in the business of educating poor black and Hispanic children. Indeed, anyone who has spent much time in the company of school reformers in the past decade has seen this practice turn almost comical, as when charter-school operators try to one-up one another over who can claim the most disadvantaged student population." Part of this critique is fair: KIPP has not opened schools for middle-income students or changed its pedagogical style and practices to make its schools appealing to a socioeconomically diverse group of families. And, as Hess points out, some of the foundations that support KIPP-like charter schools so view their mission as educating poor, minority children that they do not provide philanthropic support for schools with significant white or middle-class populations. The result, whether intentional or not, is that their money disproportionately supports some of the nation's most segregated schools—and charter school founders may have a financial incentive to keep them that way.

But this critique oversimplifies the issue by ignoring the different pedagogical and discipline approaches practiced by families of varying social classes and backgrounds (not to mention the long history of school segregation in many communities that predates charters). Many studies have shown that low-income families support, and employ, authoritarian forms of child rearing, including hitting children and insisting on their silence, at higher rates than wealthier families. In *African-American Women: An Ecological Perspective*, authors Norma J. Burgess and Eurnestine Brown explain some of the sociological reasons for these differences, writing that the "strict discipline style, including threats and punishments, is meant to protect the child from dangerous external forces such as drugs, fights or racial encounters." While KIPP does not employ corporal punishment, its own brand of authoritarianism—which also emphasizes clear punishments, rules, and boundaries—might be more palatable to families who use a comparable approach in their own homes. There's a difference, however, between parents disciplining their child in the home and a teacher (often of a different race, social class, and background) disciplining a student in the public space of a school. And that distinction lies at the heart of many critiques of KIPP.

Many middle-income families also decry KIPP's long school day and insistence on uniforms, arguing they stifle creativity and independence. But poorer families tend to work longer hours, lack the money for music or other lessons, and are more likely to live in neighborhoods where they do not feel comfortable letting their children play outside after school. For similar reasons, they may appreciate the cost-saving graces of uniforms. (The uniform issue can go either way, however, depending on how cognizant the school operator is of choosing styles and brands that can be conveniently and cheaply purchased.) Moreover, in New Orleans it makes sense that poorer families who work in service-industry positions with no job security acclimate more readily to a school culture based on rigid rules: They know the stakes for those who can't follow them, however unfair that may be.

"I don't think a lot of poor parents really understand the freedoms associated with a middle-class lifestyle," said Andre Perry, at Loyola University's Institute for Quality and Equity in Education. Some of them "feel that intense structure and rules are what their children need to achieve because that's all they know."

In New Orleans, exceptions exist to KIPP's general demographic patterns. McDonogh 15, located in the French Quarter, draws more white students than the city's other KIPP schools because of its location, comparatively strong arts program, and the long-standing reputation of the school (which predates KIPP by decades). And by no means do all black parents from tough backgrounds gravitate to KIPP's rules and routines. In a 2010 NPR interview, Ronald McCoy, a New Orleanian raising his fourteen-year-old grandson, shook his head at the sight of tape along each side of a school hallway. "This walking the line?" he asked skeptically. "I have been incarcerated, and that's where I learned about walking behind those lines and staying on the right-hand side of the wall."

It's not uncommon to hear KIPP's critics accuse the organization of a form of cultural imperialism. They point to the fact, for instance, that KIPP schools force students to express their approbation through snapping while many of the students come from communities more accustomed to joyous claps and shouts of praise. KIPP could clearly do much more to understand and honor the cultural context in which it seeks to educate. But those same critics can be guilty of a type of imperialism of their own through their expectation (implicit or explicit) that poor families should favor the less authoritarian, more egalitarian and flexible teaching styles progressive middle-class families tend to support. At times, both KIPP's staunchest supporters and its fiercest critics insult and demean the very families they purport to protect by assuming they, and they alone, know what is best for other people's children.

Further, poor families do not have as many options as their wealthier peers. Faced with a choice between a school they perceive as safe and focused on college and one they perceive as unsafe and disorganized, they usually, and understandably, select the former. Children from wealthier homes are more likely to test into selective-admissions schools and can also more easily afford private schools or move to the suburbs if dissatisfied with their public options in the city. KIPP's critics have attacked it for finding ways to avoid or shed itself of the most low-performing, disruptive pupils. While such practices would undoubtedly color KIPP's claims and results, it's worth nothing that many of KIPP's most devoted parents in New Orleans favor "zero-tolerance" policies and a screening of prospective students. (Several said KIPP should observe students closely during the summer orientation sessions and not invite apparent troublemakers back in the fall.) Moreover, many self-proclaimed liberal and racially tolerant white parents who criticize KIPP for "creaming" stronger students have been using their money, power, and social capital to influence the demographic makeup of their children's schools for generations—moving to a neighborhood where the schools are "better," for instance, or choosing schools with selective admissions policies—and in ways that many KIPP parents cannot. In cities like New Orleans, where some schools have historically enrolled greater numbers of students who are tied into the drug trade and its attendant violence, poor parents would not be mistaken to perceive some degree of "sorting" as a means of keeping their children, and particularly their sons, safe.

KIPP is a symptom of long-standing educational inequities governing who has access to school choice and a safe learning environment. And it is a symptom of persistent and perverse norms surrounding who should be taught to question critically—and who to follow the rules. But to consider it the cause of either of those injustices is akin to denying history.

Brian Dassler, KIPP Renaissance's principal, seemed to be a living embodiment of KIPP's emphasis on "grit," a "growth mind-set," and the idea that great leaders are not born but made—and sometimes from unlikely materials. His unrelenting self-discipline and Gatsby-like focus on self-reconstruction and upward mobility match the values many KIPP schools try to instill in their students.

Dassler grew up in the Miami–Fort Lauderdale area, the son of an IT manager at a health laboratory and a school secretary. Throughout his adolescence and teen years he was overweight and unwilling to let many others (including his parents) know him intimately as he grappled with issues related to his identity and self-image. He worked hard to ingratiate himself with teachers and other adult authority figures, but kept his distance from the conventional teenage social scene.

Even as a child he was relentlessly ambitious. In middle school, he found a niche in student government and drama. He also started imitating the habits of those he perceived as leaders. "If someone said, 'This is what a leader does,' then I did it," he recalled. "If someone said, 'A leader writes thank-you notes,' then I wrote thank-you notes."

By high school, Dassler's years of deliberate self-cultivation began to pay off. He devoted less time to drama and began to focus on student government full-time. At the end of his freshman year, he lost in his bid for class president to a popular cheerleader. But he defeated the girl the next year, and then again before senior year. Looking back as an adult on those victories, he could not fathom how a nerdy teenager edged out a pretty cheerleader and wondered if the teacher-advisor had rigged the election. She had since passed away, so he would never know. His senior year, Dassler served as the student representative on the Broward County School Board, where he started hobnobbing with the school district leadership and local media. Later that year, his classmates voted him most likely to succeed.

The summer before starting at the University of Florida, Dassler decided to lose as much weight as possible; he weighed more than three hundred pounds at the time. Every day at eleven he went to the gym and worked out while watching *The Price Is Right*. He arrived at the University of Florida at a significantly reduced size.

Dassler continued his focused energy and drive toward perfectionism in college, where he served on countless committees and studied to become a teacher. After graduating in 2002 with a master's degree, he went to work teaching English at Stranahan High School in Ft. Lauderdale. Along with a group of other teachers, he created a pseudo charter school inside Stranahan. In exchange for working with the lowest-performing students, the teachers received greater autonomy—an original purpose of charters.

Professional success and personal tragedy defined his five years at Stranahan. His work in the classroom, and his networking skills, attracted the attention of KIPP's founders, who talked with him about leaving Stranahan and training to be a KIPP principal. Leaders of new KIPP schools complete one-year Fisher Fellowships, named after the Gap founder and KIPP benefactor, through which they learn about the organization's principles and strategies. While at Stranahan, Dassler decided to apply for a Fisher with the aim of opening a KIPP middle school in Florida.

In 2004, Dassler's mother died of lung cancer. Just three years later, his father died of colon cancer.

At the end of 2006, Dassler learned he had won a Fisher Fellowship. KIPP would not be opening many schools in Florida right away, so Dassler had to choose between Houston and New Orleans, cities where the network was growing rapidly. At first, he ruled out New Orleans. He had attended Jazz Fest there and disliked the dirt, heat, and smells. He also wasn't sure how he could help the city recover from Katrina's devastation. But on the advice of a mentor, he agreed to visit New Orleans again before making up his mind. During the whirlwind trip he toured KIPP Believe, the young and thriving middle school whose fifth graders, including Geraldlynn, would make up much of the founding class of Renaissance. He met KIPP New Orleans' executive director, Rhonda Kalifey-Aluise, and other members of KIPP's leadership team. New Orleans—a city hellbent on recovery—felt like a place where he could heal from his own painful losses. Dassler made his decision quickly.

He would move to New Orleans, where he would stay for at least ten years and build a school that would help send one thousand students through college. During the taxi ride back to the airport, he texted friends the news and set his sights on that single goal.

The KIPP model is built on strong principals. While the fellowship educates them in KIPP's tenets, and the organization reserves the right to yank the KIPP name from an underperforming school, in practice school leaders have autonomy as to many specifics.

Part of Dassler's philosophy is that "talent" and "intelligence" are social constructs rather than fixed attributes that control our destiny. Your IQ does not matter as much as how hard you are willing to work and how nice you are; the KIPP slogan is "Work Hard. Be Nice." If visitors compliment Dassler on the smartness of his staff, he reminds them to say hardworking, not smart. He is, after all, a once socially isolated fat kid from a modest background who grew into a poised and accomplished adult who scarcely resembled his teenage self. In KIPP's world, but even more so in Dassler's, there is only one fixed thing and that is the ultimate vision, the end goal: the thousand first-generation college graduates by 2022. Through all obstacles, he retained an absolute conviction in what could be—what would be. This focus became his greatest strength, but also his deepest flaw.

While her principal tried to stay focused on the big picture, Gerald-lynn, like most fourteen-year-olds, took life one day at a time. When KIPP Renaissance opened on August 11, 2010, she had four all-consuming concerns, only the final, and least of which, related in any way to college or academics. First, she agonized over the large size of her uniform, which on her looked more like a floor-length dress than a knee-length skirt. Geraldlynn was petite in every respect: short, slender, narrow, small featured. Second, she worried about tripping over a cord of some kind and bringing a school-wide event, or opening class, to a crashing halt. (There was no precedent for this, but the image terrorized her mind nonetheless). Third, she hoped to make some friends. And fourth, she wanted to start the year on a good note with her teachers. She woke up so early on the first day of school to do her hair and try on her uniform one last time that she fell back asleep again and nearly missed the bus.

During the first weeks of the school year, Geraldlynn spent most of her nights and weekends at her aunt's house in the 7th Ward. Langdon, her stepdad, was temporarily out of work. That meant his car was temporarily out of juice. The entire family worked or attended school in the city, not the suburb where they rented an apartment. In a car it usually took at least thirty minutes to drive from the apartment to Geraldlynn's aunt's house; on the bus it could take over an hour and involved multiple transfers. Money was tight, too tight to pay for very many bus tickets back and forth. And too tight for Geraldlynn to buy the school notebooks her teachers told the students to purchase over Renaissance's first weekend, which cost less than five dollars. She asked for, and received, an extension.

Geraldlynn often felt as if she split her time between two different worlds: her more free-spirited, rural existence at the River Ridge apartment, where she traipsed about with other neighborhood teens, and her structured, KIPP-focused existence in the city, where she barely left school or her aunt's cramped house. She liked having two distinct sets of friends, but never let them meet for fear one group might cast judgment on the other—and on her as a result. Raquel's hectic work schedule troubled Geraldlynn more than anything else. Between the night shifts at the Gumbo Shop restaurant and the full-time job at the French Quarter hotel, with its rotating shifts, Geraldlynn went for days at a time without talking much with her mother. When Raquel's work schedule was most hectic, Geraldlynn had to get up at four A.M. if she wanted to

Raquel Dillon has always been very close to her two daughters and tries to spend as much time with them as possible. When Geraldlynn and Jasmine were young, Raquel started working two jobs—one in a French Quarter hotel and the other in a restaurant—out of financial necessity. Photo by Susan Poag.

have an extended conversation with Raquel. "Sometimes I get mad because I don't really spend time with my mama," she said.

Geraldlynn made an effort to get involved in the first few weeks of school. In her roundtable group, which functions as an elaborate homeroom with about fifteen students assigned the same teacher-advisor for all four years, she befriended the quieter students and tried to draw them out. She ran for class treasurer (and lost). She contemplated trying out for the majorettes but never got the money together to purchase a baton set. ("What am I going to do? Twirl with my hands?") She joined the ceramics club, which did not involve any out-of-pocket expenses. (It fell apart after a few weeks.)

The Renaissance teacher Geraldlynn grew to know best was Mr. Saltmarsh, a Massachusetts native who, at twenty-nine, was one of the school's more experienced teachers. He taught Renaissance's required "college-readiness" class and served as Geraldlynn's roundtable advisor. Geraldlynn felt a little nervous at first because Mr. Saltmarsh was white and a man, and she worried he might be quick to judge his students. But she trusted the sincerity of his intentions more than many of her classmates. In the first month of the school year, Mr. Saltmarsh made home visits to meet each of his advisees' parents. Geraldlynn was used to such practices from her middle school years and took it in stride. Other students in the roundtable bombarded him with questions: *What you coming to my house for? My house not clean! You coming to say something bad about me? You coming by yourself? I really want to make sure you coming alone . . .*

When Mr. Saltmarsh asked one student if she was afraid to have him in her house, she responded: "I'm afraid for *you*."

In the opening weeks of Geraldlynn's eighth-period college-readiness class, Mr. Saltmarsh had the students take an online test that analyzed which of their "multiple intelligences" were most pronounced, research careers that suited their strengths, and write letters to colleges requesting information. The different intelligences, so labeled by psychologist Howard Gardner, are kinesthetic, interpersonal, intrapersonal, linguistic, naturalist, existential, visual, logical, and musical. When one student ranked low in naturalist intelligence, she shouted, "Mr. Saltmarsh! It says I'm not naturally smart. I'm smart as hell!" Geraldlynn took the test and wrote a letter to the University of Southern California asking for a brochure. But she wasn't sure what to make of the information that while she ranked high in interpersonal, intrapersonal, and naturalist intelligence, she fell lower in musical and visual. "I don't know if this is supposed to help us in high school or college or where," she said. Geraldlynn had two main criteria about college. First, she wanted diversity—ideally 25 percent African-American, 25 percent Caucasian, 25 percent Hispanic, and 25 percent Asian. Second, she hoped to leave New Orleans.

"Whenever I see these abandoned houses, it turns my mood."

On the second Friday in September, Mr. Saltmarsh gave the students in his roundtable their first progress reports. Before handing them out he stressed their importance, noting that research showed that students who earn at least a B average in their freshman year have more than a 95 percent chance of graduating high school. "This is most important to *you,* not me," he told them. "You are a mature young person. You are proactive. You have it in your hands. The world's not going to wait for you. We don't have all those manufacturing jobs we used to. You need skills. You need information." As he handed out the reports, students asked the significance of an A/B grade or an I (incomplete), muttered about how a poor grade in one class could destroy a GPA, and woefully recited out loud some of the teacher comments, which in one case included "disobedient," "disrespectful," and "never does homework."

Geraldlynn, however, took one look at the sheet of paper and then waved it over her head as she shouted, "I'm smart!" in a way that implied the question had been in serious doubt until then. Her highest grade was an A-plus in physics, and her lowest a B-plus in Spanish. She strode out of Mr. Saltmarsh's room and declared to the students in the hallway, "I got all As! Almost." Then she went in search of her Spanish teacher, a supremely organized and reserved Teach For America alum who seldom smiled in class. (In an effort to get her to smile more, the students, at the administration's urging, began marking down how many times she smiled per class and then reported the results.) Geraldlynn wasn't upset about her grade; she wanted to ask about a demerit her teacher had recorded on the progress report. The teacher told Geraldlynn she had been talking in class a few days earlier. Geraldlynn started to respond but turned away, walked off, and continued to wave the sheet of paper with glee.

She remembered a fable Mr. Dassler had told the students during orientation—reportedly based on a tale told by a Cherokee Indian elder to his grandchildren. According to the legend, two wolves live inside every person, one good and one bad. The good wolf stands for joy, compassion, and faith while the bad wolf represents fear, anger, and greed. The wolves constantly fight each other for food and nourishment. When the grandchildren of the old Cherokee asked him which wolf won, he replied, "The one you feed."

Geraldlynn wanted to protest the demerit and tell her Spanish teacher that it was only fair to inform students of infractions instead of quietly recording them in her KIPP-issued iPad. But, thinking of the fable, she bit her tongue and "let the good wolf win."

(Unlike many of the strategies KIPP Renaissance used to motivate and discipline students, the Cherokee fable took on a life of its own; even the most rebellious students occasionally reminded their classmates to "let the good wolf win" or "remember to feed the good wolf." The fable's power over their actions seemed to suggest that appealing to a person's higher self, no matter whether they are young teenagers or adults, carries more influence than rules or demerits ever could.)

That night, Geraldlynn rushed into her aunt's house, dumped her bag, and showed her stepdad the report card. He congratulated her (although Geraldlynn thought he could have been a *little* more enthusiastic after harping on her about schoolwork and college for so long). She stayed up that night until her mother returned from work and could admire the near-perfect grades. Then, well after midnight, a happy but exhausted Geraldlynn fell asleep.

Not everything was going so well at Renaissance, however. As the school year progressed, Dassler continued to "sweat the small stuff" but struggled to address bigger problems that threatened to undermine the whole school. He obsessed over minor transgressions like sloppiness with uniform ties and scratches in the wall paint, calling them "micro-abrasions against our culture." Meanwhile, students sometimes cursed out teachers or made cruel remarks to classmates with impunity. The school's application of the broken-windows theory took on a tragic absurdity.

Geraldlynn became a particularly astute observer of her high school's trials and shortcomings—a kind of Greek chorus of one, since she rarely played a direct role in Renaissance's biggest dramas. Just a month into the school year, she could sense a negative vibe. Students who talked back to teachers were sometimes cheered and egged on, not shunned. Fights broke out too often. Few of her classmates did their homework. It wasn't uncommon to hear a student exclaim at the end of the day, "Detention be popping today! We got beaucoup people there." Already, Mr. Dassler had made announcements at school assemblies about "teammates" who wouldn't be coming back to Renaissance anymore. He rarely mentioned a name or gave out any details, leaving everyone wondering who had done what this time.

"As a school we're struggling," said Geraldlynn the weekend after she got the news about her grades. She had returned to her alma mater, KIPP Believe, to help out with some community-service projects that Saturday and could not help but contrast her middle school's structured warmth to the floundering Renaissance. "We're having fights, disobedience, homework problems. If we're starting like this, I don't think we'll build stronger."

THE PRINCIPAL
"Our efforts should be spent on creating a school that's worth fighting for."

Throughout the fall, O. Perry Walker's band ended each performance with a heart-wrenching finale. Those with keen eyes and ears could tell something was different whenever the band began playing "I'll Be Missing You" by Puff Daddy. There was an extra trace of emotion in the chords, an aching sadness in the young musicians' faces, a sense of longing in their forceful, poignant sound.

The band's rendition of the song had been a favorite of twenty-two-year-old Brandon Franklin, Walker's popular assistant band director. Under the leadership of director Wilbert Rawlins (whom Laurie always referred to as Maestro), Brandon helped build a powerhouse band program at Walker in the years after Katrina.

Brandon, a Walker graduate, was sweet-faced and friendly even to strangers. The students worshiped Brandon for his charisma and talent as a musician—but also for his empathy as a teacher. Walker student Azania Briggs said Brandon gave her the gift of musical literacy. She had performed in school bands for years without the ability to read music. When she asked different musicians for help, they inevitably played a whole song for her, beat out the rhythm, or hummed a tune. Only Brandon took the time to break it down into pieces, showing her how to read the notes to "Stars and Stripes Forever" by John Philip Sousa. "It was like uncovering ancient ruins, finding a trunk of gold," Briggs said. "That was the best gift anyone has given me."

Rawlins, forty, had hoped that someday his protégé would replace him as the band's leader, helping keep alive the tradition in New Orleans schools. During a chance conversation he had with Brandon, Rawlins had joked that his wife might neglect to have the Walker band perform at his funeral.

"Brandon, make sure the band is at my funeral," Rawlins said.

"But if *I* die . . . ," Brandon replied.

"You're too young to die," Rawlins told him.

But Brandon continued, "If I die, I want *all* the bands at my funeral."

Memory of the conversation haunted Rawlins months later, in May 2010, when news hit that Brandon had been murdered. His ex-girlfriend's more recent boyfriend shot him in the heat of a domestic dispute.

Rawlins set out to fulfill Brandon's wish: He issued an all-call to high school marching band players and alums from across the region, trying to assemble a megaband to perform at the young man's funeral. In the days before the services, hundreds of musicians of all ages, experience levels, and high school affiliations descended on Walker's campus to practice for the event. Rawlins had to stand on top of a chair to see the back rows of a band unparalleled in its size.

"One person cannot stick out," Rawlins told them during a rehearsal. "You hear me? One person cannot stick out." Because of the sheer numbers, the band had no problem making itself heard. But Rawlins reminded them that sometimes even the loudest voices fall flat.

"A lot of people think that loud makes drama, but loud does not make drama," he said. "You need to come from one extreme to the other. That's what makes drama."

On a sweltering morning in May—out of their love for music, marching band, and Brandon—all the bands came. Wearing crisp white shirts and black pants, they gathered in the parking lot outside a modest church in eastern New Orleans toward the end of the funeral ceremony. They carried flutes, clarinets, trumpets, French horns, saxophones, trombones, tubas, cymbals, and flags from just about every high school in the area that still had a marching band. As Brandon's family and pallbearers exited the church, all they could see in every direction were the sad, earnest faces of hundreds of young musicians whose brass instruments gleamed in the midday sun.

The players stayed stoic for the first song, "Total Praise." But by the second, Brandon's beloved "Missing You," the heat and emotion began to overtake them. Sweat poured down their faces and mingled, in some cases, with tears. During a section when the tubas alone carried the beat, voices cried out, "We miss you! We miss you! We miss you!" As they waved their instruments in the air, the shining brass almost seemed to touch the low-hanging clouds. During the song's resounding finale, all the musicians played in unison as if they had performed together their entire lives. Not a single instrument stood out.

Walker had already lost several students to gun violence at the time of Brandon's death. Such losses were part of the reason Mary Laurie hoped to carry out the work of not only a school at Walker but a social service agency. Walker stays open for longer hours than most schools and its staff members serve as teachers, grief counselors, social workers, youth advocates, and parents. "I think we've done good work, but I don't know that the numbers (test scores, attendance and graduation rates) will always reflect our good work because of the kids we take on," said Laurie, referring to the fact that the school accepts some of the city's most challenged and challenging students. At any given time, the school has about fifty female students who are pregnant or new mothers, several students involved in the criminal justice system, and more than one hundred students with a special need. "Walker's a twenty-four-seven school. We believe we've got to find a way to give kids a safe place to be," Laurie said. "And that's not spoken for in those numbers."

Within the charter school movement there are those who favor a holistic approach to combating poverty, and those who contend educators must keep their focus narrow and their goals neatly defined. Geoffrey Canada, a supporter of charter schools, helped popularize the former approach through his work at the Harlem Children's Zone, which introduced early-childhood, parent-training, mentorship, and asthma prevention programs within an established geographic area. Only after several of those programs were up and running did Canada tackle education directly, opening a charter school. In New Orleans, most education leaders have taken the latter route, focusing exclusively on the schools and avoiding any meaningful effort to expand access to public pre-kindergarten programs, bolster the city's mental health services or drug treatment infrastructures, improve health care for families, or increase the number and quality of recreational opportunities available for their students. (It isn't uncommon to hear community leaders complain of how charter school leaders sometimes impede those efforts by keeping kids in school after the start of summer camp programs, for instance.) Recovery School District superintendent Paul Vallas pledged upon his arrival to make schools more like community centers, with parent-resource rooms and health care available. But little of that vision transpired, and what did failed to take root as Vallas steadily handed over the RSD's schools to charter school operators. Vallas received much of the praise, blame, and publicity for the successes and failures of the New Orleans charter schools. But at most of them he was an increasingly remote figure toward the end of his four years in the city, relevant mainly in that he controlled school building assignments.

Mary Laurie is a supporter of Canada's approach. She dreams of having the philanthropic support to offer the programs of the Harlem

Children's Zone, whose work is heavily subsidized by private money, including donations from Wall Street hedge fund managers; or the SEED School in Washington, D.C., where the students, mostly low-income, spend the weeknights staying on campus in an effort to isolate them from the dangers and distractions of their neighborhoods. SEED also receives significant philanthropic support for its near 24-7 approach. While Walker receives next to nothing in private dollars compared to the Harlem Children's Zone or SEED, it does benefit from some outside financial support. In partnership with Louisiana State University Health Sciences Center, the school hosts a health clinic with a full-time nurse practitioner and part-time psychiatrist and pediatrician. But most of the school's supplementary programs must come out of Laurie's budget.

Since Walker aspires to be a holistic, community-focused school without the luxury of many extra financial supports, Laurie has to rely on outstanding individuals more than programs or bureaucratic systems. Of Walker's many counselors, social workers, coaches, and "interventionists," one of the best known is Big Mike. His official title is academic and behavioral interventionist for ninth graders. But really his job is to understand the children: where they come from, what they need, when a fight is about to break out, which boy likes which girl, whether she likes him back, who has no support at home, why a student is crying. As he tells the incoming ninth graders, "You will discover soon just how well I infiltrate myself." Big Mike is like a big kid—but a seemingly indestructible one. One time, a six-foot-tall student athlete leapt straight into Big Mike in the middle of a school hallway, as if attempting a diving tackle. He bounced off Big Mike's chest and back to earth like a rubber ball. Then he picked himself up and tried the same tackle two more times before Big Mike sent him back to class. According to Anthony Johnson, a Walker defensive tackle who became the number-two college football recruit in the country, "If you lose Big Mike, you might as well count off everything."

Big Mike withholds only two pieces of information from the students: his age (every January he tells them he is turning twenty-nine again) and his weight (one can only guess from his dimensions—a girth that comes close to filling a doorway, a face shaped like a soft, round pillow, and hands that look like giant, lightly padded mitts). The lack of specificity adds to his mythical quality, the sense that, in more ways than one, he is larger than life.

Big Mike grew up in New Orleans in the 1980s and '90s, the oldest of eight children. At the age of thirteen, he walked into the family's living room one day to find his mother crying, clutching a light bill in her hand. Already working full-time, she could barely afford to pay her bills. Raising eight children without much support, she fretted about their being alone for long periods if she worked more hours. "I got it," Mike remembers telling his mother. From that day on, he looked after his siblings like a father. Big Mike attended high school in New Orleans before moving to Texas for a few years and continuing his education. After he returned to New Orleans, he began tutoring students at Woodson Middle School. The school's principal saw Big Mike's rapport with the students and quickly expanded the young tutor's duties to include child advocacy and counseling. Big Mike had little formal training in either.

Laurie first heard of Big Mike when she became principal of Guste Elementary in the 1990s, the elementary feeder school for Woodson. When Guste alums returned from Woodson to say hello to Ms. Laurie, they invariably told her stories of Big Mike. Even though she did not meet him in person until she took the helm at Woodson a few years later, she sensed his name had just as much to do with his big heart as his size.

Big Mike spent even the worst of Katrina's aftermath inside a school—although not on purpose. When he was growing up, his elders had always told him that "if a storm come, go to the projects," because the projects would always stay standing. Heeding their advice, Big Mike brought his family to the B. W. Cooper project in Central City after it became clear Katrina would be fearsome. When the winds ceased, he returned to his house to pick up provisions. The water started rising on his way back to the B. W. Cooper, so Big Mike took shelter in the old James Derham Junior High School building at 2600 South Rocheblave Street, which he had attended years earlier. The days he spent trapped on the building's second floor were the worst of his life. Other people from the neighborhood took refuge with him as the waters continued to rise. Within a few days they had finished off all the food and water they had on hand. An older man died of dehydration and want. Tempers flared. Some of the school's temporary inhabitants began to fight. A helicopter rescue finally ended the refugees' misery.

He spent the next several months in Texas, where he stayed in the Houston Astrodome for three weeks, and then Texarkana, a small town on the border of Texas and Arkansas. Big Mike appreciated the peace and quiet of Texarkana, but he missed home. When Ms. Laurie called to say she would be heading up O. Perry Walker and wanted him to help her, he jumped at the chance to go home.

One of Big Mike's greatest strengths is the ease with which he communicates with Walker's teens, even the most troubled and abrasive ones. One afternoon, a girl stormed through the school's courtyard, shouting over her shoulder at a teacher, "Screw you!"

"Come here," Big Mike said, enveloping her in a hug. "Start being nice."

He picked up the girl's hand and sniffed it, to see if she had quit smoking. They joked that the best advice her therapist had for quitting was to call 1-800-QUIT-NOW.

The therapist had phoned Big Mike not long ago because he wanted to talk to the only person who could calm the girl down. The teen had reported during one session that whenever she is about to "go off" at school there's only one solution: "I go sit by Big Mike's fat ass."

Big Mike only seems truly frustrated when a child fails to communicate with him, and that gets them into trouble. He once drove that point home to two students whose latest fight nearly got them put out of Walker. Big Mike told the students he would do everything in his power to keep them at Walker as long as they avoided each other and kept him in the loop.

"Let me even see you look at each other and I'm going to put you out," Big Mike said as they both stared at the floor. "This is a school, and this is foolishness. What do I tell you? Everything is big to me. Tell me. You talking to Mike. Mike know you, Mike know you. Put your head up, look at me."

When he had both of their eyes on him, he added, "I tell you, I know y'all from top to bottom. And I'm the only bully here. The only one."

Walker is one of a significant but shrinking number of schools in New Orleans run and staffed predominantly by veteran African-American educators who, like Big Mike, grew up in the city. Many of the displaced and demoralized teachers and administrators who worked in the pre-Katrina New Orleans Public Schools did not reapply for their jobs after their mass dismissal in Katrina's wake. Others could not get rehired, some because they failed the required skills test. Veteran educators like Mary Laurie ran most of the first charter schools to open in the city after Katrina. Several veterans continue to run successful schools, including

Sharon Clark at Sophie B. Wright Charter and Doris Hicks at Martin Luther King Jr. Charter. But the new schools that opened after 2007 were disproportionately led by young white transplants.

The vast majority of Recovery School District charter schools are overseen by either white male or black female principals, with a comparatively small number of black male or white female school leaders (which in and of itself sends an interesting message to New Orleans schoolchildren about who has authority in their community—and who does not). The black female principals tend to hire veteran New Orleans teachers, while the white male administrators rely more on younger teachers brought to the city through alternative recruitment programs such as Teach For America and teachNOLA. The latter program is a local affiliate of the New Teacher Project (now known just as TNTP), which works in more than twenty-five cities; Michelle Rhee, the controversial former school chancellor in Washington, D.C., created the organization in 1997. Like Teach For America, it focuses primarily on low-income communities and provides alternative paths toward teacher certification. But TNTP places more priority on recruiting established professionals who want to switch careers than Teach For America.

Although there are exceptions (Mary Laurie employs predominantly veteran teachers but always has at least a few Teach For America corps members or recent alums working at Walker), the results of this polarization in hiring practices are striking. One set of schools runs according to traditional New Orleans paradigms that emphasize relationships, neighborhood allegiances, a hierarchy based on age, years of experience, rank, and educational degree, and a reliance on the fixity of things, including school names, professions, institutions, and political dynamics. At these schools, the past is always present, sometimes to stifling effect. The other set of schools runs according to a mixture of corporate and Silicon Valley paradigms that emphasize data, placelessness, a hierarchy based on ambition, perceived talent, institutional prestige, and an idealization of the concept of "flexibility" in which nothing is static or fixed. At these schools the past is sometimes treated with callous disregard. Both the veterans and the newcomers often look askance at the other—sometimes for obvious reasons, since livelihoods are at stake. The result, however, is that too few schools benefit from a healthy mixture of the two philosophies and staffing profiles.

Adrienne D. Dixson, an associate professor of education at the University of Illinois–Urbana Champaign who taught in New Orleans

through Teach For America in the 1990s, notes that a vital "intergenera-
tional exchange of wisdom and energy" is lost when teachers are segregated by experience level, as they are when veterans cluster at some
schools and newcomers at others.

Josette Ripoll, a longtime Orleans parish educator (whose grandson is
KIPP student Tyrin), has negative feelings about both the pre- and post-
Katrina hiring practices. For years she tried to get hired as a principal in
the Orleans Parish school system. But the principalships always seemed to
go to those with political or personal connections. "An area superintendent told me, 'It's not what you know, it's who you know.' I said, 'Well, I
must not know the right people.'" She listened to rumors of jobs going to
the "baby mamas" of top district officials, and tales of principals who had
bribed higher-ups for their posts. "I used to say, maybe this is not for me.
I'm not selling my soul to the devil. I'm not making no deals."

After Katrina, Ripoll was appointed principal of Schaumburg Elementary, one of the Recovery School District's few remaining traditional
schools. But then she watched as charter organizations steadily took over
schools like Schaumburg, usually laying off the principal and staff and
then replacing them with younger staffs recruited partly from out of
town. As someone who had grown up in New Orleans and worked for
decades in the system to earn her position as school leader, it pained her
to watch this process. In the spring of 2010, the charter group ReNEW
Schools assumed control at Laurel Elementary, removing one of Ripoll's
friends as principal and replacing her with a recent graduate of New Leaders for New Schools. The organization, whose name has since changed to
just New Leaders, selects aspiring leaders who want to work in high-
needs schools in New Orleans and other cities, bypassing the traditional
career ladder and certification process. After watching her friend displaced, Ripoll was cautious when asked to mentor one of the program's
administrators-in-training. "I don't have problems with training
someone," she said. "But I don't want to train them to go kick my co-
workers out."

Like Mary Laurie, Ripoll rose from a humble working-class background. Her mother worked as an examiner at a factory that made men's
suits. Her father worked at a shipyard but lost work during hard times.
To keep the family afloat between unemployment checks throughout
those periods, he sold dirt from Almonaster Salvage Yard. "We had grits
and eggs sometimes for dinner, but no one went hungry. We never went
on food stamps," said Ripoll. After Katrina and the firings, everything

her parents had worked and prayed for seemed to evaporate. The firings "made you feel like they really didn't care, like they didn't respect us as professionals. You were hearing stories about people who were working at McDonald's who were still getting paid, and people teaching in St. Bernard Parish [adjacent to New Orleans] never missed a paycheck. But here we had been working with a system, a business, a company for years and they were like, 'Just go to Western Union and get your last paycheck.' That was a slap in the face."

The firing of New Orleans school employees was an attack on the city's black middle class, even if not intended as such. Like Mary Laurie and Ripoll, many of the fired educators were in the first generation of their families to reach America's middle class, an income level that finally permitted them to buy homes and cars and send their children to college. Their success represented the culmination of more than a century of battles fought and freedoms won, starting with the abolishment of slavery and continuing through the decades as African-Americans attained the right to attend public schools, the right to vote, the right to hold public office, and the right to live, travel, and move throughout the country as they chose. The whole world watched as Katrina and the failed government response dispossessed the poor black population of New Orleans of their homes, lives, and dignity. But far fewer paid attention over the following months as the school board and state dispossessed much of the city's black middle class—ironically the more invisible class in this instance—of their livelihoods and any remaining sense of security. It's not hard to understand why teachers took the firing not only personally but as a direct political assault on the power and stability the black population of New Orleans had worked for generations to accrue.

Most teachers knew as well as anyone that the pre-Katrina schools failed too many of the city's children. And all but the most extreme would concede that, in some cases, subpar educators were to blame. Taxpayers, state officials, and school system leaders set up even good teachers to fail at times, however, by starving the schools of resources or squandering them. New Orleans public schoolchildren had been criminally neglected for decades. But no single villain perpetrated the crime.

Members of the black middle class and traditional civil rights organizations are among the more vocal critics of efforts to overhaul the schools not just in New Orleans but in New York and Washington, D.C., two other cities where school district leaders have made controversial attempts to expand charters and curtail the power of teachers' unions.

As in New Orleans, the black middle class of those cities has much to lose by way of jobs and political clout. Most experts and pollsters agree that the failure of former Washington, D.C., mayor Adrian Fenty's bid for reelection stemmed at least in part from his support for his schools chancellor, Michelle Rhee. Supporters credited Rhee for her take-no-prisoners approach to improving the city's notorious school system, arguing she acted in children's best interest (if not always that of adults). But in critics' eyes, she epitomized the aggressive, unfeeling school reformer: shuttering schools, weakening teacher tenure provisions, supporting nonunionized charters, and inflating the importance of standardized tests. In New York, the NAACP sued along with the teachers' union to block the city's expansion of charter schools. In an e-mail sent in June 2011, NAACP leader Hazel Dukes accused a Hispanic mother who supported charter schools of "doing the business of slave masters," echoing the language used by Jerome Smith when he rebuked the charter operator who wanted to take over Craig school in New Orleans' Treme neighborhood.

Those seeking to transform the country's school system often describe and defend their agenda in terms of the economic development of the nation's poor. However, they rarely if ever include the stability of the teaching corps and black middle class in their economic calculus. Some of them maintain that for too long public school districts have been viewed as jobs programs for adults at the expense of children. Indeed, that can be true at times. But the firing of thousands of the city's most established middle-class workers carries an economic impact all its own.

The state takeover of New Orleans schools after Katrina and the wholesale firing of the city's teachers provoked long-standing tensions surrounding self-determination in education and the extent to which a community should be able to control the fate of its own schools. As much as Laurie liked working at Walker, she sometimes regretted the loss of Woodson Middle School, which she led until Katrina. When the city reopened in the fall of 2005, Laurie visited the Woodson building with some of her colleagues. The air stunk of spoiled food, a glass mural had shattered, and water gushed out from a broken pipe. But the flood line wasn't as high as they had feared, and the New Orleanians who took refuge in the building during the flood caused little damage. "They pushed out some windows for air, but otherwise it was exactly as we left it," said Laurie. One of her colleagues declared Woodson could be fixed up with some bleach and a good hard scrub.

School and FEMA officials had a different take. The final FEMA report described the buildings that made up Woodson's campus as "catastrophically damaged" from mold, mildew, and rust. A few years later, the buildings were demolished. Laurie drove past the empty grounds late one evening. Staring at the space where Woodson had once been, she could not help but regret the unfinished work she helped start there. In her eyes, the school's absence left a big, gaping hole in the heart of Central City. Around that time, Laurie learned KIPP would probably take over the Woodson campus. In a settlement, FEMA had agreed to give the schools $1.8 billion for repairing and rebuilding flood-damaged facilities. Part of that would go toward building a brand-new school at the Woodson site.

The school had been named after Carter G. Woodson, an African-American historian who in the early 1930s authored *The Mis-Education of the Negro*. The book contends that the white-led American public schools of the early twentieth century indoctrinated black students into positions of inferiority in society. Woodson wrote, "The Negro will never be able to show all of his originality as long as his efforts are directed from without by those who socially proscribe him. Such 'friends' will unconsciously keep him in the ghetto." Woodson argued that African-Americans had to take charge of their own educations or risk constant oppression. "If the Negro is to be forced to live in the ghetto he can more easily develop out of it under his own leadership than under that which is super-imposed," he wrote.

In many respects, Woodson's philosophy matched that of Jerome Smith and stood in stark contrast to the views of contemporary school reformers. Woodson believed whites, even the most well-intentioned and compassionate, should not take charge of the education of black children because their aim is to turn them into "good negroes" whose values are acceptable to the white majority, not fully actualized black Americans well versed in their own language, culture, values, and history. While many present-day charter school educators joined the movement partly because they felt that too few African-American students continued on to higher education—a college-for-all mantra has since come to define the movement—Smith and Woodson before him view America's higher education institutions, particularly the most elite, as corrupting in some respects. Woodson, for instance, described Harvard,

Yale, Columbia, and the University of Chicago as "the products of roll-top desk theorists who have never touched the life of the Negro." His thinking represented an evolution, and radicalization, of W. E. B. Du Bois's philosophy, which emphasized black empowerment through political rights and educational attainment. Both men disagreed with Booker T. Washington's accommodationist approach to the white power structure and his belief in an education program for blacks that prioritized economic development over intellectualism. But Du Bois, the first African-American to earn a doctorate from Harvard, put his faith in higher education while Woodson doubted blacks could ever thrive within institutions created by those who had once enslaved them.

The context has obviously changed since Woodson's book was published in 1933: Segregation is no longer legal, and minority students attend and teach at the nation's colleges and universities in far greater numbers. But that said, it's striking how prescient Woodson's critique seems in the twenty-first century. Woodson died in 1950 before the *Brown v. Board* decision, and no one will ever know how he would have felt about changing the name of New Orleans' Carter G. Woodson Middle School. But one can guess that he would probably have wanted his name to disappear with the building, since what happened in New Orleans after Katrina represented a repudiation of everything he believed in.

The philosophy of Carter G. Woodson echoed in a few of Mary Laurie's own sentiments as she surveyed the young educators who descended on New Orleans. It discouraged her and other veteran educators that many of them installed their own vision without enough regard to what had come before or the uniqueness of the place. She could not fathom, for instance, why some of the new charter high schools did not start marching bands. Horns were like extensions of schoolchildren's hands in New Orleans. In neighborhoods like the Treme and the 7th Ward, where the city's musical traditions had their deepest roots, youngsters borrowed their mamas' kitchen equipment to form makeshift bands and parade through the streets at dusk. By high school, marching band drum majors were as revered as football quarterbacks, if not more so. "I think a lot of people who come to New Orleans want to change New Orleanians," said Laurie. "We are poor, but we are not void of. Culturally we may be different, but we are not void of.[6]

"You don't have to lockstep our children," Laurie continued, referring to the intense structure at many of the new charters. "You can't take away the music. Literally what you're saying is that our children are not equal to; that there is just this one narrow way of educating the poor. Poor is not a culture. It's not . . . They believe there's a culture of poverty. They are not even conscious of it. But it plays out in all their actions."

Laurie often remarked, with mixed feelings, that schools were run more like businesses than ever before; businesses where test scores were the bottom line. And like a business, Walker had to compete: for students, teachers, attention, private funding, an inhabitable building, even for respect. The competition forced schools to up their game. But it also left educators at some schools constantly worrying about their survival—if test scores did not continue to go up, for instance, or if they lost their appeal to families.

In January, the state board of education would vote on whether to renew Walker's charter contract, and for how long. The state issued charters for five-year terms. At that point, schools had to show they had met their numbers—enrollment numbers, test-score numbers, and financial numbers—or the state could shut them down.

Numbers now equalled destiny for New Orleans public schools. No longer were schools treated like community fixtures whose future was virtually guaranteed (barring an extraordinary event or dramatic decline in student population). Now schools were like stocks in a portfolio that could be dropped at any time for poor performance. Cities across the country were shifting toward a similar model of running schools, called "portfolio management"—a term that suggested a vision of schools as virtual, abstract entities that could be bought and sold with little human toll.

No city has taken portfolio management so far as New Orleans, however. Both critics and advocates of the concept make compelling arguments: Supporters point to the hundreds of schools across the country that have grossly failed children for years, sometimes generations, with little consequence. Skeptics maintain schools should not be closed like McDonald's franchises that fail to sell enough hamburgers. Officials need to shore up floundering schools, not shed them.

Despite her concerns, Laurie felt at relative peace about Walker's future in the fall of 2010. The school would probably not receive a five- or ten-year renewal on its charter when the state board voted in the winter—its test scores weren't that high—but Laurie could not imagine the board would revoke the charter or close the school completely. She remained optimistic that after years of delay, the Recovery School District contractors would soon start work renovating the campus, particularly the auditorium.

Two of the schools' most promising recent graduates, Cornelle Carney and Richard Comeaux, had returned that fall to work as part-time assistants at Walker while they studied at local universities. Cornelle was the student who had been so distrustful of Walker when he enrolled there in the months after Katrina, wary of its violence and racial isolation. During his years at Walker, he had stopped filtering out the bad memories of suburban St. Bernard Parish, where his old school, Chalmette High, was located. He recalled the racial epithets people used to shout at him virtually every time he rode his bike down the street. As a kid, "I thought one of my names was nigga," he says. Cornelle also remembered how, in the weeks before Katrina, he had started cutting up more than ever before—smoking weed, breaking glass bottles, sneaking into the movie theater. Such typical teenage transgressions were usually harmless for the white teenagers who surrounded him at Chalmette. But Cornelle had watched several black males move quickly from minor misdeeds to ruin, the result of tenuous safety nets, racial stereotyping, and perverse incentives. "I was heading down a road where I knew I could end up in jail or killed," he recalled.

By his senior year at Walker, Cornelle had embraced Walker, realizing the school had something to offer him that Chalmette High School never could. It helped that at Walker, students and staff typecast him as a "good kid," not a bad one. Cornelle did not believe Chalmette's predominantly white staff would have known how to provide him the nurturing he received at Walker. As a young teaching assistant, he hoped to help pass on that gift to another generation of students.

Walker could strengthen its academic program, but it had a solid base from which to grow, with one of the city's more diverse teaching staffs, an increasing number of Advanced Placement courses, and dozens of students participating in dual-enrollment programs with local colleges. The range and quality of its extracurricular activities were unparalleled in the city. And its football team appeared poised for greatness with top recruit Anthony Johnson and a cast of other star players preparing for their senior seasons.

Plus, Laurie herself was back at Walker full-time. The previous school year, 2009–2010, she was forced to spend several weeks in the winter away from Walker while recovering from surgery for breast cancer. Doctors caught the cancer early, and the surgery and subsequent radiation treatments seemed to work. But the news jolted the school community, leaving the students and staff rudderless and ill at ease. Not a day went by when someone did not ask after Ms. Laurie or lament her absence. Laurie, forced to stay quarantined in her house just a few miles from Walker, did not take inactivity well: She had no real hobbies. (She often wished she could find comfort in church or distraction from sports like so many others she knew.) By the time doctors told Laurie she could return to Walker in the spring, both she and the school had settled into a state of relative malaise. Her return reinvigorated them both.

The Walker community still mourned Brandon Franklin's passing the previous spring, but the pain had eased. Laurie and the rest of Walker's students and staff prayed that violence and tragedy would not mar this school year as well—that they would make it through without the entire Walker community collapsing into grief. As the fall wore on and the 90-degree-temperature days came to an end, they settled into their work. Mark Bailey, one of Walker's assistant principals, had made an observation that resonated with the school's leadership team, including Laurie. "Instead of spending time and energy fighting for the continued existence of Walker," he told them, "our efforts should be spent on creating a school that's worth fighting for." They all hoped that would be enough.

PART IV

Trouble

(Fall/Winter 2010)

THE TEACHER
"I want to go to a normal *school."*

At Sci, they called it the October Slump.

Throughout New Orleans, students and teachers fell into a state of general orneriness just as the rest of the city started to enjoy the cooler weather and relax over the approaching end to hurricane season. By the start of October, most schools had been in session for nearly two months and the adrenaline had worn off, yet the Thanksgiving holiday still loomed far off in the distance.

At Sci Academy, the novelty of intense structure and relentless ambition dissipated as the temperature dropped. It was a season that proved particularly difficult for the first-year teachers and students. "October is hell," said teacher Kaycee Eckhardt. "Things stop being fun. Kids are like, 'We still have two hours of homework a night. We still have to stand in line. We still have to be silent. This sucks. I want to go to a *normal* school.'"

After the honeymoon period concluded, Aidan's ego started to take a beating. He no longer considered himself "the bee's knees," as he sometimes had during his final year at Martyn. At Sci, the expectations for lesson planning, classroom decorum—just about everything—were far higher. He felt as though his class was below average. As he had during his first year at Martyn, Aidan struggled most with delivering his lessons and keeping the class on task. Some of it stemmed from inexperience and

Aidan Kelly talks with Jerel Bryant and Emma Donley, his colleagues at Sci Academy. In their first year at the school, teachers often work more than seventy-five hours a week and receive constant feedback on their performances in the classroom. Photo by Daymon Gardner.

the adjustment to a new school and kids, but Aidan himself was also an acquired taste. The students were amused by his bow ties, occasional stutter, and Harvard accessories. It took time to get past all that to see how much he cared. "Not everyone took him seriously at first because he's such a character," said Sci student Marquisha Williams. As hard as Aidan worked, parts of the autumn felt defined by individual lessons gone wrong and individual students with whom he could not connect.

In his writing class for sophomores he tried, for instance, to teach the students about parallel structure the way he had learned it. One of his high school teachers compared understanding parallel structure to appreciating good music: You developed an ear for it after you heard it enough. So Aidan showed his students example after example of sentences that followed the same grammatical pattern, thus adhering to parallel structure, and ones that did not: "Bruce likes swimming, water polo, and scuba diving" versus "Bruce likes swimming, water polo, and to go scuba diving"; "The committee studied all parts of the problem: educational, financial, and political" versus "The committee studied all parts of the problem: educational, financial, and politics."

But the students did not catch on.

In his first-period class, a male student shut down completely when in a bad mood, refusing to communicate with Aidan or even look him in the eye. Aidan struggled to get him talking. Meanwhile, in his fourth-period class, a group of girls talked over him and their classmates. Aidan struggled to get them to be quiet.

One of the most challenging students Aidan taught first semester was Lora. Most kids admitted when they had done something wrong, even though they might try to finagle their way out of a punishment or occasionally explode in anger at being caught. But Lora lied up and down to avoid her fate. No matter what Aidan told her, Lora had a "What you saying?" response ready. When Aidan spotted Lora using her cell phone one day, Lora argued her defense like a pro. At Martyn, Aidan wasn't expected to do anything when he saw a cell phone, since there were few school-wide expectations and rules. But at Sci, teachers were told to take a cell phone for a week the first time they saw it, a month the second time, and the entire school year after a third sighting.

"I have to take it," Aidan said.

"No, it was a watch," Lora protested.

"It was a phone."

Lora started her cross-examination. "What kind of phone? What did it look like?"

Aidan told Lora she was being disrespectful.

"What do you mean, disrespectful?"

At Sci, each misstep or shortcoming was subject to exhaustive, well-intended scrutiny. In Marcovitz's opinion, Aidan overintellectualized his decisions in the classroom throughout the fall instead of acting on his instincts. "There are so many things to think about in a Sci Academy classroom," he said. Aidan "was not effective at internalizing one so that he could move on to the next." Aidan was so excited that some of his students participated eagerly in class from the get-go that he did not pay enough attention to the silent (or defiant) ones who contributed little in class discussions. Marcovitz and Margo Bouchie, Sci's director of curriculum and instruction, encouraged him to "cold-call"—call on students who did not raise their hands—to engage the quieter and more recalcitrant students in his lessons.

While observing a few minutes of Aidan's teaching on October 5, Bouchie tapped out 190 words of real-time feedback, nearly all focused on student behavior and Sci's expectations. The e-mail arrived in the in-boxes of Aidan, Marcovitz, and Jerel Bryant, the dean of humanities, while the lesson was still in progress.

("Lvl" was the abbreviation for different student volume levels; "ss" for student scholars. TIOS stands for "this is our school" and often refers to a moment when a teacher attempts a "full group reset" in an effort to turn around a struggling class.)

Key lever: cold call
Goal: 100% of cultural expectations 100% of time

You cold call Lora—while she answers she says shut up to a peer. You don't address. TIOS moment!

You release to lvl zero to try a couple on own. You get it. Nice.

Enforce uniform. rochelle and kendrionne both wearing outside sweatshirts-it's picking up on little things like that and enforcing every single day that will show you mean business

Brian(?) in front constantly talking to rochelle. Notice this and give consequence- every time.

Lots of open seats in front- I feel like it would be better if everyone was pushed up to first 3 rows- some in back 2 rows feel no heat.

When u are questioning one student, your focus still needs to be on other students to make sure they are tracking and only focusing on class material (many rummaging through bags, etc instead of tracking)

The quad of girls in back doesn't seem like a great seating arrangement- constant lvl 1 chatter

I think bringing in pictures and objects to use comparative and superlative adverbs and adjectives about could make this fun!

That same week, Marcovitz was more brief when he stopped by for a quick observation of the same class. He began his feedback by restating the same goal and "key lever," and then continued:

Right off the bat you're in trouble. Three ss reclining in chairs. Rochelle not doing anything. Kendrionne not tracking when u ask. Nobody in front row except Brittany is really tracking.

You're on the verge of this getting out of control. Set expectations strongly at beginning of each class and don't get distracted from your goal.

I've seen u call on 6 ppl none of them cold called.

Aidan had experienced similar struggles during his first semester at Martyn. But this time he was working even harder, his trials were more public, and the expectations were higher—both his own and the school's.

His psyche hit a low late one morning. The skies opened up over the city, unleashing a characteristically intense New Orleans rainstorm. Sci still did not yet have canopies over the outdoor walkways on its new campus, so when it rained everyone clustered under umbrellas or got drenched. The rain made students irritable, brazen, stressed—sometimes all three. On this morning it came accompanied by soul-jarring thunderclaps whose sound and fury seemed to underscore the flimsiness of the classroom modulars and the craziness of the entire endeavor. When it rained, the partially deserted section of the city where Sci resided felt very much like swampland. In Aidan's fourth-period class, some students milled around the room, declaring, "I am *not* going out in that rain!" Others walked out into the torrent without permission. One student asked to go to the bathroom, then disappeared for a half hour. Despite all of the tips and advice he had received, Aidan could think of no "tools" he had learned that would allow him to fix this situation. If Sci's opening day two months earlier had epitomized order and neat perfection, this day seemed to represent its opposite: a wet, sloppy, ungovernable mess. He doubted any of his colleagues' classrooms looked so chaotic. Over and over he tried to regain control by counting down to level zero: 3, 2, 1, silence. But inside the kids kept talking, while outside the thunderstorm raged. If he could not thrive at Sci, Aidan worried he might not be cut out for teaching at all.

Over the last several years, a growing bipartisan coalition has argued that rigid contracts, seniority-based reward structures, comparatively generous pensions and retirement benefits for those who are fully vested, and not enough focus on "results" have combined to keep too many weak and mediocre teachers in the profession for too long. (Only the most extreme and shortsighted of these critics believe most teachers are overpaid or enter the profession for mercenary reasons. And Democrats such as Arne Duncan and Barack Obama tend to emphasize the "results" part, while Republicans home in more on the benefits and pensions.) The most frequently cited examples focus on cases in which it has been difficult to fire incompetent teachers under existing union contracts. The New York City "rubber rooms," for instance, infamously served as holding pens where the small fraction of teachers accused of misconduct sometimes spent years collecting their full salaries while the arbitration process dragged on. The tragicomic absurdity of the rubber rooms became a cause célèbre for leaders like former New York Schools chancellor Joel Klein, who was hell-bent on making it easier to fire teachers.

Critics of charter schools like Sci, on the other hand, claim that young teachers like Aidan often burn out before they have time to realize their full potential—or even determine whether they are good teachers. A state-commissioned study in Texas found the annual teacher turnover rate in new, open-enrollment charter schools averaged about 38 percent compared to an average of 15 percent for traditional schools statewide. Moreover, while one might expect the turnover rate to decrease as charter schools mature, the Texas study found the rate actually increased as the schools aged: At charter schools that had been open for at least four years, the average turnover rate hit 41 percent. A widely disputed study of the Los Angeles Unified School District reported similar findings: Charter schools serving middle and high school students lost about half their teachers each year, a turnover rate nearly three times that of other public schools.

The primary sin of skeptics on either side of those arguments is one of omission: They each view the issues through a narrow, distorting lens. Those who say union contracts are biased toward older teachers and make it too hard to fire the weakest performers have a point. But in focusing so relentlessly on what they see as the intransigence of teachers' unions, they gloss over a priority that should rate just as high: finding ways to make teaching sustainable as a career (something unions have been enormously successful at). In contrast, those who bash Teach For America instructors for their brief commitment—or liken top-performing charter schools to sweatshops—are right at times, too. But they often overlook the importance of attracting more top college graduates into teaching.

One side talks obsessively about recruiting young superstars into education but not enough about keeping them there. The other rightly views education as a career and not a way station, but for too long has avoided conversations about teacher quality (disdainful of the very term) that might challenge, and even upend, the status quo.

While Marcovitz bristled at those who doubted Sci's mission on the basis of sustainability, he nonetheless spent a lot of time thinking about how to keep his teachers. Compared to other young charter schools in the city, Sci lost few teachers—two or three each year it had been open. Marcovitz hoped to keep the attrition rate small. Since he hired teachers based partly on their growth mind-set, he tried to find ways to keep them learning and growing at Sci. Most Sci teachers took on an expanded role in their second or third year at the school, perhaps becoming a grade-level chair or subject-matter dean. (It wasn't unusual in New Orleans to meet twenty-seven-year-old charter school teachers who worried that they were still, on the far side of their twenties, *just* teachers answering to curriculum directors a year or two their junior.)

Isaac Pollack, a science teacher, was the only instructor at Sci with a child. He made it work, but not without sacrifice. Isaac's wife, a nurse, had been pregnant when Sci opened for its second year in August 2009. Isaac arranged to take a week off from teaching to spend with the newborn. But his wife conveniently gave birth on the Saturday before Thanksgiving, right before a vacation week for the entire school. Isaac was back at work after the holiday along with everyone else, without having missed a single day of classes. Throughout those first few months, Isaac's wife almost always got up when the baby cried or needed food in the middle of the night since her husband's intense work schedule afforded him less than optimal sleep already. "She was amazing at taking almost the full burden of the night stuff," Isaac said. On a typical week, Isaac sees his daughter and/or wife for a few minutes each morning. When his wife is off, she spends the evening with their daughter. When she is working, Isaac watches the baby from five thirty to seven thirty P.M., spends the next hour and a half with his wife, and then works from nine P.M. to midnight or one A.M. Because he is an observant Jew, he does not work over the Sabbath and uses that time to recharge and bond with his family.

By the fall of 2011 Isaac and his wife expected a second child, but his work schedule was, somehow, busier than ever. In addition to teaching a full slate of classes and serving as the science dean, he participated in a teacher-coaching program run out of MATCH charter school in Boston.

His advisory, all senior males, took up still more time. Sci's leaders had asked teachers to avoid suspending students whenever possible. Instead they wanted advisors to put in place a "growth plan" that would allow any of their advisees who were in serious trouble to remain in school. The school had suspended 38 percent of its students at least once the previous year (the state average fell just under 10 percent). According to Isaac, the message was, "The advisor has full authority and needs to exert it. You need to own any problem. And solve it." Isaac struggled most with how to help Mark, an advisee who had been expelled for forty-five days the previous school year for bringing drugs on a school trip. (Isaac tutored Mark during the expulsion period, and the teen still took and passed the state's standardized tests at the end of his junior year.) Mark had returned to Sci for his senior year, at which point he promptly stole a set of headphones in front of three other students—declaring, "I'm a gangsta, I do what I want"—and required an immediate "growth plan."

Isaac devised several individualized lessons in morality for Mark. One day, he had his advisee assist one of the school's most severely disabled students in an effort to teach Mark empathy. Another time he asked Mark to take notes on every positive and negative behavior in a class, and then analyze how they affected the classroom dynamic and the students' ability to learn. He required Mark to read *The Chosen*, a coming-of-age story that follows two Jewish teens as they learn about compassion, religion, and faith in 1940s Brooklyn. Before giving Mark the book, Isaac reread it to gauge whether he thought it would feel relevant to an African-American teenager coming of age in post-Katrina New Orleans some seventy years later. (He decided it probably would.) Isaac spent at least three or four hours a week thinking about ways to help Mark. In his first couple of years as an advisor, he had relied more on Sci's rules and systems than individual relationships when dealing with his advisees. Now he felt as if he was paying the price. "I hid behind the systems," Isaac said of his first years as a teacher at Sci. "Now I have to backpedal and try to become more of a father figure."

Isaac had thought about leaving Sci and finding a less time-consuming job. But Marcovitz had given him a pep talk, telling Isaac he did the most important work in the world and asking if he could ever be happy in a less meaningful job. The speech succeeded. "If I didn't believe that this was the most important thing I could be doing with my time, I would leave in a second," he said. (As his second baby's due date neared in the fall of 2011, Isaac hoped his wife delivered during the Jewish holidays so he could once again avoid taking off extra days for a paternity leave.)

Other staff members could not find a way to balance Sci's rigorous demands with their personal lives. Former college counselor Liz Rainey arrived at Sci in the middle of the 2009–2010 school year, glad to find a job in the same city as her fiancé. She admired Sci's goals and accomplishments but found the pace relentless. Throughout the year her thoughts drifted to her many relatives who taught in public schools very different from Sci, including two aunts. Despite thirty years of experience and stellar reputations, they would not have lasted a week at Sci. At the end of the school year, Liz resigned to take a less exhausting job as a counselor at Loyola University New Orleans, where she could continue working to help low-income students make it through college in a different capacity.

Looking ahead, she said there was no way she could have raised a child while at Sci. "Not in the way that I'd want to be a mom," she said. "I don't know how you could breast-feed. I think I'd have trouble being pregnant and working there based on what friends of mine have told me about pregnancy and being tired all the time and not able to be on your feet as much." She paused, and thought about the puppy she and her now-husband had adopted a few days earlier. "I'm not sure if I could have gotten a dog if I still worked there," she said.

At the age of thirty, Liz had been one of the school's oldest staff members. In her early twenties, she might have felt more comfortable with the grueling pace and esprit de corps, she said. But older and newly married, she valued her time away from work more.

Other Sci teachers found the only way to make the job sustainable was to resist the pressure to take on additional responsibilities. Like Liz, Kaycee Eckhardt was also a few years older than most Sci teachers. She had tried in the school's second year to serve as freshman dean in addition to teaching. But she felt as though she was "on a seesaw," doing neither job justice. For the 2010–2011 school year, she dropped the administrative position. That still meant working a few hours on the weekends and in the evenings. But she could go to yoga class twice a week and block off five P.M. on Friday until eleven A.M. on Sunday as uninterrupted personal time. Kaycee, who grew up in Louisiana, has an infectious passion: Watching her preach the virtues of school at a student ceremony or event feels akin to attending a religious revival. She taught at Clark High School, a traditional school in the Recovery School District, for a year before joining Sci's staff. Kaycee liked Sci from the start: She felt as though she had a say in what happened. The administration acted quickly in response to student and teacher needs. Stuff got done.

"For me this is sustainable," she said. "I don't know that it is sustainable for everyone. Many of our teachers don't know how to draw lines and say, 'No, I am not doing that.' It's totally okay to say no and go home at four thirty."

One afternoon that fall, the Sci community trooped over to the nearby Greater St. Stephen Full Gospel Baptist Church to watch Marcovitz's appearance on *Oprah*. Most of them had no idea what their principal could possibly be doing on the talk show. But there he was standing beside teacher Jerel Bryant and representatives from five other schools from across the country, all of them charters. Oprah opened the segment by announcing that she was dissolving Oprah's Angel Network, a viewer-supported charity, since her show was entering its last season. "I know that thousands of kids . . . are waiting to get into your schools," she told the charter leaders. "I value nothing more in the world than education. It is the reason why I can stand here today. It is an open door to freedom." For that reason, Oprah said she had decided to award the final round of grants to the assembled charter schools. "One million for you, one million for you, one million for you," the megastar said as she went around the semicircle distributing the enormous, made-for-TV checks. "I know you will spend it well." Watching in New Orleans, the students shrieked and celebrated with a brass band.

A few students weren't invited to the celebration, however. They included one of Aidan's advisees, Gabe, a sixteen-year-old freshman who suffered from an emotional disability. The decision to leave Gabe behind that afternoon eventually generated a small storm of negative publicity when Bloomberg News ran a story with the headline OPRAH-BACKED CHARTER SCHOOL DENYING DISABLED COLLIDES WITH LAW. The story quoted the boy's great-uncle, who recalled Gabe saying, "They left me, they left me out," when the rest of his classmates departed for the church to watch Oprah. Marcovitz called Gabe a "beloved member of our school community" and said he was banned from the ceremony to protect the safety of other students. But the story left readers with more questions than answers about the circumstances surrounding the incident, and never quoted the teenager directly.

Perhaps the most oft-cited critique of charter schools is that they do not serve the neediest students. In New Orleans, there's some truth to that—particularly when it comes to children with severe, diagnosed disabilities. In 2010, for instance, charters educated about 60 percent of New Orleans public schoolchildren. But they served only about 38 percent of the students with autism, 37 percent of those with an emotional disturbance, and 23 percent of the students with multiple disabilities. The lion's share of students with the most intense disabilities attended non-charter schools run by the Recovery School District, which posted the worst results in the city. The reasons for these gaps were varied: Some charter schools break the law by turning away students with more severe special needs. Other times, parents do not even bother approaching charter schools because they assume they cannot meet their child's needs, decide the schools are too rigidly focused on college, or the Recovery School District central office assigns them to a non-charter school. As the number of non-charter schools dwindled in the years after Katrina, they served ever higher concentrations of students with challenging behaviors. The district increasingly used them as the depository for students coming out of alternative schools or juvenile corrections. And some charters, although not all, forced or encouraged their most challenging students to leave midyear. Since no centralized, student-level tracking system existed, schools could easily get away with forcing withdrawals or refusing admittance to students with special needs or chronically disruptive behavior. The unethical behavior of some tainted the reputation of all.[1]

An equally pervasive problem is adequately serving students with special needs and challenging behaviors while they are enrolled, a task that extends to schools of all types. In the fall of 2010, the Southern Poverty Law Center filed a federal discrimination suit that featured the stories of ten named plaintiffs, including Gabe. Based on their experiences and other data, the lawsuit alleged that many New Orleans schools deny admission to students with disabilities; systemically fail to create plans to serve special-needs students or implement existing plans; and punish students for behaviors that are "manifestations" of their disability, a practice prohibited by the federal Individuals with Disabilities Education Act.

The life stories and educational histories of the students featured in the lawsuit illuminate how difficult it is to assign clear blame for their struggles, particularly those with emotional disabilities, like Gabe. Most of the students were between the ages of three and thirteen when Katrina hit. Not only did they endure the immediate trauma of the storm, including lost homes and relatives, but afterward some bounced between schools for years. Meanwhile, study after study has shown that Katrina's effects on children's mental health did not abate within a year or two of the tragedy and persist today.

A shortage of community mental health services, including drug treatment programs for teens and in-patient beds for those in severe crisis, exacerbate the schools' challenges. Kathy Kilgore, a veteran special education administrator who opened a citywide special education support center after Katrina, said New Orleans has very few programs that provide ongoing therapy to families, particularly in their homes. As a result, poor families that do not own cars often cannot take advantage of the free or reduced-rate services that exist. Moreover, very few counseling centers guarantee that a child will meet with the same psychologist or social worker during each visit, which makes it much harder to build trust and basic understanding.

But Kilgore said we let schools off the hook by putting the blame too much on poverty, Katrina, and a shortage of wraparound mental health services. The high number of young teachers in some New Orleans schools—the vast majority of whom have never been parents themselves—makes it harder to confront challenging student behavior early and effectively, she says. As a result, unchecked inappropriate behaviors can morph into chronic conditions. Or, on the flip side, a novice educator might mistakenly assume challenging students have a mental illness when, in fact, they just need to talk to a trained social worker. "We have elevated the number of serious mental health issues among our schoolchildren because they weren't addressed early on," Kilgore said. "We wouldn't have as many problems if we were doing a better job with the language, climate, and culture of schools." She said her staff frequently gets called out to schools when children are having a crisis, only to discover no one on staff knows whether the children are on medication, any specific details about their home life, or whether they see a doctor regularly. Employing veteran teachers does not necessarily solve these problems, said Kilgore. But they are more likely to be familiar with the social context in which their students live and have the experience and confidence to redirect negative behaviors at their onset.

Gabe's story, as outlined in the lawsuit, illuminates these complexities. He moved to Augusta, Georgia, with his family after Katrina, where he was diagnosed with an emotional disability. Gabe returned to New Orleans at the start of the 2008–2009 school year to live with his great-uncle and enrolled at Craig Elementary, a non-charter school in the Treme. Over the course of his first semester at Craig, Gabe failed all of his classes, received a total of forty days of suspension, and was recommended for expulsion twice. He then returned to Georgia in January 2009 to live with his grandmother, who died four months later. Back at his uncle's house that summer, Gabe was shot while playing outside with friends in the Lower 9th Ward. He spent a month at Children's Hospital, then returned to school. In the 2009–2010 school year, the Recovery School District shuffled Gabe between four schools (Craig again, Drew Elementary, the eighth-grade academy inside Douglass High School, and an alternative program run by the RSD called Hope Academy) but allegedly never gave him the behavior-support or special education services required under the law. The schools suspended him a total of thirty more days, and the police arrested him on campus several times for fights, threats, and a host of other issues.

Gabe was a particularly challenging case. But many New Orleans students arrive at school with intense, often unmet, needs. Students have witnessed murders, lived through Katrina's chaos, passed in and out of alternative schools, lost close relatives to shootings, spent time in jail, and attended more schools than they can remember. One of the sophomores Aidan taught, a genial student named Bobby Calvin, spent two years at Schwarz Alternative School partly because of a paperwork mistake. "I had a fight a long time ago and ended up staying there longer than I was supposed to," he said. At that abysmal site on the city's West Bank, the RSD housed students in a crumbling, termite-infested building with spotty air-conditioning, rookie teachers, few supplies, and a single full-time social worker for, at times, more than three hundred students. For part of the period Bobby attended Schwarz, a private company brought in by RSD superintendent Paul Vallas ran the school. The company, called Camelot, fielded its own security force, which routinely slammed misbehaving students—including a pregnant girl—into floors and walls to maintain control.

Much younger children also exhibit signs of stress, trauma, and insufficient health care services. At Akili Academy, which serves only the lower grades, one troubled kindergartener could, and often did, destroy an entire classroom in seconds: knocking over chairs, throwing piles of books on the floor, trying to tip over a computer. A first grader sometimes made sexually explicit comments, referring to "titty bars" and telling classmates to "suck my dick." Two third graders who displayed all the symptoms of autism had never been diagnosed or treated. Another third grader openly and vocally complained of her anger, tensing when she said that sometimes she felt like tearing materials off the classroom walls.

No-excuses charter schools sometimes back their way into these issues. They have such an overtly academic focus, they tend to deprioritize any issue they perceive as extraneous to their mission of sending all their students to and through college. Many of their leaders believe that schools, like businesses, must adhere to the Hedgehog Concept and find the one service in which they can excel rather than dilute their programs with too many diverse goals. Meanwhile their aim of "reacculturating" their students into a more school-focused orientation can cause them to overlook the need to understand the nuances of their students' pasts, home lives, and neighborhoods. They are guilty, at times, of erroneously viewing their students as "blank slates."

Some, although not all, of the city's new school leaders and teachers grew more sensitive to their students' mental health needs over time. They learned, like Isaac Pollack, that at the end of the day relationships mattered more than systems. Their reasons were both expedient and idealistic. Increasingly, they grasped the impossibility of achieving their primary goal without more of a focus on "the whole child" (even if they would never use that term). At Akili Academy, an initial screening of the school's students by a team from Tulane University flagged nearly half as possibly having a serious behavioral, emotional, or social need. Principal Sean Gallagher had told his teachers during orientation that he did not intend for Akili to be like the Harlem Children's Zone. But by mid-fall, he lamented the dearth of mental health services in the city and continued his search to find a social worker for the school. With no social worker or counselor on hand, teachers had to text the name of a child who acted out in class to an administrator or aide. That person removed the child, then talked or walked with them until they calmed down. Everyone agreed it was an imperfect solution, since it meant taking the child out of class and did little to address the root causes of problems the way professional, ongoing counseling would.

Marcovitz's wife worked as a school psychologist, so he was more attuned to the need for mental health services than some others. Sci has had a social worker on staff since it opened and received support with psychological services from a partnership with Tulane. Over time the school also hired another part-time social worker and a full-time psychologist.

But in some cases schools did too little, too late, and in others their efforts alone would never be sufficient. By the time Gabe arrived at Sci Academy in August 2010, he had, in the last two years, lost his grandmother, experienced a half dozen school transitions, spent more than three months out of school, and very nearly been killed. He read at a second-grade level and performed math at a third-grade level. He had been failed by school after school. Sci hired a full-time mentor for the teenager. But even Marcovitz admitted that was not enough. "He needs and deserves a full-day therapy program that does not exist in the state of Louisiana," said the principal.

Aidan had internalized a conviction that defines the contemporary education reform movement and the Teach For America mission: that a student's success or failure in the classroom can almost always be traced back to his teacher. He fervently believed it was a teacher's job to meet all of a student's needs, whether that meant tutoring late into the evening or connecting them with community counseling services. "If you're stubborn and thoughtful enough, the number of things that you would file 'out of my control' shrinks dramatically," he wrote in one e-mail. "Almost everything can be attacked in some way if you remind yourself that *you* are responsible for your students' outcomes." He hoped Sci succeeded with Gabe. It would help the teenager. But it would also, he thought, show that his school could educate just about any child who came through its doors.

Eventually Aidan learned how to communicate more effectively with Lora, and she acted up less in his class. Lora thrived on sincere, precise praise, so Aidan made a point of giving her a quick thumbs-up sign or verbal accolade when she did something well. He retaught the lesson on parallel structure, this time introducing the concept in a more explicit way: He showed the students John F. Kennedy's inaugural address, and they dissected the speech and its verb-any-noun pattern together: "Let every nation know, whether it wishes us well or ill, that we shall pay any price, bear any burden, meet any hardship, support any friend, oppose any foe . . ." Aidan asked other staff members what they would have done to handle the classroom debacle during the rainstorm. They advised Aidan to "reset" the entire class if a similar situation arose again, which meant sending the students back to the entryway to walk in again, take their seats once more, and start the lesson anew.

But despite his colleagues' advice and support, as well as incremental victories, the job still did not feel right. He could not accuse the school of false advertising. Teaching at Sci was exactly what Ben had said it would be: intense, all consuming, with no time to rest on one's laurels. But Aidan did not feel like a "fully actualized person" anymore. "I didn't feel happy with myself," he said. "It felt like I was running, always running, and I never had time to stop and reflect."

It didn't help that during the fall, thieves broke into the house he shared with friends in the Treme. A houseguest had inadvertently left the metal gate covering the door unlocked. The thieves struck during the day while Aidan was teaching. They took Aidan's home computer, but at first it did not seem like much else: a bottle of Yukon Jack, a bunch of coins, the packaging for a fake mustache. It wasn't until the next morning that Aidan realized they had also taken his spare car key, because his car was gone. Around the same time, Aidan's work laptop died and he mistakenly dropped his cell phone into the toilet. The events added to his feelings of unsettledness and flagging confidence. (The robbers abandoned Aidan's car not far from his house in the Treme within a few days.)

Aidan never once thought about quitting; that wasn't in his DNA. But he made up his mind early in the fall that this would be his last year teaching. He might stay at Sci, but not in the classroom. He remained resolute for several weeks—including the day Oprah Winfrey bestowed $1 million on Sci.

He waited until a mid-October check-in to tell Marcovitz about his decision. Marcovitz told Aidan to put such thoughts out of his mind for now, pointing out that he could not act on them for months and should try to improve as much as possible before then. "If you become a really great teacher this will all feel different," Marcovitz said. If Aidan still felt this uncertain in the spring, then they could talk.

THE FAMILY
"KIPP be trying to change us."

Just hours after the start of fall break, the teachers at KIPP Renaissance High School analyzed two pie charts whose bright, geometric shapes seemed to encapsulate all their failings.

The charts broke down the 3,075 demerits the school's thirteen staff members had given to about 140 students in the first two months of the school year, an average of twenty-two demerits per student and 236 per teacher. Students who earned four demerits in a day had to stay for detention. The first pie sorted demerits by the offense the teachers had recorded in their KIPP-issued iPads: 379 for "disrespect-minor," 830 for no homework, and 1,147 for "disobedience/insubordination." The second chart broke the demerits down by teachers, who had doled out as many as 661 demerits and as few as fifteen. When Allison Luzader, the school's earnest young physics teacher, saw she had given out the second-highest number, she moaned, "I feel like a terrible person." Her 601 demerits, color coded in bright aqua, accounted for nearly a fifth of the pie.

KIPP Renaissance had just finished a rough last week of a rough first quarter. Several of the all-freshman students did not seem to want to be there. In classes they covered their uniforms with hoodies or jackets, talked when teachers told them to be quiet, insulted their classmates, ignored instructions, and complained that some teachers did not know how to pronounce their names. Luzader had tried to cut down on demerits by sending disruptive students to another classroom for the remainder of the class period. But that backfired when some students, perceiving banishment as a privilege, asked her over and over again: "Can I go to another class?" Renaissance's marching band—typically a source of pride and prestige for New Orleans high schools—struggled to get off the ground. After lackluster turnout at the first few practices, music teacher Lionel Williams temporarily suspended efforts. On the Wednesday before fall break, he hung a handmade sign in the school's main hallway that read: NO PRACTICE. WILLIAMS. Shortly before the staff meeting, a group of boys put their arms around each other's shoulders and literally skipped down the hallway toward the school's exit, chanting "Fall break! Fall break! Fall break!"

After the teachers digested the pie charts, the conversation turned to the subject of "emotional bank accounts," a term the school's college-readiness teacher had recently introduced in his class. The concept came from a book called *The 7 Habits of Highly Effective People*, and it held that human relationships are like bank accounts to which we can make deposits that build rapport and trust, or from which we can make withdrawals that erode them. The more deposits a person makes with another, the more likely the other is to forgive a mistake, but a relationship dominated by withdrawals is fraught with mistrust. Brian Dassler, the school's principal, suggested the teachers make more deposits with the students, including taking them out to lunch at nearby restaurants—particularly, he said, those whose behaviors are "already negatively impacting their path to college."

"I feel like I've already made so many withdrawals that if I made that offer to some, they'd say, 'Get out of my face,'" Luzader responded.

"No, they wouldn't," Dassler told her.

"Make more deposits," urged Jason Saltmarsh, the college-readiness teacher.

"If you really feel like it's overdrawn, kids know that conversation from Mr. Saltmarsh," Dassler added. "Just say, 'I know it's overdrawn and I want to fix it. How can I do that?'"

Two days later, Geraldlynn sat in her aunt's 7th Ward home, bemoaning her school's troubles. Without knowing about the pie chart, Geraldlynn agreed some of her teachers were too quick to hand out demerits: She had received one earlier in the week for talking out of turn. But unlike many of her classmates, Geraldlynn could count her recent demerits on one hand.

"In some classes, if they say, 'Look up,' and we was trying to finish up a sentence, we get a demerit for not looking up," she observed. She sat in the living room beside her stepdad, Langdon, and cousin on the small bed where she slept when her family stayed over. Her mother pulled up a stool to join the conversation.

"So a demerit is like a punishment or something?" Raquel asked.

"No, it's not like a punishment. It's like a—"

"Like a mark or something?" her mother said.

"Yeah," Geraldlynn agreed.

Geraldlynn conceded the school had to do something to maintain better order since the endless iPad marks weren't working. She was struggling in geometry because of all the outbursts and distractions. Some of her classmates came to classes red-eyed and "beaucoup hungry" every day from smoking pot. Rumors swirled that when school resumed in three days, at least a few of the most disruptive students would be gone. "Some days we're doing well," she said. "The next day it's out of control." Deep down, Geraldlynn wanted KIPP Renaissance to succeed just as much as her teachers, even though she might not have admitted that to her parents. (On this evening she informed them, "If we have a KIPP college, *please* don't sign me up for it.") She did not want to spend the entirety of high school showing up and taking care of her business just because that's what her mother wanted. "I want KIPP Renaissance to lead *me* to be wanting to be at school," she said. But that would only happen if the classes grew more interesting and the worst-behaved students weren't allowed to hijack the entire school.

Raquel had not expected the school to be so chaotic. "The last few days, Geraldlynn's been coming home saying they are smoking marijuana in the school. It seems like they do whatever they want to," she said. "I like the school, but I don't want anything really, really bad to happen before I decide to take her out. I don't want her to get caught up with the wrong friends."

Raquel and Langdon are by nature patient and generous-hearted people. They weren't about to give up hope yet in KIPP, whose middle school program they had loved. Indeed, their faith exceeded that of some KIPP Renaissance teachers. "I know it's going to take a minute before they get things in order," Raquel said.

Langdon remained convinced the school would turn around if the principal stayed consistent in enforcing rules. "Kids that don't want to do right, you don't even have to put 'em out because the rules are going to make them leave," he said. "The school just opened up. It's going to be fine by next year. All that man [Dassler] got to do is stand his ground, keep his ground, and watch how that school changes around. I got faith in that man."

Geraldlynn, too, tried to stay optimistic. Her grades were good. In just two months she had made lots of friends. She liked many of her teachers as people. But Geraldlynn understood the chaos at Renaissance was preventing it from thriving academically. Demerits clearly couldn't keep some kids in line. And the fourteen-year-old wasn't sure what the teachers should try next. She acknowledged the emotional bank account, with all its fancy language, confused her more than anything else.

"I really don't know the purpose," she said. "When they go on about it, I'm just not sure what they are talking about."

KIPP Renaissance's struggles increased as the holidays approached and 2010 drew to a close. A group of about a dozen students acted out on a daily basis, particularly in the classrooms of a few of the school's young white female teachers. In a not atypical scene, Geraldlynn's physics class descended into chaos one morning right after members of a national school-review team from KIPP left the classroom. A few students used markers, erasers, and a large container of moisturizer as projectiles, hurling them at enemies—or just for fun—whenever Ms. Luzader's back was turned. Ms. Luzader tried to get the suspected offenders to stay after class for a talk. But one of them turned his back and walked off with a quiet, steely "Fuck you." When Ms. Monsour, the guidance counselor, warned that he was on the verge of suspension, the teen replied, "I don't care," and continued on his way.

Every few days it felt like there was a new problem: fights (including one in which a male student with special needs started choking a female classmate, and another that started in front of KIPP's New Orleans leadership team), a pernicious Facebook slam page, a knife found in a student's shoe. Worse, the misbehaviors of only a few caused a general negativity to spread throughout the school. Geraldlynn was embarrassed on behalf of her school, but she admitted she was not immune from low-level disrespect herself. If a classmate said or did something funny, even at the expense of a peer or teacher, she sometimes joined in the laughter. Few fourteen-year-olds, after all, want to seem like a Goody Two-shoes.

The school's shortcomings were not for lack of trying. Teachers like Allison Luzader and Jason Saltmarsh spent hours planning classes they hoped would be engaging enough to keep students focused. The most maligned teachers not infrequently burst out with impassioned defenses of even their most merciless tormentors. The staff meetings almost always ran long because the teachers brainstormed over how to connect with challenging students. Teachers skipped doctor's appointments, came to school when they were sick, and worked through many weekends.

At the staff meetings and in long private conversations, the teachers agonized over individual failures and classes gone wrong. In October, sensing the need for help, principal Brian Dassler hired Nathaniel Lang to handle discipline. Most recently Lang had worked in Douglass, the school KIPP Renaissance replaced, and for years before that in the pre-Katrina school system. He grew up in what was once New Orleans' St. Thomas public housing development, and he seemed to speak the kids' language. Before hiring Mr. Lang, only one of the school's thirteen staff members, Lionel Williams, had grown up in the city. The black staff members now included Lang; Williams, who taught music; and Kia Childs, an English teacher and Teach For America alum from Philadelphia. The other ten staff members were white and came from across the country. They grew up in Florida, Massachusetts, Ohio, Illinois, Wisconsin, Michigan, Maryland, Georgia, and northern Louisiana. Several had lived in New Orleans before they started working at KIPP Renaissance, but in most cases only for a year or two. Three of them moved to town not long before Renaissance's professional development started.

Initially the school had a fourth black staff member, but Dassler fired her two months into the school year. She had resisted teaching the school's lowest-performing students in her geometry classes, saying she wasn't there to work with students who did not even grasp basic math. Dassler told the teacher she had two weeks to improve, in the middle of which, deeming her effort insufficient, he gave her the option of resigning or getting fired. She chose the latter.[2]

Even with Lang on board, KIPP Renaissance remained at sea when it came to discipline. Teachers and staff had no idea if the solution was to give out more demerits or fewer, to send disruptive kids out of class or to keep them there, to slacken the rules or to strengthen them. An us-versus-them mentality began to develop between the students and staff—and, to some extent, between the staff and the principal—a disconnect that appeared to worsen every week.

Individual teachers and students had plenty of private opinions about what was going wrong and how to fix it. Some put the blame on failed systems, others on failed relationships. Ms. Bard, the school's Spanish teacher, thought the staff needed to make more of an effort to follow through: "We need to do what we say. If a kid gets four demerits, that's a detention." Mr. Williams lamented the cultural gap between the predominantly African-American, low-income teenage students and their predominantly white, middle-class, twentysomething teachers who, he said, tried to coddle the students when in fact they needed a tough-love approach.

Tyrin, one of the students, thought the school was too strict, particularly during lunch—the only time during the day the students could talk among themselves—when they now had to sit with their roundtable groups. "I think they try to control us too much, that there's not much freedom," he said. "In the beginning of the year it was reasonable, you could deal with it. Now it's . . ." He paused. "Too tight."

His classmate Moira was even more blunt. "KIPP be trying to change us," she said. "No offense, but we a school full of black people. Some people are going to be ignorantly ghetto."

Too often, these conversations occurred on parallel planes. Rarely, if ever, did the staff and students discuss together the ways in which students felt that KIPP was trying to change them, much less address the complicated set of feelings and beliefs that led to the last part of Moira's assertion. (How, after all, are you supposed to realize KIPP's goal of lifting students from the ghetto to the Ivy League if you don't have conversations that establish an understanding of what students think it means to be "ignorantly ghetto" and why they feel some of their classmates are doomed to remain that way?) Instead, most KIPP Renaissance students spent the late fall wondering why the school had to have so many rules while their teachers wondered why the students refused to behave.

Even as the school floundered, Dassler's vision remained compelling. He wanted to build a school "that I'm proud of and would want to send my kids to, one that's not unfairly punitive or arbitrary and that's rooted in respect." He praised the teachers for "working very hard and doing the best they know how." He believed when students acted out that "a good number of their behaviors come from academic frustrations that don't have an outlet." He acknowledged the cultural gap between the students and the staff, saying, "We cannot graduate students who don't know themselves, don't respect themselves, and haven't learned their histories."

But he struggled to execute that vision, and his actions sometimes failed to live up to his words. "I have a few real sadnesses," he said that winter. "The first is that we're not a good enough school yet and the second is that I'm not a good enough principal yet for all of our kids." If his best effort was not good enough, he would have to find additional means of putting Renaissance on a more positive track. Thinking of the shoving and fighting that had become all too prevalent between students, he said, "We've got to get rid of it . . . It's going to mean some kids aren't at our school anymore."

By November, Geraldlynn had settled into life at the school, albeit at a remove. Renaissance's heavy emphasis on college preparation during freshman year baffled her. When students had to fill out copies of the common application for practice in college-readiness class, Geraldlynn failed to see the point. She never found an extracurricular activity she liked, and socialized in her free time mostly with other teens who lived near her family's apartment in River Ridge. She skipped the first school dance because she did not feel as if she had anything to wear. Raquel was also annoyed that students had to pay for the nachos and other food at the dance. The family missed the school's Convocation ceremony, a fall event designed to welcome the students and expose them to collegiate rituals. Raquel had to work that Saturday morning, Geraldlynn was out in River Ridge, and the school did not provide transportation. Student attendance at Convocation was bad and parent attendance even worse. About fifteen parents showed up (out of well over one hundred) to watch their children receive a tassel—presented as a symbol of academic and collegiate ambition—from one of dozens of local African-American college graduates the school recruited to serve as mentors. The emptiness of the auditorium that morning showed the disconnect between the school and its families. But parsing out the causes of that disconnect remained difficult: Had families failed to show up for pragmatic reasons (lack of transportation, work schedules, short notice), philosophical reasons (a lack of buy-in, flagging support for the school, little interest in the very concept of a convocation), or some combination of the two?

Raquel and Geraldlynn often discussed the causes of KIPP Renaissance's problems, debating the factors that made it so different from Geraldlynn's middle school. They talked about challenging students, disengaged families, inexperienced teachers, a first-time school leader, and, for a few students, the growing lure of drugs and guns. But easy explanations eluded them as well.

Raquel had a day off from both of her jobs one Wednesday in November. Geraldlynn wasn't feeling well, so she stayed home from school for the first time that year and the two spent a rare full day together. They tried to sneak out in the afternoon to do some shopping at a local mall, only to discover that Raquel's most recent paycheck had not yet cleared, meaning they had no money to buy anything. They arrived back at Roxanne's house dejected by the failed outing. Later that evening, Geraldlynn grew more animated, however, as she told her mother about recent events at the school. Those events included a cafeteria fight that ended with a girl from Geraldlynn's roundtable group withdrawing, allegedly under administrative pressure, from the school.

Over time, the administration tried to convince a handful of the more challenging students to leave, according to teachers and families. Few knew exactly what was said in such conversations. But as one staff member frustrated with the practice put it, "Kids withdraw when we want them out . . . [Administrators] go around telling the kids and others,

'We're looking to get rid of you.'" Dassler saw the actions differently, but said he could understand why some teachers might view it as "coercion." In certain cases parents initiated the withdrawals, he said. "Some kids need a fresh start. If that can happen, it should—otherwise we know the consequences."

KIPP Renaissance had recruited widely: Dassler visited Wicker Elementary and Booker T. Washington, two of the city's lowest-performing schools, in search of potential enrollees. (Wicker was the middle school that Geraldlynn's stepsister, Mary, had left on her own initiative.) But now, teachers feared, KIPP Renaissance was living up to a common critique of the city's charters by finding ways to "push out" troublesome students without going through a formal expulsion process. State rules require schools to hold a hearing before expelling students and allow for an appeal. Encouraging, cajoling, or threatening families into withdrawing voluntarily wasn't illegal per se, but it wasn't always ethical.

Raquel wished more of Renaissance's freshmen had come from KIPP middle schools, where they would have learned KIPP's rules.

"At the [other] schools they came from they so used to cutting up," she said.

Geraldlynn agreed, rattling off some of the city's lowest-performing schools. "By students coming from Carver, John Mac, Wicker—"

"They probably used to being in an I-don't-care environment," Raquel interrupted.

"That's why there's not stability," said Geraldlynn.

"If Mr. Meinig was over there he'd have control," said Raquel, recalling the tight ship Geraldlynn's middle school principal ran at KIPP Believe.

Geraldlynn wasn't so sure.

"Mama, we're talking about *high school* compared to *middle school*," she countered. "Mr. Dassler, he dealing with people who are fourteen, fifteen, sixteen, seventeen, and eighteen going on nineteen compared to eleven, twelve, thirteen, fourteen. At high school, you got people doing drugs, shooting guns, beefing, and fighting."

"They expect more of us," Geraldlynn added a few minutes later. "And we're giving them less."

But her mother maintained the difference had more to do with leadership than the age of the students.

"To me, it looks like [Mr. Dassler's] more easygoing," she said. "He's like, 'Well, as long as they don't burn the building down . . .' Mr. Meinig was more of the 'You either come in this classroom and learn or you don't' mentality. And you got kids coming from all over who are used to cutting up, thinking, 'Hey, I'm going to take it to another school.' You have girls coming from other schools who are used to getting flip—"

She stopped suddenly. Despite KIPP Renaissance's troubles, Raquel still held out hope.

"It takes time," she said quietly.

"Mom, if you don't see the school improve can I go to 35?" asked Geraldlynn. Her older sister, Jasmine, was a junior at McDonogh 35 High School, a legend in the city. Before Katrina, several of the city's schools were named after John McDonogh, a nineteenth-century businessman and slaveholder who left most of his extensive fortune to the cities of Baltimore and New Orleans to build schools for free black children and whites. Before McDonogh 35 opened in 1917, no public high school for black students existed in New Orleans. African-Americans who wanted a secondary education had to attend one of the city's few private high schools for black students. School officials opened McDonogh 35 partly with the goal of cultivating and sustaining a small black professional class in the city, since many white professionals did not serve blacks. Initially, McDonogh 35 functioned as both a high school and a "normal" school tasked with grooming educators to teach in the state's all-black schools. Because of its history and reputation for attracting more motivated students, New Orleanians had, for generations, considered it a cut above the city's neighborhood schools and instrumental in cultivating a group of college-educated black leaders in the city. Its alumni include Ernest Nathan "Dutch" Morial, the city's first black mayor. After Katrina, McDonogh 35 relaxed its admission standards, a change lamented by some of its graduates, who felt the school's quality dropped as well. Raquel probably would have sent Jasmine to KIPP like Geraldlynn. But since KIPP Believe and KIPP Renaissance started with just a grade at a time, Jasmine was too old to attend either one. Jasmine was happy to avoid KIPP's long hours and mandatory Saturday sessions.

In conversations with her mother that winter, Geraldlynn vacillated on whether she wanted to join her sister at 35. Sometimes she liked being off on her own at KIPP, and she worried that at 35 she would feel even shorter and younger than she already did, since the school enrolled more than just freshmen. "Everyone would call me a shrimp," she said. But other days she thought attending a long-established high school like 35— with a full array of sports and extracurriculars, more than one grade, and decades of traditions—sounded like a whole lot of fun she was missing out on. She wanted to be a cheerleader, but KIPP Renaissance did not have a squad yet. (The school had more extracurriculars than most first-year charters in the city, with active cross-country, basketball, and lacrosse teams as well as a marching band and a few different clubs.) Her mother had the final say, though, so Geraldlynn's views on the matter were largely academic.

Both Geraldlynn and Raquel understood the Catch 22 KIPP Renaissance's teachers faced on a daily basis.

"If they give out too many [demerits], the children fuss, and if they don't give out enough, the children do whatever they want," said Geraldlynn.

Lately her teachers had tried to make the issuance of demerits a more clear and public process. Instead of quietly making note of them in their iPads, many teachers wrote half a student's name on the board when they broke a rule. Geraldlynn might be denoted as "Gerald," for instance, or Brice as "Bri." With a second infraction, the teacher filled in the remainder of the name. A third problem brought a check mark beside the name, and the fourth a D for demerit.

The school was trying to tighten up all of its rules and procedures, including what kinds of jackets the students could—and could not—wear over their uniforms, how much students could talk at lunch, and how little fights would be tolerated.

"In classes they are becoming more strict," said Geraldlynn. "At lunch they are becoming more strict. At breakfast they are becoming more strict. Going down the hallway they are becoming more strict. I think they becoming more strict everywhere . . . When you strict, it gives you order. But sometimes people feel like they being controlled."

The irony was that Geraldlynn could not think of a single teacher who always had control over his or her classroom. She ran through the list of teachers in her head. "Mr. . . . No one. No one. Literally no one at all." A few of the teachers—although not all—were "too weak for a classroom, just not strong enough," Geraldlynn concluded.

"You have to build your heart up," said Raquel. "If you're too nice, they are going to run over you. If you're too mean, they are not going to like you. It's a lose-lose situation."

The teachers expected the students to change their behavior, dress, and language to become KIPP students every day. But several of them seemed at a loss over how to play their own parts as teachers. Thinking of one of them, Geraldlynn said, "If you actually go in her classroom to talk to her, she is really sweet. But during class she makes us be silent all the time. And when we keep talking the only thing she know to do is say, 'I'm not playing.' We keep talking and the next thing we know she is in tears. We are like, 'Oh my God. Soft. Weak.'"

It sometimes felt to Geraldlynn as if the students and staff were at war for control of KIPP Renaissance. The students appeared to be winning, yet Geraldlynn worried that if the fight persisted, everyone would lose in the end.

Those who only knew Brice on a superficial level often dismissed him as nothing more than trouble. At times they were right. Brice had started to hang around with drug dealers in his neighborhood that school year. He chose to attend KIPP Renaissance because he had bigger ambitions, but he often brought his tough persona to school with him. Through his own distinct brand of civil disobedience, Brice could bring down a class—at his worst moments, the whole school. Some days he spent entire class periods cocked and edgy, refusing to sit down or take off his backpack; he stole WET FLOOR placards from the hallway and calmly placed them on his desk; he once refused to take an interim assessment designed to see how Renaissance students compared to their peers elsewhere, prompting other students to join his rebellion; he could curse out teachers until they cried. The fight that led to the forced departure of a girl from Geraldlynn's roundtable had been a romantic dispute over Brice. Where he led, other students followed.

But Brice wielded his power for good as well as mischief. One afternoon, a fed-up teacher sent Brice to sit in a different classroom. Listening to a girl berate an overweight classmate in his new room, calling him a "fat fucking retard," Brice intervened. "Why y'all don't just let the good wolf win and say nothing?" he asked. The fable Mr. Dassler told during orientation had stayed with him. At the first KIPP Renaissance dance, a popular student named Trey tripped over the power cord for the sound system, bringing an abrupt halt to the bounce recordings the students were dancing to (bounce is a New Orleans variation of hip-hop, inspired partly by the call-and-response chants of the Mardi Gras Indians). Trey retreated in shame to the upper row of the bleachers, where he bowed his head and refused to make eye contact with anyone. He ignored multiple entreaties to come down from his exile. Then Brice approached. "I don't know why you lookin' like that," Brice told him. "You straight. You straight." With Brice's approval, Trey returned to the dance.

Brice had a rare capacity to serve as a cultural broker. At times he tried to explain the students' feelings and frustrations to the teachers. And he had the confidence to call out the teachers when he did not think they were being fair or had overreached. When his favorite teacher, Ms. Childs, started writing half names on the board to signal a rule violation, he shook his head as he told her, "That's not your swag, Ms. Childs, that's not your swag."

At the end of one long fall day, Mr. Saltmarsh struggled to capture the attention of his eighth-period college-readiness class, which included both Brice and Geraldlynn. Brice, in particular, would not stop talking, walking around and pounding his hand with his fist. Mr. Saltmarsh railed into Brice all of a sudden. "How would you feel, Brice, if you were trying to talk, to give out information, and people wouldn't let you talk? They wouldn't let you say what you needed to say?" At this point, Brice quietly interrupted him and, in an inversion of the teacher-student dynamic, motioned for Mr. Saltmarsh to join him in the hallway. Once outside the classroom, Brice did his best to explain why the students were so talkative and edgy that afternoon. "There's just been a fight," he said, gesturing broadly with his arms as he spoke. "Everyone wants to talk about it. We're concerned. You got to understand we're hyped. We have all this energy. All this energy."

Mr. Saltmarsh realized Brice was attempting to clue him in, to tell him as politely as he could to back off. "He was trying to help me," he said, adding, "If you win with Brice you've done so much. He's either going to be a loud protestor or a vocal defender of the status quo. He was both at times. He could turn a class."

Brice might have driven his teachers crazy and called them out on their missteps. But the teachers did the same to him. What's more, the Renaissance staff members were not, like their students, asked to shed their identities at the schoolhouse door every morning. Brice had adopted his bluster partly because he thought he needed it to survive on the street. He would not part with it easily. One weekend, a few of Brice's teachers learned someone had shot at the teenager, although he escaped unharmed. Brice moved between a world where teenagers routinely risked their lives to supply their families with cash and one where he had to snap his approbation, always remember the good wolf, and silently track the speaker. One world taught authority backed up by guns and money, the other compliance with comparatively meaningless penalties. It gave new meaning to code switching.

Brice resembled a truth teller in a tragedy: low on the totem pole when it came to socioeconomics, more clever than most, uttering truths that eluded the powerful, a curious mixture of loyalty and rebellion, and, for all these reasons and more, particularly vulnerable.

Renaissance had an abundance of rules by the end of the fall but, as parents, teachers, even students, complained over and over again, little discipline. Discipline, as both a word and concept, had positive connotations for many New Orleanian educators and families (despite the city's famous reputation for permissiveness). Students chose to refer to beloved figures like Big Mike at O. Perry Walker as "disciplinarians." And Mr. Williams once remarked that "discipline is a beautiful thing." But they spoke of a kind of discipline founded in respect and trust, not rules alone. Mr. Williams saw all the rules as a failed substitute for true discipline. "We're punishing all of them because of our weaknesses as a staff," he said.

As the school year continued, Raquel and Geraldlynn developed their own ideas about what might improve the situation. It had been obvious for a while that many students failed to take seriously their young teachers' reprimands, and that the endless demerits and detentions were fruitless. But the next level of punishment—a time-out or an in-school suspension with Mr. Lang—did not frighten students either. The kids viewed it as a break from class, not an unpleasant consequence. (Often, students *asked* Mr. Lang to take them out of class.) Raquel thought the school needed to make in-school suspension so miserable for the students that they would behave in class to avoid it. At KIPP Believe, students spent in-school suspensions in Mr. Meinig's office writing letters to him, their teachers, and themselves about their mistakes and how they would do better. Each letter had to be copied several times. By contrast, at Renaissance, the students sometimes slept during in-school suspension. Geraldlynn believed more strong male teachers would help, particularly with the boys. In the meantime, staff members should "put some bass into their voices" so they didn't come off as too soft, she said.

Most of all, Geraldlynn thought the teachers needed to talk with the students more about their home lives. She liked the fact that roundtable advisors met each of their students' families—or tried to, at least. She just wished the school did more of that kind of outreach. "Say if a teacher focuses on one kid who comes to school with bruises, and that kid is taking out their anger on another kid," she said, describing an actual situation at the school. "If the teacher can just talk to them about it and say, 'Just because it happened to you doesn't mean you have to do it to someone else. I can get you help.'" Besides, only through individual conversations could teachers learn their students' strengths and gifts, Geraldlynn concluded.

"Talking to someone one-on-one, you are like, 'I didn't know this person was that intelligent,'" Geraldlynn said. "I can be smart in my own way."

"We all can be," said her mother.

KIPP Renaissance's administration increasingly seemed to conclude that some students were beyond their reach, however. One December morning, several students were out on suspension. Dassler had given Brice and another student thirty-to-forty-five-day suspensions, which would keep them out of school until after the holidays. He threatened to suspend a third student for an equally long term. Brice's family did not realize (or at least did not protest) the possible illegality of the suspension. Students suspended for more than ten consecutive days are entitled to far more due process rights than those suspended for shorter terms. And in Louisiana, state regulations suggest administrators should find alternative placements or provide homebound instruction for students who receive long-term suspensions. Dassler said the decisions were made in consultation with the students' families, and teachers checked up on the teens and provided them with schoolwork. He regretted, however, that he had not been able to "create conditions so every student can be successful" at the school. Brice's mother said her son received little, if any, homework during his suspension.

The teachers were confused about the punishments. According to their accounts, Devon, one of the students with a long suspension, had teased another student, Jamar, who then hit him, prompting a fight. Jamar received a much shorter suspension, however. Brice's case was also ambiguous. He was suspended for trying to start a fight with a student named Floyd. But few knew whether he had touched Floyd or just threatened to do so. Staff members described the incident as "the fight Brice might have tried to start."

No one thought the suspensions would be beneficial to Devon or Brice. Telling teenage boys who already lived on the cusp of full-fledged thuggery not to show up at school for a month sounded an awful lot like tempting fate. As Raquel said, "It's just too many days idle."

It's not uncommon for urban school leaders to use some mixture of suspensions, expulsions, and forced midyear school "transfers" to shed their buildings of the most troublesome students. KIPP Renaissance's parents, after all, had cried out for Mr. Dassler to enforce zero-tolerance discipline measures at the school's very first parent meeting. Edward Wiltz, Tyrin's father, said he had been surprised the school did not do a better job "checking out" the incoming students during orientation. "What happened was they got a bunch of students from outside schools who didn't act the same way the KIPP students did.

"Sometimes," he said, "a melting pot is a bad idea."

But parents who favored zero-tolerance policies, like Wiltz, still put part of the blame on the school's own failings. Wiltz had loved just about everything about KIPP Believe middle school, including the young teachers from across the country and the strict discipline. At Renaissance, however, the same features no longer seemed to work. "A young female teacher who doesn't have children may not know how a fifteen-year-old [male] acts," he said. "They expect them to sit there like robots: Go home. Pass my test.

"With all the detentions, they will get used to being institutionalized and having someone be on their neck all the time," he added.

Even teachers who stood to benefit from the extended absences of their most unruly students sharply criticized the long suspensions. Why had Devon been given a much harsher sentence when he had not even thrown the first punch? they wondered. Certain students may have been fair targets because of their long history of interrupting the educations of their peers. But they were easy targets, too, in the sense that they lacked parents who understood the rules and could fight for them. All of the school's parents cared about their children; but not all had the time, wherewithal, and knowledge to protest if they felt their child suffered an injustice. Those students without advocates (or with insufficient ones, such as the mother who had recently called her son a "bitch" and a "hoe" in front of the school's staff) were at a disadvantage at Renaissance—and in nearly every other aspect of their lives. Wasn't it those students the school could most help?

Moreover, some of the teachers feared that any effort to push out Renaissance's most challenging students played right into the hands of charter school critics who alleged that schools like Renaissance weeded out low performers. Challenging black teenage males formed a significant part of the high school population in New Orleans and in most American cities. If KIPP Renaissance couldn't, or wouldn't, serve them, what business had it to open its doors in the 9th Ward of New Orleans and call itself a community school? The young educators, most of them intensely idealistic, had not come to the city to perpetuate the inequities and failures of the pre-Katrina schools; they had come to lead an educational renaissance. But increasingly they worried the school might be creating its own inequities and failures—just under a different name and banner.

During KIPP Renaissance's inaugural months, education experts debated the merits of charter schools, teacher tenure, and "value-added" teacher rankings ad nauseam. But, considered in the context of a student like Brice, such issues felt at times like rearranging deck chairs.

From an educational perspective, several factors contributed to KIPP Renaissance's struggles. It opened with a first-time principal and a crew of relatively inexperienced teachers, most of whom had little firsthand knowledge of their students' lives and backgrounds. Teachers had scant time to build course curricula, which they had to develop largely from scratch and on the fly. Although groups of KIPP officials evaluated the school on occasion, the staff had little in the way of consistent, ongoing support from experienced educators. (At times the school leadership seemed to prefer it that way.) Renaissance had no curriculum advisor, academic dean, or even a lead teacher in its first year. Dassler, one of the more experienced educators, was often busy dealing with emergencies and rarely observed entire lessons.[3]

In some respects, the education-reform movement had asked KIPP Renaissance to accomplish the impossible: to educate teenagers traumatized both by Katrina and the daily realities of life in a city with decrepit physical infrastructure, bare-bones welfare services, inadequate health care, grossly oversubscribed mental health and drug treatment programs, one of the nation's highest violent crime rates, and corrupt—at times, racist—law enforcement. Even after decades of neglect in these other areas, the most die-hard advocates of educational change believed schools should be able to compensate for all; that they could, acting in isolation, educate poor children into college and mainstream, middle-class lives. As one Renaissance teacher put it, "What we are trying to do is teach kids the 'middle-class code' so they can succeed both in their own world and the middle-class, capitalistic world."

Some New Orleans charter school leaders taught teachers to compartmentalize the myriad forces that got in the way of that objective. They called them the "brutal facts," an expression borrowed from the book *Good to Great*, whose author wrote that successful companies always focus on "the brutal facts of reality" rather than idealistic dreams. During professional development, Dassler had the KIPP Renaissance staff plaster a sheet on the wall with brutal facts the school faced in its first year: many of the families' phone numbers failed to work, incoming student skill levels ranged from the second to the twelfth grade. They wrote them on Post-it notes, acknowledging their existence while simultaneously minimizing their importance.

Dassler used the expression in ways that suggested Renaissance, and Renaissance alone, could save its students from lives of poverty. In his depiction, whether the students continued on to successful college careers depended almost solely on the quality of their teachers and school. "That's one of the brutal facts," he told his young staff. "It's always on us."

One can hardly fault KIPP Renaissance's staff for not working to improve the city's police force, health care, public housing, or job conditions. They had their hands full. The fault lay with the system and leaders who in effect set them up to fail, at least with some of the kids, some of the time; who let many of society's greatest injustices be reduced to scribbles on Post-it notes; who led them to believe they could, and should, attempt to redress so many historic wrongs alone.

As the school year progressed, the teachers' doubts grew. They felt less self-assured concerning their role in New Orleans, less convinced of the path forward, less destined to be saviors. Many days, they just felt helpless.

THE PRINCIPAL
"I thought all the stories would be good stories."

Mary Laurie did not understand football. She spent most of O. Perry Walker's football games in a quiet state of agitation, unable to sit still or relax. Even when Walker seemed certain of victory, as it did by halftime of its November 12 playoff game, she paced and averted her eyes at critical moments. Laurie cut an odd figure for a school principal: lurking behind the bleachers of Walker's neighborhood stadium, covered from head to toe in a knit cap and layers of bulky shawls, with the school's initials—O.P.W.—emblazoned in orange face paint across her cheek. Walker, seeded fifteenth in the state, played eighteenth-seeded Minden High School in the first round of the state playoffs that night. The visitors, who drove six hours from a small town in northwestern Louisiana, never held the lead. When Walker was up 28–6 with only a quarter left, Laurie finally ventured out by the sideline to watch a few minutes uninterrupted. But she looked nervous right up until Walker's marching band led a victory parade back to the school. Walker always paraded home, even when the team lost.

Laurie's anxiety wasn't entirely unjustified. She had seen Walker's football squad blow large leads in the fourth quarter before. She also hated to watch any kids lose—even Walker's opponents. Walking back to the school after the Minden blowout, Laurie grimaced as she thought of the deflated visiting team driving home across Louisiana in the dead of the night, their season now over. Laurie wasn't a football fan like her husband, a police officer known as Sarge, who came to Walker's games. She sometimes had to attend meetings of the Louisiana High School Athletic Association, where the men who set the rules for football play held forth with the self-importance of those negotiating for world peace. The beauty and thrill of a well-executed play eluded her, as did the names of just about every football player, living or dead, apart from Walker's own. When the New Orleans Saints won the Super Bowl nine months earlier, she celebrated because of the joy it brought to the city. She appreciated the way in which the event united New Orleanians of all colors and walks of life. Similarly, she relished Walker's victories for the glory and esprit de corps they brought the school. In a landscape where schools had to compete for everything, fielding a powerhouse football team helped attract new families and students. She pragmatically saw it as a part of rebuilding a strong Walker the community would value.

Laurie also believed that at their best, football teams taught players to hope against hope, even when the odds were stacked against them and even when all effort felt in vain. She knew that as black men from poor families, many of Walker's players would face long odds throughout much of their lives. Football might convince some of them never to stop trying.

By the start of winter, O. Perry Walker was in a groove, both athletically and academically. Over Thanksgiving weekend, the school secured a spot in the state football semifinals after defeating seventh-seeded Bastrop High School from northern Louisiana in the fourth overtime.

That same week, the Algiers Charter Schools Association, which oversaw Walker, scheduled a press conference to announce Walker and several other schools in the association had posted the highest possible "value-added" test score results on a scale of 1 to 5. A rating of 5 meant that Walker had in a year advanced most of its students significantly more than their projected growth compared to similar Louisiana students. Value-added measurements look at the growth schools make with individual students based on where the students start, not their absolute results. So in most cases, a school that moved a ninth grader from a fourth-grade to an eighth-grade reading level would score higher than one that moved a student from an eighth- to a ninth-grade level. A national debate brewed about the use of value-added results to assess individual teachers' job performance at that time. Louisiana and several other states embraced pilot initiatives linking students' value-added test scores to teacher hiring, firing, and salary decisions. Race to the Top, a competitive federal education-grant program, gave states points in their application for incorporating student growth in teacher evaluations, prompting some of the surge in support. Proponents of value-added argued that for too long teachers had been paid based largely on longevity, regardless of whether they were "adding value" (business speak that in and of itself rankled some educators because it implicitly likened children to widgets). Critics countered that myriad in-school factors (multiple teachers, peer behavior, school leadership, per-pupil spending) and out-of-school factors (parental support, stability of home life, presence or absence of physical and emotional trauma) contribute to how well a child learns to read over the course of a given year. No matter how mathematically sophisticated and all-encompassing, they claimed, no formula could ever account for all those variables.

Walker's score of 5 reflected the school's growth as a whole and determined the overall amount of performance-based bonus money to be distributed across the staff. Teachers who taught subjects the state tested, such as English and math, also received their own individual value-added scores based on how far they moved their students over the course of a year. An individual teacher's share of the bonus pot depended partly on the school-wide score, partly on qualitative observations of their teaching, and partly on their own value-added score (if they had one). Given the large number of students who arrived below grade level, Laurie preferred value-added metrics to comparisons based on absolute test scores, although she understood why each needed to exist.

On December 1, the evening before the press conference about the value-added test score increases, Walker hosted a basketball game. Students, staff, and alums milled about the campus well into the evening, cheering on the basketball players and revving themselves up for the football semifinals in two days. Laurie was in the campus's main building finishing up some paperwork while all the activity swirled around her. Just before eight P.M., she left her office hoping to catch the end of the game between Walker and nearby Helen Cox High School. As Laurie approached the gym, she heard a series of loud pops that sounded like gunshots coming from the opposite direction. Inside the gym, the roar of the crowd drowned out the sound of the blasts, so the basketball game continued unabated for a few more moments. But Laurie stopped in her tracks.

A few minutes earlier, nineteen-year-old Torrance Massey, a 2009 graduate of Walker, stood talking and laughing with friends in front of the school. Just after eight P.M. he climbed into a black Chevy Equinox with a companion, promising to return to cheer on his alma mater in the state football semifinals on Friday. As he pulled away from the school, a volley of bullets rained down, striking Torrance in the torso and his friend in the wrist, elbow, and calf.

Torrance, whom everyone called Boogie, had been the team's star quarterback during his years as a Charger. He led Walker to its only other recent state semifinals in 2007, when the team fell one step short of the championship game. A consummate ladies' man, Boogie always dressed with flair; he had a terrible voice, but liked nothing better than trying to imitate Usher's smooth tones.

Boogie wielded his considerable social capital at Walker with grace, paying particular respect to teachers he admired, never hesitating to lend less popular classmates some of his cool through public approbation. Some mornings his mother would find her living room full of sleeping teenagers because Boogie had brought home classmates and friends who had no other place to stay.

Unlike some families who had a contentious or detached relationship with the public schools, Boogie's family made it clear how much they valued education, Walker, and its teachers. Boogie's older brother, Thomas, was Walker's first salutatorian after Katrina. That night he came straight from his college finals in Baton Rouge to the scene of the shooting. Boogie's mother, Catina Massey, was the kind of parent who showed up at school in an instant if one of her kids had a problem. Some parents defended their children no matter what they had done, but Catina Massey treated teachers with an old-school deference. In any dispute at the school, she shushed her children until all the teachers or administrators had their say.

At the urging of some of his mentors, Boogie left New Orleans after high school graduation to attend the Apprentice School in Newport News, Virginia. They worried he was caught up in neighborhood-based rivalries that had the potential to turn violent. In Newport News, everyone called the teen Ace Boogie. He played football, studied shipbuilding, and took a photo when he saw his first snow in Virginia to show Walker's staff. He knew they would appreciate the novelty of all the white flakes. Boogie was exceptionally close to his family. Homesick for his mother and siblings in Virginia, he had a neck tattoo made with his little sister's name, Moneisha.

Boogie and his roommate ran into some financial problems, however, and within a year he returned to the city and made plans to enroll at Southern University for the spring semester of 2011. That fall, he found work welding and building Mardi Gras floats and went to every Walker football came he could. As happy as they were to have Boogie home, many of those who cared about the teenager could not help but wish he had stayed away.

As the basketball game ended, the crowd emptied out of the gym and into the parking lot, just a short distance from Boogie's car. Since he had graduated less than two years ago, many of the students knew Boogie personally, as did most of the staff. When they came upon the scene, their excitement turned to despair, their shouts of encouragement to cries of grief. Walker teachers, students, and supporters held each other as they sobbed behind the yellow police lines. To many, he had seemed invincible: an exceptional athlete, an honors student beloved by girls and his teachers alike, the support of a strong family behind him.

Just an hour earlier Boogie had parted from his family, begging a few dollars from his mother so he could get into the basketball game. Catina Massey and her daughter went off to buy Christmas decorations, which they planned to put up with Boogie's help after the game. But a little after eight P.M. they started getting phone calls from family and friends telling them to get to Walker as quickly as possible. There had been a shooting, and it looked bad. They caught a ferry across the Mississippi River and made their way to the school.

Catina Massey sensed the truth as soon as she saw all the cars, people, and police clustered around Walker. But she pleaded with everyone who came up to her, their faces breaking the news without words: *Just tell me that's not my son. Tell me that's not Boogie.*

When police informed Catina Massey the victim—the one who wasn't going to make it—had the name Moneisha tattooed on his neck, she finally knew for certain. Her son was dead.

In 2010, New Orleans had the highest murder rate of any American city, at about 51 murders per 100,000 people (with 175 total confirmed). Unlike many cities, where the vast majority of murders occur in specific quadrants or sections, New Orleans killings are distributed across the crescent, with clusters in a handful of particularly tough neighborhoods. Also unlike other cities, about half of New Orleans murders take place in broad daylight, a brazenness law enforcement officials attribute to the fact that many are executions. Moreover, since so few perpetrators of violent crimes get caught in New Orleans, murderers may be less concerned about concealing their bad actions under the cloak of darkness. As in other cities, the vast majority of New Orleans killers and victims are young black men. In 2008, for example, 79 percent of the city's murder victims were black males (by contrast, 8 percent were black women, 6 percent white men, and 2 percent white women). More than three quarters of the victims were under the age of forty, and a full half of them fell in the eighteen-to-twenty-five age range, like Boogie.

New Orleans does not have a gang problem like Los Angeles or Chicago. Some have theorized that may give it a worse murder problem, though, since countless neighborhood-based cliques compete for a share of the port city's thriving drug trade without the structure and defined turf imposed by established gangs. A large number of murders are only loosely connected to drugs, however, if at all. The violence on New Orleans streets sometimes calls to mind the bloody family feuding memorialized in the tragedy *Romeo and Juliet*: born of domestic disputes, petty grudges, and perceived slights; wrought largely by impetuous adolescent boys and young men; devastating in the collateral damage it leaves behind. But the ancient combatants fought with fists and swords. Today they destroy with guns that can spray dozens of bullets in a matter of seconds.

As with many New Orleans murders, rumors circulated on the street about who had killed Boogie. Friends say the gunman was upset at people close to Boogie and shot him in retribution. They whispered of vengeance exacted on the streets. But through some combination of fear, distrust of police, and inadequate investigation, the rumors never rose to the level of evidence that could be used to make arrests. The case, it increasingly seemed, would go unsolved, and the motive would never come to light.

Catina Massey did not want street justice, which, she knew, would only break another mother's heart. She hoped to see her son's killer held to account in a court of law. Massey sometimes worried detectives did not take the case seriously, that to them Boogie was just another young black male mixed up with trouble. She ached for news of developments on the case—something to show her Boogie's death mattered so "my heart won't hurt as much." But developments were few and far between; months after the shooting, police had no solid leads.

In the wake of Boogie's murder, Laurie did everything she could to help comfort his family and keep her composure in front of Walker's students. She knew they would be looking for reassurance, for someone to tell them everything would be all right. For that reason, she did not want them to see her cry. But the murder had unsettled Laurie deeply; she wasn't sure of anything at the moment. The details of the killing— its location so close to the school, its victim so well-known and full of promise—were troubling. But the killing of any young person troubled those with a conscience. Laurie had come to believe that until communities reckon with the broader psychological toll exacted by gun violence, they will not see it end. How could students fully commit themselves to school, college, and dreams of a brighter future, she wondered, when part of them worried about living to see age twenty-one?

The murder of a young person had the power to kill not only the dreams of the deceased, but those of everyone who hoped or cared for him. When many people hoped and cared, it magnified the destruction. Officials might define and measure school safety through the number of weapons, fights, and violent incidents on a given campus. But increasingly Laurie came to understand violence's steep cost through the immeasurable loss of dreams deferred.

Two days after Boogie's murder, Laurie and a large group from Walker piled into a caravan of school buses to drive north about seventy miles to Franklinton, Louisiana, for the semifinal game. A police escort led the four buses, which contained dozens of staff members, the band, the color guard, the cheerleaders, the Walkerettes (flag team), the Chargerettes (dance team), the majorettes (baton twirlers), and the Perryettes (who carried the school's initials). The Walker contingent left campus with only minutes to spare in order to arrive before kickoff; the football team had traveled on its own earlier in the day. As the blue sky morphed into the brilliant pinks, oranges, and reds of a southern Louisiana sunset, the buses chugged over the twenty-four-mile Lake Pontchartrain causeway, the second-longest bridge in the world. On the other side of the lake, they passed through the comparatively suburban and tony villages of St. Tammany Parish and, as darkness descended, farther up north into the small, less prosperous farming villages of Washington Parish. Franklinton had a population of about four thousand, half white and half black. Its football team was also racially mixed. Because it was unusually cold for Louisiana—the low neared freezing that night—even the fashion-conscious baton twirlers accessorized their tights and sparkly boots with practical white headbands that kept their ears warm.

As the buses pulled up beside the Franklinton High School Demons' football field just after six thirty P.M., a cry went out to "Suit up!" (or finish any final wardrobe adjustments). Then all the bus riders bowed their heads and quietly recited the Lord's Prayer in unison before disembarking. Franklinton supporters had already filled the home-team stands to capacity, making the Walker stands look comparatively barren. The Walker football team, too, looked frighteningly outmanned, its sideline of reserve players significantly more shallow than Franklinton's. Walking to join the visiting fans, one color guard member looked worried. "It looks like the whole town of Franklinton came out," he said. "At least our band will win," replied his classmate, referring to the battle of the bands, a staple of New Orleans high school football games Walker dominated. Laurie, who wore a sweatsuit and wrapped a large blanket over her, took her usual spot alone by the side of the bleachers.

Unlike Walker's home stadium on the West Bank of New Orleans, Franklinton's Demon Stadium featured a functional scoreboard and bathrooms with hot water. In a town with a household median income of about $20,000, Franklinton had invested considerable resources into football. After losing the state championship game in 2009, Franklinton was determined to bring home a title this time. The school had suffered its own tragedy that football season: In August, Damien Jenkins, a senior at Franklinton High, had climbed up a fence behind the stadium's bleachers and fallen to his death. Detectives never ruled on whether it was a suicide or an accident.

A Franklinton student opened the game with a prayer and a brief tribute to Boogie. As usual, Laurie stayed out of sight during the first half of the game, which offered Walker's fans no respite from worry. Franklinton won the coin toss. Although the home team failed to score on its first possession, the Demons kept control of the football for most of the first quarter, which featured Charger penalties, incomplete passes, and a Franklinton interception. It ended with the home team up 7–0.

Walker fans began to get antsy when the second quarter began on a bad note as well. Watching the Walker quarterback clock a teammate in the head while trying to complete a pass, they wondered why the team did not use its run game more. The passes were so clumsy. During Walker's last two playoff games the team had performed flawlessly by comparison. The final seconds of the first half ticked away with two joyous eruptions from the Franklinton stands: the first when their defense sacked Walker's quarterback, and the second when a Walker player dropped an interception. Walker held Franklinton's lead at 7, but failed to score. Yet as expected, Walker's band, auxiliary, and dancers walked away with the halftime show.

As if seizing on the momentum, the Chargers upped their play in the second half. Quarterback Devin Powell threw a touchdown pass, putting Walker on the scoreboard. The team tried for a two-point conversion, which would have given them a one-point lead over Franklinton, but failed to convert. Walker never chose the easier extra-point option because the team had no kicker. The Chargers' lesser numbers became a liability as the second half wore on. Franklinton's team roster included more than eighty players compared to Walker's forty-two. Many of Walker's stars, including defensive lineman Anthony Johnson and defensive back Cortez Johnson, doubled up on offense and defense. Running back Robert Kelley suffered from a thigh contusion throughout the game. And offensive guard Isaiah Webster went down on the fourth play of the game and hobbled uncomfortably through the rest. Toward the end of the third quarter, Walker had possession at the Franklinton 9-yard line. But after four downs, the Demons stopped them one yard from the end zone. The fourth quarter began with the Demons still up by one.

Midway through the final quarter, Walker melted down. The players never stopped trying, but the flubs that had held them back all evening grew increasingly pervasive. Chargers tripped, fumbled, dropped snaps, and fell over when the ball hit them in the back of the head. The Walker players looked ready to keel over from exhaustion. In the last five minutes of the game, Franklinton scored touchdown after touchdown. All but the most die-hard Walker fans began to drift toward their cars as the point gap widened and a come-from-behind victory grew out of reach. The supporters who remained shivered on the stands while the temperature plummeted, and the ratio of human flesh to aluminum seating diminished. With a minute left in the game, the Demons led by 25 points. The Franklinton announcer started to give instructions for how fans could purchase tickets for the championship game next week in the Superdome. But Walker's band played on. And so did the limping players.

Mary Laurie emerged from the shadows only when the loss was final and the scoreboard read 36–6. Sarge called out to his wife on her way to comfort the players, his eyes full of tears. He wanted to see if she was all right. But Laurie felt better than she had at nearly any point in the last two days. This was a loss she could handle. In the center of the field, she formed a tight circle with the defeated players. From the stands the band struck up the O. Perry Walker anthem while Laurie and the team held their arms up toward the dark sky, as was tradition. Then Laurie thanked the football players for never giving up. Even as their hearts were breaking and defeat grew inevitable, they left everything they had on the field. Just as she had hoped they would.

Laurie devoted as much time as she could the next week to helping Boogie's family make funeral arrangements. She proofread the obituary that would appear in the paper, which noted that Boogie left behind not only his mother and siblings, but also a baby daughter. And after school let out on Wednesday that week, Laurie piled into a van with Walker's athletic director, Coach T, to scope out possible sites for Boogie's repast, the traditional meal held after a funeral. Accompanying Laurie and Coach T were Cornelle Carney and Richard Comeaux, the two recent Walker alums who had graduated a year before Boogie and now worked part-time at their alma mater while they pursued their undergraduate degrees.

Cornelle drove that night as the group looked at sites for Boogie's repast. They started at the Craige Cultural Center, a funky space located near the school that featured artistic murals and white billowy sheets hanging from the ceiling, decor that made it feel perfect for a poetry slam. Laurie thought the cultural center would work well for the repast, but Coach T could not reach Boogie's family to clear it with them. So they continued on. "We're giving them options, T, just giving them options," Laurie repeated. As the evening wore on, Laurie and the crew scoped out the OJ Dunn Lodge in nearby Gretna, the VFW, and a small music club. At some point in the travels, Catina Massey called to say that Craige would be fine, but Laurie urged Cornelle to keep driving.

Arriving back at Walker after eight P.M., Laurie found the front foyer still packed with kids who had stayed late for extracurriculars. They clustered around Big Mike, laughing and telling jokes. Laurie instructed Coach T to present the four options to Catina Massey so she could think on them overnight. Then she entered the throng of students. Joining Big Mike at the pulsing center of the quiet commotion, Laurie told him of the search. "I just want to give the mom peace," she said.

A couple weeks later, Laurie would answer her phone after midnight when Boogie's older brother, Thomas, needed someone to talk to about his pain. In the coming months, she reached out regularly to Catina Massey, reminding her how many people in the world still cared about her son. And she would be there on the first anniversary of Boogie's death, standing beside his family at the site of the murder, quietly saying a prayer.

Mary Laurie understood a mother's grief as well as anyone. Seventeen years earlier, as she worked her way up through the city's school system, she struggled with Wayne, her second-oldest son. Wayne always seemed to be in trouble.

One day in 1993, Laurie gave Wayne a ride home, and he told her that he had learned his lesson and planned to lead a different kind of life. The twenty-one-year-old had a baby of his own due in a couple of weeks and knew he would not become the father he wanted to if he continued down the same path. "Mama, I am *going* to do better because my baby is coming," Laurie remembers Wayne saying. She could hear a new determination in his voice and felt cheered by the words. Years later, she would remember the exchange as a small gift from God, an encouraging memory to hold on to when she thought of her son.

That night, Laurie learned an unknown acquaintance had shot Wayne dead inside his Uptown apartment. She did not feel anger so much as incomprehension. She wondered why Wayne never had the chance to act on his newfound maturity, or if God was punishing her for some past sin.

Laurie assumed Wayne's death was the worst thing she would have to experience. Anything else she lived through would pale in comparison, she reasoned. But tragedy struck her family again just three years later when a gunman murdered Roy, her oldest son, in front of his 9th Ward home. He was twenty-five. Roy had done nothing apart from being in the wrong place at the wrong time: His car resembled one driven by the killer's intended victim.

Roy, a hardworking family man, left behind three young children—a kindergartener, a four-year-old, and an infant—babies who would never know their father. When Laurie remembers her eldest, she usually thinks of the small, ordinary moments that seem unremarkable at the time but actually define family relations: like catching him cooking turkey necks and gravy as a penny-pinching adult even though, growing up, he griped about being served that same meal.

For the longest time after Roy's death, Laurie could not bring herself to pray and dreaded church. Over the next ten years, she threw herself into her work as principal of Guste, Woodson, and O. Perry Walker. She never felt comfortable, however, when people implied her success as an educator stemmed from the tragedies she had experienced—or that she would not have possessed the same passion otherwise. Why should a person have to live through tragedy to feel empathy? That would leave the world with little hope.

But the events certainly shaped her work. One can see that on a daily basis when Laurie insists on staying at Walker until well after midnight on game nights to make sure every student has a ride home, when she proposes keeping the school open until eleven P.M. so students have a safe place to hang out, and when she drives around a dark city looking for a site to hold Boogie's repast, to spare his mother the trouble.

"I hope that I've been integral to Guste and Woodson and Walker," she says. "But I don't know that folks will ever know just how integral this work has been to me . . . It's all part of filling a void, that void that exists in my life because of the losses I've experienced. That's some of my drive, I know it. I've got the passion. I would always have the passion. But some of it is just trying to make it right. Just trying to make it right."

Laurie's windowless office at Walker features few adornments and serves primarily as a spot for leaving her coats, bags, and half-eaten sandwiches before heading out into the rest of the building. Unlike more modern school buildings, Walker does not have individual thermostats or temperature controls in the rooms. On the rare occasions when Laurie shuts her door for a series of meetings, the office becomes either uncomfortably hot or cold. The room's walls are made of dark wooden panels and a worn-looking PRINCIPAL sign hangs above the door. Laurie keeps a shelf of books behind the desk: a signed copy of Harry Potter (whose popularity she admits she will never understand), a nonfiction book about New Orleans featuring Walker's band director, Wilbert Rawlins, and several books about education. There's also a printout of the old adage: "When you get there, remember where you came from."

She sometimes looks over at the wall immediately to the right when entering the office. Photos from the past five years cover most of the wall: snapshots of couples posing at homecoming and prom, photos of football stars kneeling on the field, images of Laurie standing smiling beside graduates, clippings from the local newspaper that mention Walker students and their victories. The wall looks like several pages of candid photos from a high school yearbook spliced together.

Walker stayed open the week before Christmas so students who had fallen behind could catch up on credits or coursework. Whenever Walker was open, Laurie tended to be there, her big old boat of a car parked on the grass out in front of the school. She always talked about getting away during vacations—maybe taking the train up to Memphis so she could see some new scenery—but she rarely seemed to travel much farther than her own house down the street. She tried once or twice that week to stay home and rest; it had been an emotionally exhausting month. Yet most mornings found her at the school, working on something.

One morning that week, three days before Christmas and three weeks after Boogie's murder, Laurie seemed preoccupied with the pictures on the wall. Each of them told a story. Three of them haunted her.

She looked over at a photo of a Walker student named Arthur, shot dead in 2007 before he could earn his final high school credits. In the photo, a serious-looking Arthur wore a tie and the blue cap and gown he should have donned again on his graduation day. He had failed to graduate on time with this class. But the summer he died, Arthur had been coming to summer school. So Laurie brought a high school diploma to Arthur's funeral and gave it to his mother. How she wished he had lived to see it through.

Laurie could think of a dozen stories like Arthur's, most of them reduced to a few lines in the newspaper—tersely written paragraphs that focused solely on the demise, with nothing on the life lived.

She continued to scan the wall, finally settling on the image of James, who should have graduated the previous spring. James had been a good kid. His only mistake was going to visit his grandmother in Central City on Christmas night three years earlier. That night a bunch of men shot up the place, killing two teenagers, one of them James, and wounding four others.

"James wasn't a part of anything," Laurie said. "Other folk might have been part of it, but James was just going to his grandmother's house."

Searching the wall again, Laurie spotted a small headshot atop a brief obituary cut out of the newspaper. Aaron, the teen pictured in the fuzzy image, wore a necklace, long hair, and a sad face. Hot tempered, Aaron had been put out of Walker for some offense Laurie could not recall.

He had made plans to return just before someone killed him—in a dispute over potato chips.

Ms. Laurie's voice grew louder as she made another round of the photos, her expression more pained.

"Right now we should be talking about Arthur going on to be a chef." She banged the photo quickly, almost as if trying to startle the image back to life.

"Aaron, right now—"

Thwack!

"—should be going to school for drama.

"You understand what I'm saying?

"James should have graduated last year. It all gets lost.

"That was the excitement after Katrina. Every time a piece would come back, you thought it was going to be better. You thought, you know what, we going to fix this! We going to *fix this*. Children going to get their education and go off to college and get the good jobs they are entitled to and this is going to be a wonderful, super city. That's what we felt after Katrina: We going to fix this. We at Walker. We got this. Now, I think we've done a good job. *But it was supposed to be fixed!*

"I thought all the stories would be good stories. Nothing but good stories to tell."

PART V

Higher Education

(Winter 2011)

THE TEACHER

"This is the way, hey! We start the day, hey! We get the knowledge, hey! To go to college!"

Several times each day, Sci Academy's freshmen walk past a large chart with each of their names and pre-ACT scores, ranked from highest to lowest, complete with examples of colleges that might accept them based on their results. Three students placed in the top-tier 26-to-30 range, their names listed below pictures from the campuses of Yale and the University of Chicago. Ten students earned a score of 16, their names clustered by images from Xavier, Clark Atlanta, and the University of New Orleans. A full two dozen, however, fall on the far left in the "below 12" category, with only Delgado Community College within reach.[1]

Sci Academy makes no bones about its overarching goal—to send its students to and through four-year universities—or, as the very public display shows, about how far away that goal remains for some. Like other similar charter schools including KIPP, college talk, preparation, slogans, symbols, and visits infuse daily life. Such messaging and preparation begins with the youngest students, who might learn on their first day of pre-kindergarten that they are members of the class of 2028 (for the year they will graduate from college, if all goes according to plan). During Akili Academy's first year in 2008 it painted arrows with THIS WAY TO COLLEGE written on the cement outside the school for the five- and six-year-olds to follow. Teachers tell the youngsters to line up or throw out their trash "college fast." Some classes begin with students—a few of whom do not know how to read yet—chanting: "This is the way . . . hey! We start the day . . . hey! We get the knowledge . . . hey! To go to college . . . hey!" Success Preparatory Academy, another New Orleans elementary charter school, solicited local Ivy League alumni groups to "sponsor" different classes, a slight twist on the widespread practice of naming advisories or classrooms after the alma mater of the teacher.

At high schools like Sci and KIPP Renaissance, the college references become more urgent, detailed, and specific. Teachers tell the teenagers, "A college student takes notes during class without being told," or, "A college student does not talk while a classmate is speaking." Sci takes its freshmen to visit their first college within the first week of school; by the time they hit the middle of their junior year they have toured upward of twenty colleges in seven states.

The schools have scant proof they will be able to send most of their graduates to and through college. The college completion rate for Americans who fall in the bottom income quartile (as the overwhelming majority of Sci Academy and KIPP Renaissance students do) has never exceeded 12 percent; recent data put it at 8 percent. By contrast, more than 80 percent of Americans from the top income quartile graduate from college. Nationally, just under a third of Americans earn a bachelor's degree by their midtwenties.

In New Orleans, those rates are lower. According to the 2000 census, 26 percent of white New Orleans residents over the age of twenty-five had bachelor's degrees, compared to 10 percent of black female residents and 7 percent of black male residents (those figures include all income levels). About 30 percent of the city's schoolchildren attended private schools before the flood, and adult transplants to the city are more likely to have college degrees. So the rates probably would have been lower if just public school students were included in the analysis.

One Sci teacher estimated that 8 percent of public school students in the city ultimately graduated from college in the years before Katrina, using a combination of federal, state, and school district data. When she looked exclusively at African-Americans, the rate dropped to 5 percent. Using her analysis, of the approximately 4,900 black public school students who started the ninth grade each year before 2005, about 250 had earned college diplomas a decade later.[2]

Young teachers who work in New Orleans schools often express shock over the low skill levels of most of their students. The turmoil and lost school time after the flood explain *some* of the challenges. But Katrina alone could not account for why so many children returned four, five, six, even eight years behind their appropriate grade level. When speaking carelessly, teachers refer to their students' many "deficits": learning gaps that will have to be filled at super speed. They describe teaching as "adding value" to make sure the teenagers are "college ready." More thoughtful observers and teachers put it differently: They see their students' gifts as well as their "deficits." How, they wonder, could so many bright children have been allowed to fall so far behind in school? What kind of system and city had allowed it? And how can they win children's trust when so many leaders and authority figures unconscionably failed them for so long?

Most no-excuses charter schools have not existed long enough to build up extensive data—or, in Sci's case, any data at all—on college graduation rates. And those that track such data often do not share it. One of the only publicly released studies to date focused on KIPP's oldest alums, a relatively small group. It found that a third of the students who graduated from a KIPP middle school had completed a four-year degree a decade later. KIPP's critics jumped on the report as evidence that the charter school chain is failing in its mission at least two thirds of the time. Defenders pointed out that KIPP's success rate is four times higher than the norm for students from comparable socioeconomic backgrounds, and slightly exceeds the national average across all income levels.

As KIPP's experience shows, even charter schools with impressive state standardized test scores have struggled to translate that into success in the college classroom for a majority of their students. Despite their unrelenting focus on college, Sci Academy leaders worry about becoming another high-performing charter school whose graduates nonetheless can't, or don't, make it through four-year universities. Most of Sci's students pass the state tests. Among New Orleans high schools, only Lusher and Ben Franklin, which both test potential students before admitting them and have significantly lower student-poverty rates than Sci, consistently have higher percentages of students achieving grade-level test score results.

But passing the state's standardized test does not necessarily mean a student is prepared for college-level work. A student who earns a passing score of "basic" on the state's Graduate Exit Exam (or GEE) is on pace to earn about a 19 on the English portion of the ACT and an 18 in math, according to a study analyzing the scores of thousands of Louisiana students on both the ACT and GEE. ACT scores below 20 do not qualify a student for Louisiana's Taylor Opportunity Program for Students (TOPS), which gives students free tuition at any Louisiana public university. Nor will those scores necessarily disqualify a student from remedial courses once in college (students need an 18 in English and a 19 in math to bypass remedials). As a result, teenagers who just barely pass the state's exit exam, and schools that pass large numbers at the "basic" level, can be left with a misleading sense of confidence.

This paradox has defined the recent history of the school accountability movement: Accountability has raised expectations of educators and students by demanding, in theory if not in practice, that all public schools meet set standards for all students all the time. But it has also limited expectations by failing to establish those standards at a level that will prepare students for college or postgraduate employment, and by leading the public to believe that "basic" is good enough.

The college-for-all ethos embraced by school reformers has its origins in the decline of the manufacturing economy, the disappearance of low-skill jobs that supply a living wage, and a series of ominous statistics related to those two trends: Over the last thirty years, all the net job growth in the country has come from positions that require at least some education after high school. By 2008, the median earnings of workers with bachelor's degrees were 65 percent higher than those of high school graduates, a gap that continues to widen. Of the forty-seven million jobs that will open up between 2008 and 2018, nearly two thirds will require workers with some education after high school.

The debate over "college for all" epitomizes the false dichotomies that define the conversation about education in America, however. In a report issued in February 2011, a group of Harvard researchers pushed back against the concept: "The 'college for all' rhetoric that has been so much a part of the current education reform movement needs to be significantly broadened to become a 'post high-school credential for all.'" The report pointed out that new job growth will be greatest for "middle-skilled professionals" who work as dental hygienists, paralegals, electricians, and in other positions that require some post–high school education, but not necessarily a four-year degree.

Both the reformers and the Harvard report are right: For too long schools serving poor minority students have done an abysmal job sending their children on to universities. But to go to the opposite extreme risks cutting them off from opportunity in less academic-oriented fields and imposing a one-size-fits-all model on students with diverse interests and needs. It also takes the onus off universities, many of which need to do a better job reaching and serving low-income, first-generation students.

Disputes over how many—and which—Americans should attend college, and what kind of college, have persisted since the founding of the republic. During the colonial era and early nineteenth century, established college campuses featured some socioeconomic diversity but very little racial, ethnic, or gender diversity. The universities educated white Protestant males who were divided into two categories: The wealthier "commoners" came from families who could afford the tuition, while the poorer "servitors" worked in the dining halls as a condition of their scholarship. A few all-female "seminaries" or "academies" trained women to be teachers, and occasionally an African-American managed to attend university—sometimes by passing as white. Ohio's Oberlin College was one of the first to embrace both women and African-American students publicly after its founding in 1833. That ushered in a period of modest growth in higher-education opportunities for females and minorities. Cheyney University of Pennsylvania, the first historically black higher education institution, opened in 1837 under a different name; that same year, Mount Holyoke College, the oldest of the Seven Sisters, began admitting young women. Blacks and women did not see a rapid increase in college accessibility until after the Civil War, however.

In the post-Reconstruction era, Booker T. Washington and W. E. B. Du Bois famously articulated their opposing beliefs about the kind of education that would best advance their race: In Washington's view, blacks needed an industrial education that would prepare them for jobs in the nation's burgeoning economy. Unless blacks learned technical skills and trades considered valuable by the white power structure, they would never achieve parity, Washington argued. "No race can prosper till it learns that there is as much dignity in tilling a field as in writing a poem," he wrote in his autobiography, *Up from Slavery*. He also emphasized the importance of character, observing in one speech that "character, not circumstances, makes the man."

Du Bois fired back in *The Souls of Black Folk* that Washington's proposals have "an economic cast, becoming a gospel of Work and Money to such an extent as apparently almost completely to overshadow the

higher aims of life." Du Bois, the first African-American to earn a doctorate from Harvard, decried Washington's education agenda as too narrow and limiting; he argued that more blacks—especially the elites he
described as "The Talented Tenth"—needed a rich classical education in
literature and the arts and sciences if they hoped to rise in a white-
dominated society.

Du Bois grew more egalitarian over the course of his life. But in his
early writings in response to Washington, he argued that the black community should cultivate first and foremost its most promising intellectu-
als, not the latent potential of the everyman. He viewed education more as
a path to political and social change than immediate economic uplift. He
criticized the tendency, "born of slavery and quickened to renewed life by
the crazy imperialism of the day, to regard human beings as among the
material resources of a land to be trained with an eye single to future
dividends."

At first glance, it would seem that today's charter school leaders share
more in common with Du Bois than Washington. Like Du Bois, they
believe higher education plays an enormous role in social uplift. And like
Du Bois, many of them do not explicitly condone the kind of structural
inequality Booker T. Washington overlooked in his failure to make a case
for African-American civil liberties and equality under the law.

But Du Bois framed his argument for black advancement in political
and intellectual terms, and focused on the development of an African-
American elite. Washington and many of today's school reformers frame
their argument in economic terms, focusing on character building and
skills training. In many of their schools, education becomes a means to
jobs, to money, and to a rightful place in the existing capitalistic power
structure—not a mechanism for overthrowing it. KIPP's founders took
their network name, Knowledge Is Power Program, from their mentor
teacher's most popular chant: "You gotta read, baby, read. You gotta read,
baby read. The more you read, the more you know, 'cause knowledge is
power, power is money, and I want it." KIPP teachers speak of helping as-
similate their students into the economic mainstream: A KIPP teacher
said he wanted to help them succeed in the "middle-class capitalistic
world." KIPP parents often describe education in terms of its economic
benefits, as when Langdon told Geraldlynn, "You going to have to have
some kind of college up under your belt to get a job."

Even President Obama employed similar language when he said,
"African-American [and] Latino students are lagging behind white

classmates in one subject after another—an achievement gap that by one estimate costs us hundreds of billions of dollars in wages that will not be earned, jobs that will not be done, and purchases that will not be made."

Critics of KIPP-style schools today assail many schools for their rigid focus on test preparation, which can mean forgoing not only extracurricular activities but subjects such as art and civics—subjects that usually aren't tested but help constitute a broad-based education of the kind middle- and upper-class families tend to demand. (Teachers and school leaders cannot be held solely responsible for this narrowing of the curriculum, however, since the current policy environment mandates that schools, particularly high-poverty ones, boost their math and reading test scores or risk loss of funding and closure.)

KIPP's leaders preach the virtues of "grit" and have devoted considerable time and effort to figuring out how to teach character. In their depiction, almost anyone can rise within society's ranks—as long as they work hard and know the rules. Brian Dassler, for instance, prefers to describe people as "hardworking" instead of "intelligent."

The context has changed dramatically from the end of the nineteenth century, when Jim Crow prevailed. Today blacks and whites share more equal rights under the law. Segregation, de jure at least, is outlawed. Children of all races and economic backgrounds are entitled to a public education. Yet the two distinct approaches persist: One, championed by Washington, seeks to help poor black children compete more successfully in accordance with society's existing rules. The other, championed by Du Bois, seeks to change the rules. The fact that there is no empowered personification of the latter man's philosophy today shows just how modest our agenda for social change has become.

Marcovitz's advice in the fall to hold off on career decisions put Aidan at ease, freeing his mind to focus on the work at hand. He made small yet significant changes to his schedule in an effort to regain some control of his life. He committed, for instance, to finishing his weekly lesson planning on Saturday afternoons, even if that meant getting up early in the morning to do so. That gave him Saturday evenings free to relax without the specter of a rushed, frantic Sunday morning hanging over him.

In January, Aidan took over a new set of classes after a colleague's departure. He still taught English, but now exclusively for juniors; his new roster included two American literature classes and Advanced Placement

Aidan stands beside Sci Academy student Troy Lenard Simon at a school awards dinner. When Aidan started at Sci he taught mostly sophomores. But halfway through the school year, he took over a slate of junior English classes and started teaching Troy. Photo by Jessica L. Bard.

Language, which focused heavily on rhetorical devices and prepared students for the AP exam in May.

Aidan liked his new courses, particularly the challenge of the AP class. The AP student scores from a midyear practice test hung in the back of his room with student initials beside them. They included nine 1s, seven 2s, and two 3s. The tests are graded on a scale of one to five, with a score of three or above considered passing and qualifying a student for college credit. Aidan knew it would be tough to raise most of his students to 3s or above in the four months he had to work with the class. But he seized on the opportunity to teach difficult texts of the kind they would encounter on the exam.

Student behavior improved in his classes. Even though Aidan had to adapt to a new group of kids—and they to him—it helped that his new students were older and more accustomed to living under Sci's rules. He incorporated his colleagues' advice and benefited from their endless guidance and willingness to brainstorm teaching strategies with him. At Sci, Aidan never felt isolated or alone in his struggles; that camaraderie, perhaps more than any other single factor, helped him learn to cope with the inevitable setbacks and challenges. His classroom management was by no means flawless as the second half of the school year progressed. But he felt much more at peace about his life and teaching.

Aidan focused his energies on teaching Sci's juniors some of his most beloved literary favorites, including works by T. S. Eliot, F. Scott Fitzgerald, and Langston Hughes. He questioned how didactic he should be, and how much he should impose his own literary preferences on his students. His list of favorite writers featured some racial and gender diversity but tended toward the Western canon. In the end, he made the decision to prioritize the literature he found important or beautiful over books featuring contemporary characters more similar to his students. "I struggled with the racial and gender mix," he said. "But I decided if I am not passionate about something, I'm not going to teach it well."

He placed particular emphasis on generating lively class discussions that would prepare students for the give-and-take of a college classroom. Some days went better than others. After an American literature class in early January, he lamented, "My questions didn't drive discussion enough." He worried the students would not remember much about the poem he had taught that day, Wilfred Owen's "Anthem for Doomed Youth," because of his own failure to get them engaged in the conversation. "I'm taking heart because I'm building technical skills," he said. "But the technical skill of running a class discussion is not something I've mastered."

He had observed English classes at Newman and Jesuit, two elite private schools in New Orleans, as well as at his alma mater, Regis, in Manhattan. Based on those visits, Aidan concluded that the role of an effective English teacher is to help the kids make connections and ask good questions. "I am trying to come up with some better questions. My language can just be way too precise. I'm really verbose. I have to turn that down."

Later that morning, the AP students walked into class holding print-outs of a section from Karl Marx's *The Communist Manifesto*. Most wore frustrated looks on their faces as they settled into their seats for the do-now task that began each class. Sensing confusion over the reading, Aidan said he would give them until the end of class to answer the questions on the reading test he had prepared.

"I know this book was really tough and I didn't give you a lot of context," Aidan began, adding that he would provide a little background and then let the students talk. He wore a green sweater in celebration of the New York Jets' playoff victory the weekend before.

"Everything that has to do with Communism comes from this book," he said, pausing to nod his assent when a student asked if the word *bougie* comes from *bourgeoisie*. "This is one of the most important books ever written, and it is essentially an argument."

Aidan was explaining the meaning of generalizations when a tall girl named Marquisha interrupted. Marquisha never hesitated to share her thoughts.

"Mr. Kelly, would you like to know my opinion of the book?"

She continued on without waiting for a response.

"It was *dreadful*. It was hard to read. And it didn't make a lick of sense."

"What was difficult?" Aidan asked.

"We didn't really have background information or context about this . . ."

"I absolutely will give you context in the future. Do you know why I didn't?"

"The ACT?"

"The AP. The AP will not give you context."

He explained that the reading selections on the AP language exam would be presented without much background information, although most would not be as difficult as reading Marx.

Then he moved on to a discussion of the terms "means of production" and "proletariat."

"The proletariat sells their labor and then what do they get?" he asked. Silence.

"It says they work for what?"

Silence.

"It begins with a W . . ."

"Wages!" a student exclaimed.

Aidan said the proletariat's wages could be compared to Sci's "SMAc Bucks"—fake money the students received in exchange for good behavior, which they could then use to purchase school supplies or buy larger prizes at auctions. (The capitalized SMA stands for Science and Math Academy.)

"You work all day and the only place you can spend it is the company store," Aidan said.

"That's not fair," replied a student.

"Why don't they rise up?" Aidan asked.

"Maybe they are used to it?"

Not only that, but it wasn't so easy to overthrow the existing power structure, Aidan said. The bourgeoisie not only had money to hire their own security: They could also bribe the police. Moreover, no laws existed to protect workers' rights.

"Like teachers?" a student asked. "You work for two years and you can't get fired."

Aidan said he wasn't even thinking about unions or tenure, but the most basic laws shielding workers—including children—from exploitation and unsafe working conditions.

"Do the proletariat know how to start a revolution?" Aidan said.

When no one answered, he asked if they thought the proletariat, most of whom worked in sweatshops from the age of twelve, would be able to read and understand a book like *The Communist Manifesto*.

"If you were a middle-class person, who would you ally with, the proletariat or the bourgeoisie?"

"The proletariat," several students replied in unison.

Aidan said he wasn't so sure if that would happen, at least in Marx's depiction. Some of the middle-class shop owners probably sympathized with the proletariat's plight. But their fear of defying the bourgeoisie—who controlled the land, the police, the government, and the means of production—might overwhelm their desire to help the proletariat.

"If it's not going to be the shop owners, who is going to come down and help the proletariat?" he asked.

"Could it be the bourge, bourge—" a student stammered.

"Bourgeoisie," Aidan said. "But let's look at New Orleans East. Do you have a lot of rich people coming here to help?"

"I know," a student burst in. "Someone might help the proletariat so that they could become the government."

Aidan agreed.

"Why haven't the proletariat already risen up?" Aidan said.

"Because they are not educated enough," the student replied.

"So they need people like this [who want to take over the government]? Do you think it's going to happen?"

"Yes, because poor people deserve it," the student answered.

"A lot of people are going to die in this revolution . . ." Aidan countered.

"But doesn't that happen all the time?"

In subsequent conversations about the *Manifesto*, the students opined that Marx would have approved of Sci Academy because they were all from the proletariat and the school offered them training. He would not, however, have supported the school if it led them to abandon their class consciousness and join the bourgeoisie. Of that they were convinced. Mr. Kelly, moreover, seemed suspiciously bourgeois when they thought about it, with his Harvard pedigree, bow ties, colored socks, sometimes esoteric jokes, and ever-proper speech.

The students had complex feelings about Sci. Most of those who stayed bought in to the program, to some degree at least. They often talked appreciatively about how their Sci teachers went out of their way to ensure they learned the material. (Several said they felt frustrated when the pre-Katrina schools passed them on regardless of whether they had learned anything.) But for the most part the students did not see themselves in their teachers, many of whom they considered modern-day bourgeoisie. Sometimes they resisted their teachers' imposition of values, tastes, and aspirations—in ways both big and small. One morning, Aidan introduced *The Great Gatsby* to a class of juniors by describing it as "one of the greatest works in human literature." A student murmured in response, "It's just a teacher thing. I read it."

Even Jerel Bryant, one of Sci's few black teachers, said he felt "very foreign to the kids for a long time because I'm not from here." Bryant grew up in Harlem, attending the elite Collegiate School with financial assistance, and then Yale. Ironically, some students viewed him as even more foreign than his colleagues, since the teens had grown accustomed to young white teachers from other parts of the country. "I was a young black male with a funny gait and a funny accent," he said. "I didn't feel like I was taken in right away."

In the final class discussion on the *Manifesto*, the AP students agreed they would accept the school's training but never forget who they were and where they came from. That, they believed, would be what Karl Marx wanted. At the end of the day, the proletariat had to look after its own.

People often assumed Aidan came from a privileged background. Compared to many of the teenagers he taught, Aidan had had a comfortable upbringing—growing up an only child in a two-parent household in Yonkers. His parents weren't wealthy, but the family never suffered from deprivation. His mother and father met at a bar off Fordham Road in the Bronx when Martin Kelly asked Eileen Conway to dance. His father grew up poor in southeast Ireland, the second youngest of ten children, only two of whom finished high school; no one went on to college. Aidan's father left school after the eighth grade, briefly attended trade school, and then moved to England in 1965. There he worked with his brother, who died of walking pneumonia a few years later. At that point he immigrated to New York City to join some of his siblings; close to half of the family ultimately moved to the United States. In New York, Kelly found employment as a carpenter, working mostly on the interiors of office buildings for various contractors and, during one memorable project, on the inside of the rebuilt Museum of Modern Art.

Aidan says his father, aunts, and uncles "were models of how to achieve respect and security without college degrees, but it was never a question that their children would be much more educated than they were."

His mother grew up in the South Bronx and taught in that borough's Catholic schools for her entire career, including Sts. Philip & James and St. Mary schools. St. Mary charged low tuition and enrolled more low-income students than many private schools, giving her some inkling of the challenges her son would face working as an educator in a poor community. By the time Aidan joined Teach For America, his mother had taught for more than two decades.

Aidan attended Catholic elementary schools at discounted tuition, since his mother taught in the parochial system. His family always assumed he would continue on to a Catholic high school, but his admission to Regis High School came as a surprise. Regis, the only all-scholarship private school in the country, attracted an intellectual rather than economic elite; it gave preference in admissions to those students whose families would not be able to afford a Catholic secondary education without the free tuition. About 40 percent of its students are, like Aidan, the sons of immigrants. Competition for admission is fierce: About eight hundred prescreened students vie annually for 135 spots. Nearly every Catholic grammar school in the New York City region nominates its best candidates; the selected nominees must take a test and submit grades, essays, and letters of recommendation that the school uses to decide whom to bring in for interviews.

Regis helped instill a non-relativist view of the world in Aidan. The "school was always about character," he said. "They spoke from authority: There is a right way to do this; there is a right way to live." The absolutism extended not only to morality and personal conduct but also to scholarship and aspirations. He revered certain institutions and universities, not only for the training they offered, but for the excellence and values they denoted and the identity they conferred. "I was brought up to aspire to be a BC man, a Georgetown man," he said. "If that had meant changing who I was, I would have seen it as growth."

At the last minute, Aidan decided to apply to Harvard early decision. He had not yet visited the campus. Applying to a college you haven't visited is "not something I would recommend for my scholars," he says. But Harvard University represented the pinnacle of the prestige and achievement to which he and most of his colleagues at Sci had been taught to aspire. If you got in, of course you went.

Sci Academy and other charter schools like it run a risk in creating such structured, disciplined environments where students receive motivation from external rewards and punishments. The approach can backfire in the long run if students do not know how to function once all the structure and incentives disappear and if they do not learn how to think for themselves. Sci's students will not be able to call their college professors at nine P.M. if they fail to understand a homework assignment. They will not have professors who remind them to take notes, call home if they do not show up, and confer daily on their behavior and academic performance. No one will understand if they snap their approbation, use a hand signal when asking to go to the bathroom, or make a reference to SPARKing. There will be no SMAc Bucks, demerits, detention, or straight line to follow. No one will catch them if they do what Ben Marcovitz described as the default action for many an overwhelmed Sci student: "Let your body go limp and wait for someone to tell you exactly what to do."

Despite the guiding ambition to send all their students through college,

Sci's learning environment is the opposite of collegiate in many respects. Marcovitz describes it using the borrowed term "progress trap": To make progress, a school puts a series of structures in place. But at a certain point those structures become impediments, and the same expectations and systems that helped bring students to grade level prevent them from becoming, in one of the reformers' favorite buzz phrases, "college ready."

Sci attempts to peel back some of the structure as its students progress through high school. The sophomores and upperclassmen do not walk in straight lines. Teachers try to refrain from giving demerits to students who doze off in class or fail to turn in their homework so they will learn the ultimate consequence is a failing grade ("non-negotiables" such as uniform violations or cursing still result in demerits for the upper-grade students). They attempt to foster more free-form, student-driven discussions of the kind the students will encounter in college.

Yet even with the adjustments, Sci remained defined by rules and endless support. Je'on Domingue, one of Sci's top students, said the teachers struggle to let go of the structures. "They say they've loosened up, but if you go against things you will still get a demerit," she said.

The students had more nuanced views of Sci's approach than either the school's biggest champions or its fiercest critics. Almost without exception, they said they hated all the rules at first. Some left as a result. Other students departed because they wanted more extracurricular activities and sports than Sci initially offered, because they kept getting into trouble, or because the school put them out. Sci, like many New Orleans high schools, has a significant student attrition rate. The size of its first class of students dropped by 37 percent between the fall of 2008, when the school opened, and 2010, when Aidan started. (The figure does not equate exactly to the school's attrition rate since the school holds a large number of students back and sometimes replaces departed students with new ones.)

The students who accepted Sci's intense structure and demands said they did so for two reasons: First, they felt as though the teachers made genuine—if strange, at times—efforts to explain the reasons behind the rules. A teacher might remind students that if they slouched at their desks, less blood and oxygen made it to their brains, making it harder to pay attention and stay awake.

Second, and more important, they felt as though they were learning.

"At first I felt like, 'I'm in high school and I'm still getting treated like a baby?'" said Marquisha Williams. "But when I came back for sophomore year, I saw myself progressing, so I went with the program."

Bobby Calvin, who bounced from high school to high school for years, said he found in Sci a place where he felt safe and challenged. He signed himself up after reading a newspaper ad about the school. "My mama always told me to let her know when I found the school where I was comfortable, where things were peaceful and I could see myself graduating," he said. "In the schools I was at before, I never saw much structure or organization."

During Bobby's sophomore year, his girlfriend, another Sci student, became pregnant. The two teen parents took time off from school when the baby arrived in the fall of 2011. Sci teachers brought them work at home and arranged for individual tutoring, cementing Bobby's dedication to the school.

But Bobby, who hoped someday to become a barber, thought Sci sometimes went too far. Even seemingly small rule changes could trigger his frustration, like when he discovered the school had tightened up its uniform requirements his junior year.

"The uniform rules are unnecessary," he said. "You have to wear certain kind of socks, certain kind of shoes, a certain kind of undershirt, a certain kind of this, a certain kind of that. Some people are not fortunate enough to have a certain kind of everything."

Sci led students through the college-search process with its usual painstaking didacticism. During visit after visit, they asked students how they felt about different colleges, pushing them to be as precise as possible in their praise or criticism. Aidan's father had taken the same tack when he took his son to visit Georgetown and George Washington universities eight years earlier, asking Aidan to articulate the reasons he preferred the first school to the second one. "Why? Why is one right and one wrong?" his father had asked.

Sci's teachers hoped the juniors would bring similar clarity to a series of college visits in February. On this trip, they were headed to Millsaps and Tougaloo in Mississippi, as well as Tuskegee and Birmingham-Southern in Alabama. By this point they were old hands, having visited campuses in New Orleans, Memphis, Austin, Atlanta, Montgomery, west Florida, and Baton Rouge, among other places. Two and a half years into their high school careers, they had toured more universities than most Americans see in a lifetime.

Sci encouraged its students to leave New Orleans for college. "For a lot of scholars, I think it's important for them to get out of New Orleans and see something different," said Aidan. "There is a huge value in being out on your own. We want to create graduates who are worldly and well traveled." This ran counter to natural instincts and tradition in a city with one of the highest rates of native-born residents.

The teachers delighted in each moment of earnest self-reflection they witnessed from the students during the February trip. One junior hashed over each visit in depth with Aidan, analyzing the pros and cons of every college. Another said he could see himself excelling at a small college like Millsaps, where students got to know professors and peers intimately. A third surprised herself by falling in love with Tuskegee.

But several students had grown jaded or weary from all the visits. They no longer viewed the college trips as "rewards." Moreover, they no longer considered college the most interesting part of the trips. Some of them complained during campus visits. At Tougaloo, which some students disliked because of the drab campus, a few students "shut down" during the tour, refusing to pay attention; at Millsaps, one fell asleep during the information session. The teachers worried Sci's reputation would suffer as a result. Since no parent chaperones came along on the trip, the Sci teachers were responsible for the teens day and night. Some barely slept and returned from the four-day trip exhausted.

Sci's teachers concluded they needed to do a better job explaining not only the importance of college but also *how* to visit different campuses. Before the next round of tours in a few weeks, the teachers planned to tell their students that it was natural to dislike some colleges. That did not mean, however, that they could zone out, text, or fall asleep; instead they needed to sort out precisely what made them feel uncomfortable or bored and incorporate that into their ultimate decision about the kind of college they would apply to and attend.

For his part, Aidan planned to be much more specific about what students should look for during the visits, and the lessons they needed to take away.

"There are a bunch of teacher actions the next time that can make the student actions better," he said. "You break it down and there's a deliverable: an informed opinion on that college." Learning how to evaluate a college resembled any other skill, in his view. It fell to the teacher to make sure the students mastered it. If they failed to do so, the teachers had failed to do their jobs.

THE PRINCIPAL
"You want to go to college, baby?"

One spring afternoon, Laurie made her way out to the school's courtyard, where a lone student sat at a picnic table with a large stack of papers in front of him and a frustrated look on his face. Laurie recognized the student as Mervin, a shy, sweet-faced senior with one of the highest GPAs in his class. The documents, it turned out, were all from Tuskegee University. Tuskegee had accepted Mervin, offering him a full scholarship. But they required a $500 deposit by April 2, the next day, if Mervin wanted to secure his spot. He had no idea what to do.

"If that's where you want to go, let me know," Laurie said. "I'll try to get the five hundred dollars."

Mervin said nothing.

"You want to go to college, baby?" she asked gently.

Mervin nodded and wandered off, a confused look on his face.

If one of Walker's top students struggled to navigate the college-admissions and financial-aid maze, Laurie worried about how less motivated students were faring. Earlier that winter, she had decided Walker needed to do a better job helping its students sift through the process. Now she saw how far the school still had to go.

Walker employed two college counselors, but they had their hands full helping caseloads of hundreds. Laurie wanted someone to create a comprehensive data system so the school knew, at any given moment, how many of its students had taken the ACT, been accepted into colleges, and qualified for the state's main college scholarship program, known as TOPS. Data had not always been Walker's strongest suit. More intangibly, Laurie hoped to do a better job ensuring "everyone was speaking the same language" when it came to college admissions and financial aid.

Laurie also wanted to start tracking how the school's alums fared after graduation, an undertaking she wished the school had started years earlier. She had an anecdotal sense of which students made it through college and found stable jobs. Few school days passed at Walker without one or two recent alums returning to chat with Laurie, Big Mike, Coach T, or another staff member. They came bearing babies, whom Laurie inevitably cooed over, and telling stories of current adventures at work or school. "That's honest work, baby," Laurie would say, whether the visitor described running a business or cleaning trash off the streets. Other Walker graduates, like Cornelle Carney and Richard Comeaux, remained fixtures at the school. But every year some students departed after graduation and were never heard from again. Laurie often wondered how they were doing.

She hired Andrea Smith Bailey, the wife of assistant principal Mark Bailey, to help with these new tasks. Andrea had taught at Guste Elementary the final year Laurie served as principal. Andrea so admired Laurie she encouraged her husband to apply at Walker once Laurie became principal there. Andrea finished her master's degree in counseling psychology that winter while working part-time at Walker. Her job could have kept a team of full-time employees busy.

Creating a data system was the easy part, even though new information about college acceptances, ACT scores, and grade point averages poured in daily. Translating the "language of college" proved far more difficult. The labyrinthine rules and processes surrounding scholarships, loans, and financial aid did not account for the messy realities of poor families' lives. One senior, for instance, qualified for a state scholarship that provided full tuition at a two-year technical or community college. The student couldn't access the money, however, because he lived on his own and had no parent or guardian to sign for him. Andrea tried to register him as "homeless" so he could sign his own paperwork. She discovered it took mountains of paperwork even to qualify as homeless, particularly since one of the boy's grandmothers had erroneously claimed him as a dependent on recent tax forms. "We have a lot of kids who just don't fit in the federal government parameters of what's a family, what's a parent," Andrea said.

The scholarship parameters weren't designed with low-income students in mind either. TOPS promised qualifying students a free ride if they earned a 2.5 grade point average and scored at least a 20 on the ACT. But the scholarship failed to cover numerous expenses. One Walker student named Jamal planned to attend the state flagship, Louisiana State University, through a TOPS scholarship. But the grant did not cover the $150 he needed to get on a wait list for a dorm room, or the $500 housing deposit. Andrea delved into Jamal's financials, trying to figure out when his next paycheck from Taco Bell would clear so that he would not miss the deposit deadline and find himself homeless in Baton Rouge. Such challenges kept many low-income students from even starting college.

The communication barriers extended in all directions: The federal and state government bureaucrats little fathomed the complexities of low-income students' home lives. But the students, most of them first-generation college aspirants, often did not understand what a "loan" or "interest rate" meant—much less how to make sure they maximized their TOPS and Pell Grant payouts if they qualified for both. (For nebulous reasons, some students received full payments from both while others did not.) Andrea had worked as a family case manager for Habitat for Humanity between several education-related jobs. Countless times she encountered applicants with outstanding student debt who never realized they had even signed for a loan. She grew convinced Walker needed to include "college-going skills" as part of its curriculum, like KIPP's college-readiness class. It was too late to start those conversations senior year.

Even Walker's best students struggled to find their way through the financial aid maze. Jamal, for instance, had completed Advanced Placement courses and qualified for the highest level of funding under TOPS. Before accepting LSU, he had considered Morehouse College, an all-male, historically black institution in Atlanta. Jamal asked Andrea if he could borrow her phone one morning "to make a couple of calls about college scholarships." Andrea agreed, and a few minutes later she heard him asking someone at a college in New York for a scholarship to Morehouse. Andrea put the pieces together after some investigating, realizing Jamal had read something about a college in New York that was giving out scholarships. He had assumed that meant they were awarding grants to *any* college.

"He was just trying to do whatever he could," she said.

Walker had already forged a strong relationship with one beleaguered local university, known as SUNO, where it sent several graduates each year. Unlike other high schools that dismissed Southern University at New Orleans as subpar—a destination only for those who could not get in anywhere else—Laurie saw the historically black university as a viable option for many of Walker's graduates. In her eyes, the school's proximity to students' families, homes, and support networks was an asset for some students. "This is a small town," she said. "People don't always leave."

Arriving upstairs one morning, Walker's upperclassmen encountered a gigantic banner from SUNO. Peppy university cheerleaders wearing short skirts in the school's gold-and-blue colors greeted the Walker students with smiling faces at the recruiting fair. It was Walker's first SUNO Day, part of the growing partnership between the two schools. Table after table offered students information about the university's admissions and financial aid, degree programs and extracurricular activities, and free giveaways including Skittles packets and coin purses. Staff from both Walker and SUNO wore T-shirts proclaiming CHARGERS TO KNIGHTS, in honor of the two schools' mascots. The leaders of both institutions—SUNO chancellor Victor Ukpolo and Mary Laurie—circulated in the background, lending the event an official air. Laurie paced behind the tables where Walker students gathered information, shouting each time they approached a dean or official, "Ask those critical questions! Ask those critical questions!"

SUNO is a part of the Southern University System, the only historically black university system in the country. The school opened in 1959 during the last gasp of school segregation—a final victory for advocates of Jim Crow. Construction began two years after the landmark 1954 Supreme Court decision in *Brown v. Board of Education* declared that separate was not equal. Civil rights groups bitterly opposed SUNO at the outset, since its opening seemed to perpetuate a segregation they had long decried and the high court now pronounced illegal. The school opened in its first year with 158 freshmen and fifteen professors in Pontchartrain Park, a neighborhood of subdivisions created for middle-class blacks after World War II.

Laurie graduated from the University of New Orleans, but she took some of her education-methods classes at SUNO. She says it would have taken her even longer than a decade to finish college had it not been for SUNO's night classes, one of the many ways the four-year university tried to accommodate the schedules of working students. In Laurie's five years at Walker, she forged a friendly relationship with the college, sending dozens of graduates there each year. Laurie saw parallels between the two organizations: Both were committed to open access and serving students whom other schools would not take. Both were led by African-Americans and known for the familiar, folksy warmth with which they treated students. Both struggled at times to "keep their numbers up" in an era of strict school accountability. SUNO struggled more than Walker, though, a shortcoming that nearly led to the university's demise.

Compared to SUNO's, Walker's future seemed secure that winter. The state board of education approved a three-year renewal for Walker at its January meeting. Other charter schools received longer renewal terms—even for a decade in one case. But at least Walker did not suffer the fate of nearby Harriet Tubman Elementary School, also a member of the Algiers Charter Schools Association. State officials voted to turn it over to another charter school operator because of low test scores.

Meanwhile, SUNO's future hung in the balance. The same week the state board of education extended Walker's lease on life, Louisiana governor Bobby Jindal commissioned a study to explore the implications of a merger between UNO and SUNO, the only four-year public universities in the city. Most observers took the governor's action as a sign he supported shuttering SUNO.

SUNO's critics, including Jindal, dismissed the university in the same terms they used to describe the pre-Katrina New Orleans public schools: failing, inefficient, outdated, dysfunctional. But unlike the public schools, they added, SUNO failed to graduate most of its students *and* left many of them in crippling debt from student loans.

For years, SUNO's abysmal graduation figures made it difficult to rally political and public support for the university. In 2009, the school posted a six-year graduation rate of 8 percent, the second lowest of any urban public college in the United States. That figure represented a three-percentage-point increase over 2008, when SUNO graduated 5 percent of its students. SUNO officials acknowledged the need for improvement, but also cited their unusual student population. Most of their students worked or had children, which meant they often needed six, eight, even ten years to graduate, just as Laurie had decades earlier. The chaos and dislocation wreaked by Katrina further depressed graduation rates, they said. More important, if SUNO closed, a whole population of students—the ones only it admitted—would be shut out of four-year universities.

SUNO's students knew the historically black college lived up to both the best and worst of its reputation. They told stories of lost applications, nonresponsive administrators, classes canceled without notice or makeup. But they agreed that without SUNO, hundreds of low-income black students would miss out on the chance to earn a bachelor's degree. A merger between SUNO and UNO would be more conquest than equal union, with the historically black college's greatest strengths—including its openness and understanding of the conditions in which low-income, minority students live—lost forever. In an ideal world, merging SUNO and UNO would be cost effective and "no group would be left out," said Laurie. "But of course we're not in an ideal world."

The push to close SUNO came at a time of eroding African-American political power in New Orleans, a city where black residents still outnumbered white residents by almost two to one. Some of the shift stemmed from changing demographics: The city as a whole grew a little whiter and wealthier after Katrina. Black officials also lost some long-held positions due to unique circumstances, as in 2008 when the Vietnamese politician Anh "Joseph" Cao defeated William Jefferson in his bid for a U.S. congressional seat. Jefferson, the first black politician elected to Congress in Louisiana since Reconstruction, was facing federal corruption and bribery charges while he ran against Cao. (He was ultimately convicted of bribery.)

In 2007, whites claimed a majority on the city council for the first time in two decades. The following year, a white district attorney replaced a black one. Even the Orleans Parish School Board—which grew much more irrelevant after Katrina, when the RSD assumed control of most public schools—had a clear white majority in 2008 for the first time since 1984.

In 2010, city voters elected their first white mayor, Mitch Landrieu, in more than three decades. Landrieu had lost to black politicians (Marc Morial and Ray Nagin) in two previous bids for the position, but his family had long-standing support in the city's black community. Mitch Landrieu's father, Moon Landrieu, led the desegregation of city government during his own tenure as mayor between 1970 and 1978.

Throughout the public school landscape, African-American influence and clout waned after Katrina. Starting in 2007, two white men, State Superintendent Paul Pastorek and RSD superintendent Paul Vallas, ran the Recovery School District with unprecedented operational latitude and financial resources. They answered only to the state board of education, or BESE, where a majority of members usually supported their agenda. And they benefited from the millions in disaster aid that flowed into the district after Katrina, spending 65 percent more per pupil than the schools did before the flood. The principal and teacher corps gradually became whiter, a shift affecting not only the schools but also the political dynamic of the city as a whole.

"[The teacher firing] essentially destroyed a class of educated opinion leaders—schoolteachers—who had job security and were mostly middle-class and self-supportive," said Jacques Morial, a political consultant and the son and brother of former New Orleans mayors Ernest "Dutch" Morial and Marc Morial, respectively. "You dispersed an entire political class who played a vital role in political empowerment, and many of them still haven't returned."

A month before Jindal threatened SUNO and Walker received its three-year extension, the state board of education voted down charter school proposals from a couple of highly regarded black educators with a long history of running schools in the city. The spurned applicants included Doris Hicks, who already ran Dr. King Charter School in the Lower 9th Ward, a symbol of community resilience and resistance. She had applied to run a second school in addition to King.

In the wake of Katrina five years earlier, Hicks had been one of few RSD charter applicants to win state approval without hiring an outside management organization. The school's teachers and administrators wrote the application on their own. In the fall of 2006, the Recovery School District delayed reopening King charter because they had not yet rid its temporary location of mold and exposed lead paint. Hicks brought together hundreds of schoolchildren, local African-American politicians, and Southern Christian Leadership Conference president Charles Steele Jr. to protest the postponement. Children carried signs proclaiming, EDUCATION IS A RIGHT! Steele likened some of the white Baton Rouge bureaucrats responsible for the delay to members of the Ku Klux Klan. Hicks railed that the children had waited long enough. The protest achieved immediate results: RSD officials found a habitable building for King school within two weeks.

Doris Hicks is tall and broad shouldered, her presence imposing, her eyes piercing, her large, circular face ringed by a mass of copper-colored curls. Children stop in their tracks at the sound of her voice. She speaks with the cadence of authority. Hicks nurtures New Orleans traditions at King. The school has a vibrant marching band and holds numerous special events designed to teach students about their heritage, including visits from local civil rights icons such as Jerome Smith and an art class in which a Mardi Gras Indian chief poses for the students.

In 2010, Hicks applied to take control of Craig Elementary School in the Treme in addition to running King. Jerome Smith, who had so vociferously opposed the Recovery School District's petition to charter Craig a year earlier, supported Hicks's taking the helm at Craig—even if that meant the school became a charter. She embodied the kind of forceful self-determination he championed for the black community.

In its recommendation to deny King's second charter, a panel for the Chicago-based National Association of Charter School Authorizers, known as NACSA, wrote that the school's written application was deficient: School leaders had failed to outline the specifics of their proposed academic program at Craig or Hicks's role in overseeing the two campuses; they also left one section of the application blank. It turned out the RSD had asked Hicks to apply to run Craig at the last minute and provided her with scant support in preparing the thick application. She nailed the interview and clearly had community support in the Treme and the ability to run a school well. But from a technical perspective, the application did not suffice. The decision cemented the suspicion of some that local grassroots groups led by black educators would never gain much of a toehold in the city's charter school movement.[3]

The civil rights movement was gaining momentum in New Orleans and across the country when SUNO first opened its doors in 1959. Relegating black students to a separate, under-resourced university felt like an intolerable continuation of Jim Crow. In a letter to the New Orleans *Times-Picayune* newspaper, Willene Pulliam Taylor, a SUNO professor of English, said the school was built "for the express purpose of further perpetuating the immoral system of racism in this country." Emmett Bashful, the university's first chancellor, understood why civil rights organizations opposed SUNO's founding: "They thought it would increase segregation. After the *Brown* decision, they felt all institutions should be open to everybody."

Fifty years later, when black leaders fought for SUNO's continued existence, the context could not have been more different. The university represented one of a dwindling number of public institutions left under African-American control in a city where, just six years earlier, blacks ran City Hall, city council, the police force, the criminal courts, the schools—and now they ran none. The civil rights community that half a century earlier so bitterly opposed the university's founding now rose to its defense.

At a March 2011 rally, the Reverend Jesse Jackson mobilized the crowd by comparing the fight to keep SUNO open with the civil rights marches of the 1960s. "You weren't born when the March on Washington happened," he told the students and other SUNO supporters who crammed into the school's gymnasium, "and you missed out on the march to Montgomery. But God always gives us other chances to sacrifice."

Louisiana State Representative Austin Badon spoke for much of the legislature's black caucus when he declared that SUNO would not die without a fight: "Let the battle begin," he said.

Laurie supported SUNO, although she remained frustrated by the segregation that defined both New Orleans and American society more generally. When Laurie thought about race relations in twenty-first-century

America, it reminded her of "parallel play," the term used to describe toddlers playing side by side yet utterly disengaged from each other. It was depressing to think that the nation had come no further than self-absorbed two- and three-year-olds so wrapped up in their own lives that they remained oblivious to the range and diversity of experiences surrounding them. America had mastered the illusion of togetherness.

The Friday before Martin Luther King Jr. Day, Laurie attended a high school choir performance at Franklin Avenue Baptist Church intended to honor the man who dreamed that "one day right there in Alabama, little black boys and black girls will be able to join hands with little white boys and white girls as sisters and brothers." The event, which included performances by Walker, Clark, and McMain high schools, featured hand-holding and glorious renditions of "Total Praise" and "We Shall Overcome." King's desire for racial harmony and integration were honored, too, although in a curious way. The choir from the Ansar Bible College in Kristiansand, Norway, flew more than four thousand miles to participate in the event, as they did each year. Apart from the Norwegians, only a few whites attended. King's dream that neighbors and Americans of all colors would someday join hands felt a long way off.

A tension between community control and integration has persisted throughout American life. In the 1960s and '70s, for instance, some cities, including Boston, prioritized school desegregation over community control. Court-ordered busing effectively desegregated the schools, but it caused so much unrest and turmoil in targeted low-income communities that the suffering at times seemed to outweigh the benefits. African-Americans and the poor bore the brunt of the pain. Atlanta ultimately took the opposite path. The NAACP in that Southern city chose to forgo cross-city busing in exchange for black control over the schools.

A similar tension played out again and again in New Orleans. In the 1950s and '60s, many African-American leaders pinned their hopes for racial advancement on desegregation, as evinced in their adamant opposition to SUNO during its first decade. Desegregation meant giving up much of the community and cohesion African-Americans felt at all-black institutions, including the public schools. But for generations, the black community had been subjected to overcrowded schools, unequal pay for teachers, decrepit facilities, and insufficient programming, particularly at the high school level. Integration offered the prospect of greater equity.

By the 1980s, the pendulum had swung back to community control. The ideal of integration lost much of its luster since black families suffered most of the trauma associated with desegregation and the schools so quickly resegregated (on decidedly unequal terms). Moreover, like the early-twentieth-century historian Carter Woodson, some black leaders questioned whether their children could ever thrive in institutions created and led by whites.

By this point, blacks in New Orleans had gained unprecedented political power and effectively ran the public schools through their majorities on the school board and teachers' union. Black control of the schools was, in many respects, the educational equivalent of the "hollow prize," however. That theory holds that black politicians, including mayors of moribund cities like Detroit, often come to power at a time of inevitable decline. Black leaders took much of the blame for the failings of the public schools over the next two decades, which were legion. Defenders of the pre-Katrina system argue that white business and political leaders across the state—and white taxpayers in the city—financially strangled the New Orleans public schools. Critics argue the system strangled itself through a mixture of corruption and institutional obsolescence. Probably both arguments were true at times.[4]

In the years after Katrina, de facto segregation remained the norm in New Orleans *and* African-Americans lost much of their autonomy and authority in the city's public sphere. In exchange for promises of increased school quality, they were asked to give up both their claim to community control of schools and any hope for meaningful integration. That proposition proved divisive. If the schools continued to improve over several years, the black community would benefit. But if they did not improve significantly, the black community would be left more powerless than it had been for generations. Considered in this context, it is not surprising people clung to SUNO, which, for all its struggles, belonged to them.

Those who worried SUNO's closure could shut hundreds of New Orleans students out of the chance at a college education had legitimate grounds for fear. America's higher education system, and Louisiana's in particular, has long reinforced existing class divisions rather than promoting social mobility in several troubling respects. By 2011, SUNO was one of a dwindling number of public universities that tried to accept virtually any student, regardless of academic background. The debate over its future raised broader questions: Should universities be open to all, or serve only those with demonstrated academic abilities? Should higher education in America be more egalitarian or elitist?

In Louisiana, the Board of Regents phased in tougher admissions standards across its four-year university system between 2004 and 2014. Universities can no longer accept students who require a single remedial course. To avoid remedials, students usually need to earn at least an 18 on the ACT in English and a 19 in math. In 2011, the average composite ACT score for a New Orleans public school student was 18 on a 36-point scale. That means about half of the students who took the ACT—a select group in and of itself at some schools—will not qualify for admission to any four-year, in-state university under the new standards. O. Perry Walker posted an average score of 17.8 in 2011. Most of its graduates needed at least one remedial class.

New Orleans guidance counselors worry the tougher admission standards will disproportionately affect low-income minority students who, on average, score lower on the ACT. TOPS, the state's main scholarship program, has long been biased in favor of middle-class students. TOPS awards hinge solely on merit, since they are tied to grades and ACT scores. Critics of TOPS say an awards system based on comparative class rank— awarding scholarships to the top 15 or 25 percent of every graduating class, for instance—would ensure greater access for low-income students.

Most states devote a far higher percentage of their scholarship pool to need-based aid than Louisiana. Nationwide, states spent 23 percent of their aid on merit-based programs and 59 percent on need-based in 2008, according to a report by the nonpartisan Louisiana Budget Project. Louisiana, by contrast, spent 81 percent on merit-based and 17 percent on need-based programs. That year, the number of white TOPS recipients outnumbered the number of black students by seven to one in a state where the population ratio of white to black is roughly two to one.

The group's report concluded that much of the $1.25 billion the state spent on TOPS over a dozen years went to "those who need it least."

While SUNO's critics could not see past its low graduation rate, in the eyes of Walker's leaders, SUNO and other historically black universities worked the hardest to ensure continued access as the admissions standards took effect. SUNO, for instance, invited Walker students to ACT prep sessions and created a summer program for students who required

*Laurie smiles and claps her hands as she sends Walker's students off to classes one morning. Photo by Susan Poag/*New Orleans Times-Picayune.

remedial courses. Students who completed the summer classes could enroll as full-fledged students in the fall. "There are a lot of students who feel like the HBCUs [historically black colleges and universities] have their best interest at heart and work with them where they are," said one Walker counselor.

Walker buzzed with nervous energy as winter ended and the final stretch of school commenced. On the first day of April, hundreds of eighth graders came to visit Walker as part of its new student-recruitment campaign. Across the city, schools vied for students, since supply exceeded demand at many grade levels. They advertised on highway billboards, posted signs in the neutral grounds of city boulevards, and knocked on doors. Walker's leaders had decided they could best tout their wares by bringing students straight to the source. They fed the eighth graders grilled burgers and treated them to a series of student performances in the gym. Laurie lingered while the band performed one of her favorites: "I Want to Be in the Walker Band," played to the tune of "I Want to Be a Billionaire."

Laurie suspected most of the students would like Walker. Every Friday the school hired a DJ to spin songs during lunch—the kind of music the kids liked. Unlike many of the city's other charter schools, Walker allowed students of all grade levels near total freedom at lunch to mill around the courtyard and cafeteria, chatting with whomever they chose. After one glimpse of the older kids relaxing to the DJ's music, the eighth graders would view Walker as an exotic place far cooler than their middle schools. Convincing their parents that Walker was no longer the failing, troubled high school they remembered from before Katrina would be harder.

After lunch, Laurie made a quick stop at an honors English class taught by assistant principal Mark Bailey. She steeled her face before opening the door to the classroom. Once inside, she lit into teacher and students alike with uncharacteristic harshness.

"I am tired," she said. "I am *tired* of what y'all are writing in your journals. I am *tired* of hearing from your parents about what you are writing in your journals. I am *tired* of you complaining to your parents! On Monday you are going to have a new teacher!"

Laurie left abruptly. The confused students sat speechless in their seats. Out in the hallway, she counted to three and popped back into the classroom.

"April fools!" she cried.

Everyone laughed. Even in times of great stress and tragedy, students and staff at Walker found solace in humor.

"You are one of my favorite classes on campus," Laurie said before leaving. "I watch you engage around instruction and I am very impressed. You model what I would like to see every day at Walker."

Later that afternoon, Laurie encountered Mervin, the straight-A student who had won admission to Tuskegee with the promise of a generous financial aid package but seemed frozen by indecision.

Laurie summoned Mervin's guidance counselor, who explained that three different universities had offered him full scholarships because of his high grades. While the offers made him the envy of his classmates, the teen had no idea what to do. As deadlines loomed, he sifted aimlessly through paperwork. The guidance counselor had reached out to his mother, but the woman brushed her off.

Laurie asked if there might be a substance abuse issue.

"No . . ." the counselor said. "I guess she didn't want me to pressure her."

Laurie pondered this for a few seconds.

"Maybe if you've never been to college . . ." her voice trailed off. "She might not know. I just don't want him to miss these deadlines and end up with nothing."

"Originally he wanted to go to college out West," said the counselor. "But Mom said she didn't want him going anyplace she couldn't drive." They limited their search to Alabama, Mississippi, and Louisiana as a result.

"Tuskegee would be great for him," she added. "He could come into his own there."

Laurie thought a little more.

"I'm sure his mother wants him to go to college," she said. "She just doesn't know how it works. But at the same time, we dropped the ball. We shouldn't be at this point."

That night, Laurie called Mervin's mother. The woman said she had left the decision up to her son.

"I got the feeling Mom had probably been in a situation where she had been talked down to," Laurie said later. "Sometimes it can be intimidating to talk to someone who is telling you something and knows more about it. We are not doing a good enough job of helping them understand how college works. If one of our top students with all these scholarship offers doesn't have a sense of how to make a best choice, what about all the rest?"

Teaching students and parents the intricacies of deposits, scholarships, interest rates, and loans would help only so much. It might, for instance, have prevented Jamal from calling up a college in New York and asking for a scholarship to Morehouse. But information and knowledge weren't enough if families and students felt so disempowered they shut down whenever the subject of college came up or they faced a crucial decision. That problem had deeper roots and more complicated solutions. It required changing long-ingrained habits of mind and feelings of inferiority. You could not, after all, teach someone the language of college if he lacked the confidence to start the conversation.

THE FAMILY
"Money makes money."

From the moment Raquel and Geraldlynn walked into KIPP Renaissance's February parent-teacher-student association meeting, they knew the school had something unusual planned. A cadre of smiling, if mildly officious, strangers in business attire circulated amid the small number of parents who showed up. Each family received a glossy packet with information from the ASI Federal Credit Union. White and green balloons decorated the tables. The room looked like money.

Raquel wore her work uniform even though Geraldlynn had asked her to change before coming. Raquel never shied away from letting people know what she did for a living, and most parents arrived in their work uniforms anyway. As everyone waited for the meeting to start, Raquel scoured the credit union pamphlets while Geraldlynn fired off texts, excited to have a cell phone back in her possession. Months earlier, Raquel had found curse-laden song lyrics among her daughter's papers and had withheld phone privileges. "The first thing Mama goes for when she punishes me is the cell phone," said Geraldlynn, joking, "I love my phone—although I wouldn't take a bullet for it."

Like KIPP, the credit union and other officials did not take a subtle approach to the subject of college. Using a series of prepared slides, they tried to hammer home the importance of starting college savings accounts as soon as possible. (The woman presenting noted that she created an account in her daughter's name and made the first deposit within a week of the child's birth. Most of her audience, however, had missed that chance by about fifteen years.) One slide stated that a college degree quadruples the likelihood that a child born to parents on the bottom rung of the ladder will make it to the top. Another contained an image of a Venn diagram representing "college success" as the intersection of three traits: ability to succeed, ability to persist, and ability to pay. A third noted that even low-income students who receive full tuition scholarships sometimes have to drop out if they cannot afford university housing or textbooks.

"We don't want your kids to go through all the rigorous training Brian [Dassler] is putting them through to go to college and not succeed for financial reasons," said the woman. "*You* don't want to be the main reason they don't make it."

Several "savings tips" followed: buy in bulk, look for sales before making purchases, shop with a grocery list. Next came a recitation of the adage

"Money makes money" and an illustration of how bank interest causes dollar bills to multiply. To this end, the credit union officials said they had decided to help jump-start that multiplication process for Renaissance families, using a grant from the Keller Family Foundation and money from KIPP. For every dollar the parents put into an ASI college savings account—up to fifty dollars—they would match it with two. At that point, the officials brought out a dummy check, practically larger in size than Geraldlynn, made out to "KIPP Renaissance students" for the amount of "College." Geraldlynn and three other classmates clustered around the enormous check while the officials and parents snapped pictures. Then the mothers grilled the credit union representatives for several minutes. Raquel, for instance, wanted to know if she could open an account for Jasmine, who didn't attend Renaissance, through the same deal (she couldn't). Another parent asked if she could get her money back if her son did not go to college (she could). Eventually, Raquel and Geraldlynn departed for home, taking with them the packet of information, a handful of leftover cookies from the refreshment table, and three of the large balloons which, although they would not multiply by morning, lent a festive air to the house.

Raquel had already opened a college savings account for Geraldlynn at the start of the school year but had not yet deposited money into it. That spring, KIPP Renaissance created a public display featuring a thermometer-shaped image for each family with an account. They shaded the entire thermometer once a family had deposited $100, half at $50, and so forth. But many of the thermometers stayed empty all school year—including Geraldlynn's—with just the base colored in.

A few decades ago, in the era that Mary Laurie attended the University of New Orleans, Raquel would have had a much easier time affording college for her two daughters. That's because a dollar today buys far less than it did forty years ago, and the cost of a university education has skyrocketed. Both the Consumer Price Index and higher education costs have risen at faster rates than the minimum wage. In 1970, a student could have covered her college expenses through a part-time job at McDonald's. But in 2011, a parent working the same job, full-time, would have to dedicate her entire income to send her child to many public universities for a year. In 2011, student default rates on federal college loans reached their highest level in fourteen years, offering just one glimpse of families' struggles to afford the rapidly rising cost of higher education.

KIPP officials hoped most of their students would qualify for TOPS scholarships to in-state, four-year universities. That way, families' college expenses would be dramatically reduced. But KIPP teachers knew, without significant improvements, the ACT threshold of 20 would shut out many of their kids. Only top students from KIPP middle schools go on to earn a 20 or above on the ACT at the various high schools they attend, said Nicole Cummins, a college counselor for KIPP. Even a KIPP middle school alumna who became her high school valedictorian struggled to score high enough to qualify for TOPS. Whether KIPP Renaissance would improve on that record was an open question.

Raquel worried constantly about paying for college. But there wasn't a whole lot she could do about it besides worry. She had forgone health insurance because her take-home pay was so meager when she participated in the hotel's plan.

The "money makes money" expression could have applied to other aspects of Raquel's life as well—ones further outside of her control than college savings. For most of her adulthood she has worked in an industry whose leaders have amassed ever-increasing quantities of wealth partly on the backs of the working poor. In the late 1990s, average hotel room rates in New Orleans lagged behind just a few cities', including New York City, San Francisco, and Boston. Yet New Orleans housekeepers were paid significantly lower wages than their counterparts in other major American cities. That made New Orleans one of the most profitable places to run a hotel in the country, if not the most profitable. The average hourly wage for a housekeeper in New Orleans at the time was $5.48, compared to $10.92 in New York City and $8.66 in Las Vegas, two cities where most of the hotel workers are represented by unions.

In the 1980s and 1990s, efforts were made to organize the hospitality workers in New Orleans. The most ambitious, known as HOTROC (Hospitality, Hotels, and Restaurants Organizing Council), took root in the mid-nineties with the backing of the AFL-CIO. During face-to-face meetings with dishwashers, maids, convention waiters, and janitors in their homes, organizers described what the workers' lives would be like if they lived in other cities. They explained that if a New Orleans hotel housekeeper did the equivalent work in Las Vegas, she would likely earn at least 60 percent more. She could afford a mortgage on a decent house. She would own a car—probably not a new one, but it would run. She would not have to rely on Charity Hospital for medical services. And she could set aside some savings for her children's college education.

The effort ground to a halt with very few lasting victories. The reasons varied. Louisiana is a right-to-work state, meaning it prohibits closed shop unions. More significantly, the unions had to amass political capital virtually from scratch: For generations, the hospitality industry controlled many of the city's most influential politicians by virtue of its money and enormous clout. Nevada is also a right-to-work state, but the unions in Las Vegas have long overseen the recruitment and training of hospitality workers in the city. That means the business community has to work with them or jeopardize the quality and size of its workforce. In New Orleans, the union had fewer bargaining chips to win over politicians and hotel management. And the latter was merciless in firing workers who served as lead organizers because weak labor laws meant they would face few, if any, consequences.

In New Orleans the business community retained a captive workforce through the persistence of unconscionably bad schools that graduated many of their students to bottom-rung jobs or lives of crime. Indeed, organizers said they had to contend with the fact that many hotel workers could not read well, making it harder to spread information and flyers about the campaign. Moreover, despite the city's long tradition of longshoreman and mail-carrier unions, fewer New Orleanians had relatives who belonged to unions, adding to the challenge of communicating their relevance. There was also, at times, a cultural gap between the young, white, Yankee labor organizers imported by the unions and their target audience of mostly African-American mothers, fathers, grandmas, and grandpas who had lived all their lives in the Deep South.[5]

While the union drive never gained much momentum, labor leaders received some consolation when New Orleans residents voted in 2002 to raise the city's minimum wage one dollar above the federal level—to $6.15. Organizers had fought for six years to get the living-wage proposal on the ballot. The vote represented the first time an American city chose to impose a higher minimum wage even on private employers. Close to fifty thousand New Orleans workers, including restaurant dishwashers and hotel maids, would have earned more when the increase took effect. But the business community, led by the Louisiana Restaurant Association, fought the measure in the courts. They argued the hospitality industry could not afford to pay its workers $6.15 an hour, and they claimed businesses would abandon New Orleans if the raises took effect. Seven months after the ballot measure passed, the Louisiana Supreme Court rejected the voter-approved change, declaring it unconstitutional. The minimum wage stayed at $5.15.

The last bid to win a contract for employees at Raquel's French Quarter hotel failed in the early 1980s—years before she went to work there. She had mixed feelings about working conditions at the hotel. Over thirteen years, her pay had risen from $5.25 an hour to $10.75. She felt grateful for the steady increases but wondered why she did not make at least $13 after so many years of reliable service. Raquel watched as supervisor after supervisor cycled in and out—about one, on average, for each year she worked at the hotel. Very few people in the housekeeping department had as much history and experience as Raquel and Roxanne. They cleaned rooms when they started at the hotel, but after Katrina their main responsibility was to tidy up public spaces like the bathroom in the lobby area. Raquel often handled the cleaning in the bride's room during weddings, and regretted that she almost never glimpsed the ceremony itself. "By the time I'm finished cleaning they are always dancing," she said.

The Gumbo Shop restaurant where Raquel and Roxanne bused tables was small and family owned. The manager usually accommodated the sisters if they had to leave for a rare family emergency (although on one particularly painful day he refused to change Raquel's schedule so she could attend Geraldlynn's kindergarten graduation ceremony). At the hotel, the supervisors were less generous. "They understand it, but they don't care to me," said Raquel. "They'll let me go, but then be asking all kinds of questions about how long I'll be, and where I'm going again."

If Raquel had a complaint or query about any aspect of her working conditions, her main recourse was to put a note in an employee-concern box and hope that someone with power read it and cared. The bosses were not always forthcoming when they made changes to pay or overtime rules. Raquel found out when she received her paycheck. After she realized they had dropped time and a half for Mardi Gras day, Raquel thought about leaving a note in the box expressing her concerns. But by the time she got around to it, the box had disappeared.

Mardi Gras season is one of the busiest times of year for New Orleans hotels. For most professionals in New Orleans the holiday means slow-paced, shortened workdays and at least a day or two off. People open up their homes for parties, take their children to the myriad parades, and leave work early to avoid getting stuck in traffic behind a line of floats. For Raquel, it means virtual nonstop work and parades glimpsed in passing, if at all. For years she hoped to find the time to see the Zulu parade from start to finish. During the famed event—the city's largest historically black parade—float riders throw coveted decorated coconuts into the crowd. But Zulu always rolled early on Fat Tuesday, right in the middle of one of the busiest hotel housekeeping shifts of the year. On the bright side, the cleaning itself wasn't always too taxing during the final days of Mardi Gras. Tourists spent most of their time on the streets and in the bars, hardly visiting their rooms. The guests at large weddings spent more time indoors, and often left behind bigger messes.

When Raquel first started the two jobs in the late 1990s, she worked full-time at both the hotel and the Gumbo Shop. She had not yet met Langdon, and the girls' father wasn't much help with the bills. "I used to get up real, real early and the girls used to cry when I left because they wanted to be with me all day," she said. "They understood better as they were older and coming up: I have to do this so I can take care of y'all." Even after she went down to part-time at the Gumbo Shop, Raquel couldn't always enjoy her off hours. Some days, the hotel and restaurant shifts fell so close together it wasn't worth going home in between. Other days, she collapsed into bed as soon as she walked through her front door.

Although she still missed out on Zulu, Raquel felt more at ease during Mardi Gras 2011 than at any Carnival in recent memory. For the first time since Geraldlynn and Jasmine were toddlers, she only worked one job. She had quit her part-time position busing tables at the Gumbo Shop a few weeks earlier when Langdon found steady work as a prep cook in a takeout seafood restaurant. Occasionally, she still helped out with a relative's housecleaning business to earn some extra cash. But the shift left her with many more evenings and weekends to spend with her daughters. Raquel often said she wanted to "hold on to" her girls for as long as she could, by which she meant preventing them from befriending the wrong crowd and losing all interest in school. She worried about their wandering around the River Ridge neighborhood with other teenagers she did not know well. Building a college savings account would certainly be nice. But the money would mean little to her—or to her daughters—if she had already lost that grip.

Katrina awakened much of the country to the grim realities of poverty. But the storm opened Raquel's eyes to how much she had to lose: jobs. A home. Her family. The joys of her hometown.

Like thousands of New Orleanians, the family stayed in town for Katrina, never expecting the city would flood so badly. Initially, they took shelter at the hotel where Raquel and Roxanne worked. But as the waters started to rise outside the Quarter, the hotel shut off its power and management told everyone to leave. The family members have varying recollections of the sequence of events that followed. Most of them agree that they headed to Raquel's house in the 7th Ward, where the water already covered the front stoop and had started to seep through the floors. A passerby loaned the group—which included Langdon, Raquel, Roxanne, and all of the twins' children—a fishing boat. Using the boat, they made their way to the home of Raquel and Roxanne's mother, Diana Davis, just a couple miles away. When the boat got stuck under a bridge, they abandoned it and traveled as best they could on foot.

The family spent a day or two huddled in Diana's house, which remained relatively dry. They had a healthy supply of water and food, although Raquel worried constantly about where to go "once we came to our breaking point." That point came quickly, when their ill grandfather ran out of medicine. Fortunately, a speedboat with volunteers running rescue missions gave them a ride to a slab of dry land along the bayou in Mid-City. From there, helicopters transported them to the airport. The family spent several hours resting at the airport before officials put them on a bus bound for Houston. In Houston, they lived in a shelter and a church, whose leaders found them an apartment in the suburb of Webster.

They stayed in Webster, where all the children attended public schools, for about two months. McWhirter Elementary School enrolled a far more diverse student body than any school Geraldlynn had ever seen. She thought McWhirter was run better than McDonogh 42, her old school. But she had a hard time communicating with her new classmates and teachers, who often did not understand the way she talked and sometimes seemed to look down on the transplants.

Raquel and Roxanne returned to the city in October because they missed home and heard they could resume their jobs at the hotel.

"We went from Grandma's house to the Bayou, the Bayou to the helicopter, helicopter to the airport, airport to Houston, Houston to the shelter, shelter to the church, church to the apartment, apartment to back here!" Jasmine says.

"It was survival, you know, of the fittest," said Geraldlynn.

"I hope it never happens again," said Raquel.

"If it does, we be hitting the road *before* time," concluded Geraldlynn. The twins' mother chose to remain in Houston. Diana Davis had spent her entire adult life taking care of children, including a son who was in and out of trouble, and several grandchildren. She relished a more solitary life in a new city, where she found work as a home health care aide and opened her own catering business.

Raquel felt her mother's absence on a daily basis. Raquel and Roxanne could always trust that their kids were safe with her. "They wasn't about to play at Mama's house," said Raquel. In the years that followed Katrina, she even thought about sending Geraldlynn to live in Houston. She knew her daughter would be in good hands there, and the teen could continue at KIPP since the network ran more charter schools in Houston than in any other city. Raquel never pursued the idea, however. She could not bear to have Scooter so far away.

After quitting her job at the Gumbo Shop, Raquel pitied a young co-worker whose exhausting schedule reminded her of her own life a decade earlier. The woman worked an eight-hour night shift at the hotel, a day shift as a security guard, and cared for a baby son. Whenever Raquel saw the woman, she tried to elicit a smile or laugh by asking facetiously, "Are you working? I feel on that. Girl, someday me and you are going to Vegas."

Vegas remained a pipe dream, but Raquel did take a vacation before the Mardi Gras parades started and the tourists poured into town. For weeks she planned the trip to Houston to surprise her mother.

Raquel spent the day before her trip doing some last-minute errands and scrubbing in the River Ridge apartment. Langdon would watch Jasmine and Geraldlynn in her absence, but she could not count on him to do any hard cleaning. "Men get weak in the knees when it comes to taking care of business," she said. She hopped a bus early one Friday morning and set off on her adventure. Somehow word of her visit arrived in town before she did, so the surprise part failed. But mother and daughter spent several relaxing days together shopping, eating, and wandering around Houston.

With additional time on her hands, Raquel planned more family outings in New Orleans as well. Some evenings she took the girls to CiCi's, a restaurant in a nearby strip mall that sold all-you-can-eat pizza slices for six dollars. For years, Jasmine had been responsible for the girls' dinner. She cooked whatever the family had around—often hot dogs or instant potatoes. Jasmine so liked cooking Raquel thought about signing her up for a class, but she wasn't sure how to go about finding one.

The girls enjoyed getting out of the house and spending more time with their mother. But they remained acutely aware of the family's financial limitations. During one trip to CiCi's, Geraldlynn and Jasmine spent several minutes eyeing the electronics in a claw machine from a distance. Once they had eaten their fill of pizza and sticky cinnamon buns, they ran over to the machine for a closer inspection of its contents, coveting the iPod in particular. Raquel followed them, fishing through her coin purse for four quarters so they could try their luck with the claw. But her daughters refused to take the money. "A dollar is too much," Jasmine said as Raquel put away her coins. It wasn't worth the gamble.

What's your mascot?
   Y'all can ride your bikes on campus?
   You got a roommate?
   Y'all have ROTC?
   Where's the main building where if someone BIG come they give a speech?

All through Geraldlynn's visit to Dillard University, a private historically black college in New Orleans, she fired off questions as fast as her tour guide could answer them. Geraldlynn wasn't shy around people with whom she felt comfortable, and she liked Dillard freshman Bianca Jones from the moment she met her. Bianca, who grew up in New Orleans, managed to project a brainy coolness Geraldlynn admired. The older girl seemed just as at ease in the library, where she grew animated describing the contents of Dillard's archival collection, as she did in the student lounge, where she chatted and joked with a group of guys shooting pool.

KIPP Renaissance's staff organized the daylong excursion to give their students a taste of university life. Dillard had long-standing ties to families and schools in the 7th Ward neighborhood where Geraldlynn grew up, including her sister Jasmine's school, McDonogh 35. The teachers spent most of the day clustered together in a corner of the student lounge—deliberately staying away from the students to let them experience Dillard on their own. They made an odd sight, sitting crammed around a table bent into their laptops and iPads.

The school scheduled the trip for St. Patrick's Day, and teachers worried at the last minute that it might not be a typical day on campus. But an African-American doctoral student writing her dissertation on KIPP Renaissance pointed out the black community usually doesn't celebrate St. Patrick's Day, or take much note of it at all. The researcher later included the anecdote in her dissertation as a small but telling example of the cultural gap between the school's staff and students. She provided several other examples, including one teacher's ignorance of the meaning of the acronym HBCUs (Historically Black Colleges and Universities) and another teacher's failure to realize a student had been disrespectful in class partly because the teen came to school hungry that morning.

In the morning, the students went off in groups of twos and threes with Dillard student guides. Geraldlynn paired up with Aliyah and Brekel, two friends from her roundtable who were both quiet and reserved. She liked the challenge of drawing them out. Geraldlynn had instructed Mr. Saltmarsh to find a "sophisticated" guide for her group. But she betrayed her own giddy nervousness seconds before meeting Bianca when she frantically asked Brekel to help straighten her tie and rehearsed her introduction, extending her arm and saying, "My name is Geraldlynn." To Bianca's amusement, the three girls deferentially referred to her as "Ms. Bianca" throughout the day.

Bianca graduated from Ben Franklin High School, one of the city's top magnet programs. She wore the college uniform of jeans, T-shirt, and sneakers, moved quickly, and dispensed advice liberally to her charges. They started with a quick spin around the grounds and then made their way into the lounge area, where Bianca told the younger girls not to be scared by the guys lurking around the pool table. Geraldlynn led the way, peering cautiously around a corner at the game under way. She ducked back quickly to join her friends as soon as one of the boys spotted her.

"Hey, high school students, what school y'all coming from?" one of the young men called out.

"KIPP Renaissance High School," they said in unison, venturing out of hiding together.

"Now that's an original name."

"All the schools have these long-ass names after Katrina," said another of the guys. "Every one's a charter school."

The pool players waxed nostalgic for a few moments about their own time in high school—college could be such a grind.

"Y'all got a long time since you're freshmen," one said. "Please enjoy high school."

"I'm not going to go to college as soon as I get out of high school," Geraldlynn told Bianca as the tour continued. "It's gonna be a long four years. I want a year off."

"You better go right after," Bianca told her. "That way you still got the information in your head. I know someone who took a year off and now she's failing all her classes."

Inside Dillard's gymnasium a few minutes later, Bianca explained that students could attend all the basketball games they wanted, but only if they paid the student activity fee of $100.

"That's why you all have to enjoy high school. Everything is free. Here you pay for everything. I'm paying to stand here and talk to you."

Money dominated much of the day's conversation. Bianca advised the girls to save their dollars now because they would not want to work jobs while in college—classes and partying would more than fill up their time. She also cautioned against getting credit cards until they graduated from a university. In her experience, credit cards usually led students, particularly poor ones, into serious trouble.

"They say it's cheaper to live in a dorm than at home?" Geraldlynn asked.

Bianca corrected her gently, explaining that at Dillard students paid about $27,000 a year to live on campus and $21,000 to live off campus. Only athletes and a few others received full scholarships from the university, she said, but if you looked hard you could find all sorts of smaller scholarships.

"They got them for everything," Bianca said. "If you left-handed, there's a scholarship. If you wear glasses, there's a scholarship."

Geraldlynn took every word to heart.

"If you right-handed, can you get a scholarship?" she asked.

Bianca's friend TJ joined the group midmorning. TJ had graduated as salutatorian the previous spring from a young KIPP high school in Houston. The KIPP Renaissance students were slightly in awe. Geraldlynn spent much of the afternoon walking and talking with TJ, grilling her about Houston's KIPP schools and her experience so far at Dillard. "I've never met someone who was second in their class," she said.

The group cruised through the academic buildings as lunch hour approached. Outside a room with the word CALCULUS written on the door, Geraldlynn said, "That's the hardest part of this campus. I would never want to go in that door." When they walked past the English hall, she asked, "So you go down this hall if you want to be a poet or something?" Near the science wing, she inquired, "They do dissections in here?"

In the afternoon, the five girls ate several plates of french fries and pizza in the dining hall, twirled around in the dance studio, walked a loop on Dillard's indoor track, and admired the miniature campus movie theater and bowling alley. In the weight room they encountered an unexpected delay when Geraldlynn insisted on trying every machine. Determined to experience all the room had to offer, she stretched and strained to operate even the machines that were too big for her.

As the day drew to a close, Bianca told them she hoped to move on campus for her sophomore year and live in the Gardens, reduced-cost apartments traditionally reserved for students with high GPAs. She had earned a 3.6 in her first semester and knew she would make it into the Gardens if she kept her grades up. Whispering in the library during one of their final stops, Bianca pointed to the archives room: "I usually go in there and read when I don't have anything else to do—because I'm a nerd."

"You are *not* a nerd," Geraldlynn said. Then she gave her tour guide a hug good-bye.

After her visit, Geraldlynn recited the facts she had learned about college with a new, more definitive tone:

"It costs more when you stay in the dorms than when you go home."

"They have parties on Thursday—like really, every Thursday."

"When you are in a college class you have to be quiet."

"College is not all about learning. You gotta be on point, but you can still have fun."

She could imagine herself attending Dillard someday. "It's a college where you see a lot of people you know and then you go home," she said. "The tuition is lower—some are like thirty thousand dollars. I wonder how people pay all that to, like, them top-notch colleges."

But Geraldlynn worried about Dillard's size and lack of diversity. Small campuses, especially one smack-dab in the middle of New Orleans, made her feel hemmed in. She often said she wanted to attend a college with an equivalent number of white, black, Asian, and Hispanic students. She imagined that everyone would learn from each other. From white students the others could learn "how to act in front of people who are like major business people," she said. Meanwhile, Geraldlynn thought she could teach her peers of other races "what to do to avoid dangerous situations."

The lessons casually conveyed by Bianca and TJ—particularly the importance of saving money and that you could like reading and still be cool—stuck with Geraldlynn. Nothing she had studied in college-readiness class, seen on the walls of KIPP Renaissance, or heard from her stepfather impressed her so; such didactic lessons often had the unintended effect of dissuading her from aspiring toward college.

The trip was a bright spot in an otherwise dull March. As the school year progressed, Geraldlynn increasingly fell through the cracks left by KIPP Renaissance's disruptions. Her teachers' time and attention remained absorbed by the behavior problems that persisted in virtually every class. Geraldlynn's grades slipped (although she still earned mostly As and Bs). She played no sports, participated in no clubs, and rarely socialized with her KIPP Renaissance classmates outside of school. Her life rotated between long, uninspiring days at school and evenings and weekends spent sleeping, talking on her phone, and hanging out with her friends from River Ridge. It did not help that staff morale continued to flag: Kia Childs, the popular English teacher who handled her class more deftly than most, became pregnant and could not devote so much time and energy to the school. The school's counselor, Alison Monsour, disagreed with Dassler about the best use of her time: She wanted to focus on counseling and therapy while he wanted her to prioritize student attendance, which could be measured. Because of the persistent student behavior problems, a couple of teachers lived in constant fear they would be fired due to an inability to manage their classrooms.

The observation of Geraldlynn's old mentor Alison Drake began to ring true: People sometimes assume all is well with the teen because of her sunny disposition and decent—enough—grades. As a struggling first-year school, KIPP Renaissance was particularly prone to overlooking a student like Geraldlynn. But she would probably never be an outlier in an academic environment. Her stepsister, Mary, and cousin Maurice, for instance, represented relative extremes when it came to behavior and student performance. As a result they sometimes received more of their teachers' time and attention. Geraldlynn never earned record-high grades and paychecks like Mary, although she was proud of her stepsister's book smarts. Nor did she often seem to be in trouble like Maurice.

Mary soared at KIPP Believe with a 4.0 grade point average, comparatively high scores on Louisiana's standardized exams (one advanced, two masteries, and one basic on the seventh-grade tests), and enormous talent as a writer. She often repeated KIPP mantras: "The whole time I've been at KIPP I've never been on the Bench. I just follow directions, do my homework, and be nice."

Leslie Feingerts, KIPP Believe's high school and college advisor, thought Mary might be ready for a less structured environment for high school. "They say I need to go above KIPP right now to a school where it's all on me," Mary said. "KIPP has risen me up so I don't need it anymore."

Unlike Geraldlynn, Mary applied in eighth grade to several of the New Orleans area's top private and public schools. She even contemplated boarding school, particularly the all-girls Foxcroft School in Virginia, which another KIPP alumna attended. The summer before eighth grade, she had spent three weeks on the Deerfield Academy campus in Massachusetts participating in an intense science program designed to expose KIPP middle schoolers to boarding school life. Mary learned there that if she did someday attend Deerfield, no one would understand either KIPP's language—including the snapping—*or* the speech patterns and colloquialisms she had grown up speaking with her family and friends in New Orleans. "They said, 'People won't understand you if you don't articulate better,'" Mary recalled. She would have to change her communication style yet again.

Although Mary's confidence exceeded Geraldlynn's in the classroom, Geraldlynn had an instinctive social intelligence and capacity to connect with different people Mary sometimes lacked. Their nicknames, Scooter and Nook, captured their different personalities. Geraldlynn was curious, full of energy, and, at times, all over the place; Mary had a dreamier, more introverted quality that sometimes made it harder for her to express herself verbally.

In the middle of the school year, Mary heard she had won a scholarship from the Jack Kent Cooke Foundation, which could, if she kept up her grades, cover her education expenses through graduate school. The program awards about sixty scholarships a year to low-income students from across the country. The foundation pays for their summer and school-year enrichment expenses (art classes, summer academic programs, laptop computers, and so on) through high school, as well as private school tuition in some cases. At the end of high school, the students can ask for continued financial assistance. Ms. Feingerts helped her with every step of the arduous application, just as she then led her through the high school selection process. The two talked about Mary's future during runs after school, and Feingerts spent hours upon hours helping Mary weigh her choices and track down different documents for the various applications.

Mary agreed she might be ready for a school that offered her more independence than KIPP. But she had mixed feelings about boarding school: It sounded cool and exotic, and she had promised her friends from the Deerfield summer program that she would at least apply there. But she would not be able to visit home very often, a prospect that distressed her mother. She certainly would not be able to traipse about with Scootah on the weekends, as she liked to do.

By the middle of eighth grade, her top choice for high school was Metairie Park Country Day, one of the toniest and most expensive schools in the region, with annual tuition charges exceeding $17,000. Between the school's own financial aid program and the Jack Kent Cooke scholarship, she was fairly sure she would be able to pay for it. "I have a feeling if I get accepted into that school, I am going," she said.

By contrast, Maurice was repeating sixth grade for a second time that school year. Sometimes he went for long stretches with no problems at school. But other times the phone calls home, detentions, and stays on the Bench seemed unrelenting. Despite Maurice's struggles, Roxanne thought KIPP Believe was the best school either of her sons had ever attended in New Orleans, largely because the teachers spent so much time helping the students and gave out their personal phone numbers. Maurice also said he felt safe at KIPP Believe.

Parts of the program frustrated her, however. She did not think Maurice should have to attend Saturday school every other week, especially since school let out so late on weekdays. "There's no free time, no time for themselves," she said. Roxanne also thought KIPP Believe could do more to accommodate the schedules of working parents. If Maurice stayed after for detention, someone usually had to pick him up in the early evening. Roxanne did not own a car and continued to work both the hotel and restaurant job. It wasn't easy for her to trek across town to retrieve Maurice; many evenings it was impossible. She had to pay someone gas money, rely on one of his teachers to bring him home, or take the bus. When she took the latter route, neither mother nor son made it home until after eight P.M. Sometimes it seemed as if Maurice acted up on the days he knew his mother had to work just to inconvenience her.

Of all the cousins, Maurice's older brother, Lionel, had the most turbulent experience in the post-Katrina schools. Lionel was, like Jasmine, too old for KIPP Believe. Upon returning to the city, he finished seventh grade at James M. Singleton Charter, one of the first schools to reopen in the city. For eighth grade he then transferred to Wicker—the school whose disorder Mary fled for KIPP Believe that year. At Wicker, Lionel failed to pass the LEAP test required to advance to high school. The Recovery School District sent him to Booker T. Washington, which they described as a remediation program for students who struggled to pass the LEAP. But Booker T. Washington really functioned as an alternative school with a high percentage of students who had been expelled or incarcerated. Lionel, shy and soft-spoken, found himself encouraged to fight a classmate on his very first day. "I think everybody hated it," he said. "Students came and went. The police were always there. Guest speakers always told us the same thing: Progress and stop the violence." But Lionel had always wanted to "progress." And he never saw so much violence until the RSD forced him to attend Booker T. Washington.

Lionel made it out of Booker T. after a year and enrolled in Douglass High School. He wanted to attend McDonogh 35 like his cousin Jasmine, but was told the school was full when he applied. Despite Douglass's negative reputation and poor performance, he felt comfortable there. Compared to Booker T., Douglass was well run and safe. But after two years, the RSD closed Douglass to make way for KIPP Renaissance. That meant Lionel bounced to Cohen, the alma mater of his mother and aunt. By the time he arrived at Cohen, Lionel had attended seven different middle and high schools, including one before Katrina and another during his evacuation in Texas. Of all the different schools, he thought Westbrook Intermediate School in Friendswood, Texas, was the strongest. "You learned so much more than in New Orleans schools," he said.

At Cohen, Lionel once again made the best of it, excelling on both the track team and in an elective philosophy class. Despite his shyness, once Lionel started talking about topics that interested him, he spoke with great animation and eloquence. He loved the philosophy class's focus on complex questions, which he obsessed over long after the course had ended: "How come people come in different races and what's the difference? Why is everything this way? How do we know what's ethically right or wrong? What are we? Why do we speak to each other and why do we have five fingers and five toes? How can we make the things we make? How do we know what matter is, and why can we feel things? Why do we have different eye colors?"

Lionel thought he would like KIPP, long days and all, based on what Maurice and Geraldlynn told him. He yearned to study philosophy in college but worried he would never make it there since so few Cohen students continued on to universities. The school posted an average ACT score of 15 in 2011; Lionel scored a 12 when he took the test in the spring of his junior year. Given his intelligence, the low score showed both how little the test captured and how poorly Lionel's schools had prepared him. A new charter school opened on Cohen's third floor in 2011, although Lionel continued to attend the old program on the first floor. After he graduated, the charter school would take over the whole building. It would be the third time the RSD closed one of his schools to make room for a charter they said Lionel was too old to attend. He grew jealous because the new charter school on the second floor included the phrase "college prep" in its name, although sometimes he wondered what—apart from the different name and uniforms—would distinguish it from the old Cohen.

He would never know. "It's probably good for the kids who will come after me that the charter school is taking over," Lionel said. "But I won't be here to find out."

Brice had a new hardness to him when he returned to KIPP Renaissance after his weeks away on suspension. Alison Monsour, the guidance counselor, noticed it and asked Brice if something had happened during his time out of school. Brice started to answer, but then stopped abruptly. He changed the subject whenever Monsour raised it again.

Brice went along on the Dillard trip even though he planned on joining the military after high school instead of attending college. It struck his teachers as an odd desire, since the fifteen-year-old had such a creative and unusual mind. But, as he once told Monsour, guns and drugs were what he knew. In his limited experience, drug dealing—not college—led to success and money. His mother, Tamika, could sense drug dealers in the neighborhood were trying to pull him into their world that school year. One dealer in particular had been observing Brice for some time. A neighborhood bar owner told Tamika he had spotted Brice out on the corner. She tried her best to keep him indoors.

One afternoon in late March, Jason Saltmarsh tried to engage a group of students in the book *First in the Family: Advice About College from First-Generation Students*. The Dillard visit, only two weeks past, seemed a distant memory. The class included Geraldlynn, who had a difficult time getting into the book, as well as Brice. With much prodding, the students identified the book's major themes as "being a loner on a journey," "connecting with others who have had similar experiences," and "overcoming adversity and succeeding." When Mr. Saltmarsh called on Brice, asking him if he could relate to any of the themes, Brice demurred, saying none of them seemed relevant to his situation.

Throughout the class, Brice alternated between a kind of distraught exuberance and a total disconnect. He burst into laughter when a classmate read the line, "Her father and mother did not have college degrees, so why should she?" When Saltmarsh asked for a word to describe that character who, a paragraph later, reconsidered her decision to drop out of high school, Brice shouted out: "Failure!"

Saltmarsh tried—in vain much of the time—to draw out the students' thoughts on the predicaments facing the book's characters, many of whom came from backgrounds similar to KIPP Renaissance's students and the college kids they had met at Dillard.

He moved the class across the hallway to the library, hoping the new scenery would wake them up a bit. Once there, they sat in a circle and took turns reading and answering questions.

In the library, impatience overtook Brice. "Come on, *pick* somebody," he said when Mr. Saltmarsh was slow to call on the next student.

Geraldlynn wore a dazed expression and spent much of the class sliding her chair farther away from the circle so no one could see her face.

She perked up for a moment, however, when someone read a line about one of the characters hoping a college education would allow him to buy his aunt her first house. Geraldlynn nodded to herself.

Meanwhile, Mr. Saltmarsh continued his prodding.

"Moira, what's one word you would use to describe [this character]?" he asked.

Silence.

"I can't think of a word right now," Moira said.

"I'm not going to let you off the hook," Mr. Saltmarsh replied.

He read the passage aloud again.

"*Helpful*," said Moira.

"Way to show grit," said Mr. Saltmarsh, snapping his fingers vigorously.

By the time Saltmarsh introduced a *Jeopardy!*-style game based on the experiences of the book's characters—a game he spent several hours creating—Brice had had enough.

"I'm tired of school," he said. "I'm ready to go home. My nerves bad."

College readiness ended that day with a lecture.

"Do you want to be the type of class, the type of school, where we get to the end of a long day and you break down and talk and can't handle doing a game?" Mr. Saltmarsh asked. "We can be many great things. But you have got to decide: Are we a learning community or are we a joke? The point is, Are we going to learn together, or sink together?"

By the time Mr. Saltmarsh concluded his speech and dismissed the class, Geraldlynn was texting surreptitiously on her phone. Brice bobbed restlessly to a beat in his head, a sound he alone could hear.

PART VI

Translations

(Spring 2011)

THE PRINCIPAL
"In every child I see my children."

An hour after the end of the school day, Mary Laurie sat beside a lanky teen in her office, poring over a grammar workbook. They focused for several minutes on different types of nouns, grappling in particular with the distinction between abstract and concrete.

Laurie pointed to the word *justice.*

"Can you see it?" she asked.

"No," replied Anthony, the student.

"That means it's an . . . ?"

"Adjective?"

She reviewed the terms once more and tried again with *freedom.*

"Can you feel freedom?" she asked.

"You feel freedom. But it's still not right there . . ." Anthony said. He correctly identified an abstract noun this time.

Laurie herself had mixed feelings about the distinction. In a fair, democratic society you *should* be able to see and feel justice and freedom, at least sometimes. But she did not want to confuse the issue for the teenager. Laurie wore a flowing black sweater that looked like a cape. Prior to this tutoring session, her only impression of Anthony had been of a defiant-looking student who sat in class with his legs outstretched and a cap pulled down low over his eyes. This evening, he appeared much more humble, vulnerable even, eager for help and clinging to Laurie's every word.

She had unexpectedly become the instructor of his sophomore English class in the middle of the second semester after deciding their teacher wasn't getting the job done. The school divided the students by gender at that level, so Laurie taught only boys. That morning in class—with just days to go before the sophomores would take the state writing exam— she had issued an open invitation for individual, after-school tutoring. Anthony and one other student took her up on the offer.

After reviewing compound nouns, Anthony confided that he stayed after school every day working on his own. His grandmother picked him up each evening. He knew he was far behind, yet he still hoped to earn enough credits that spring and summer to skip his junior year and return in the fall of 2011 as a senior.

Laurie asked his age.

"Nineteen."

"It can be done, but you've got to be committed."

"That's why I've been staying after school and doing homework by myself. My grades were dropping."

"You don't have to do it by yourself. I'm here to help you."

They talked about pronouns and antecedents until about six P.M., when Anthony's grandmother called to say she was sitting in a car out front, waiting to bring him home.

"Come back about your credits," Laurie called out as Anthony left. "Tell your grandmother to come, too."

Given his age, she understood his desire to move through high school as quickly as possible. But she doubted he could pass enough classes to start the next school year as a senior. Laurie began brainstorming how to make sure Anthony could stay at Walker until after his twenty-first birthday. In Louisiana, public schools are under no obligation to serve students after they turn twenty unless they qualify for special education services. She might need to meet with his grandmother sooner rather than later and put Anthony on a specialized track. But she would find a way to keep him at Walker for as long as possible. Keeping kids around came naturally to her.

Laurie took over Anthony's English class because the original teacher had lost control of the classroom. She battled constantly with students until the power struggle consumed more class time than the lessons. Even after the switch, the class aide, Teikeshia Charles, sometimes struggled to maintain order when Laurie wasn't around. Laurie had the gift of calming down a group of unruly teens by virtue of her very presence. As Wilbert Rawlins, Walker's band leader, often told his musicians, "Loud does not make drama. You need to come from one extreme to the other. That's what makes drama." Whether through experience, instinct, or a combination of both, the principal applied that lesson to the management and manipulation of teenagers. She often trod softly, and her silence proved more potent than the loudest roar. Recalcitrant teens quieted down and sat up straight, leery of causing an eruption from Ms. Laurie.

One morning Laurie had to attend a meeting, so she left Ms. Charles to handle the first part of the class, which met in the school's library that day. Students refused to sit in their seats, cursed loudly, and threatened to fight. At one point, two boys stood up and circled each other, bumping chests lightly, daring the other to make the first move. With some help from a male "behavior interventionist," Charles finally got everyone sitting in their seats, just minutes before Ms. Laurie arrived. Learning of the disrespect and near fight, the principal stared quietly at the students for the remainder of the class, her steely gaze out-daring them all. The boys thought they had escaped her wrath once the bell rang. But on her way back to the office, Laurie spied the two students who had threatened to fight.

"Come here, both of you! You lost your minds!"

She told the students, both football players, to find their coach and captain.

"Go, so I can let Coach Powell and your captain know that you have embarrassed yourselves, your coach, and the rest of the players. Bring me your captain."

They hesitated.

"Bring me your captain! BRING. ME. YOUR. CAPTAIN!"

The students scampered off, and Ms. Laurie smiled to herself. "Both of them are good kids," she said. "They're just silly."

Within minutes the students appeared in Laurie's office with their coach and captain in tow. The three young men and coach, all tall and burly, looked uneasy as they stood there. They kept their heads slightly bowed, shifting their gazes between Ms. Laurie and the floor.

"We are trying to work with them and do all that we can," Laurie started in. "Nothing in my contract says that I am supposed to be teaching language arts. Ms. Charles here already had another class. It's disturbing to me. I left here on Friday feeling very good about this class. But today you all act like you are going to start a fight in class—"

One of the boys started to say something.

"You aren't saying anything! I never thought you would be so disrespectful in class to Ms. Charles. I never thought you would be so disrespectful to your captain. To your coach. To your team. You would prefer for someone to believe that you are thugs on the street. Inexcusable. Inexcusable."

She zeroed in on one of the students.

"You needed tutoring. Did I not sit here with you?"

"You did. Yes." The student's head bobbed rapidly up and down.

"I wasn't doing it for my benefit. I learned this forty years ago. I graduated *forty years ago*. You just disrespected all of us. You are playing into the stereotypes that exist of you. Shame. *Shame*. I want you to sincerely apologize to Ms. Charles. How dare all of you?"

"NOW!" said Coach Powell.

The students quickly apologized.

"You need to keep telling yourself that Walker's better *than* and I represent the better in Walker," Ms. Laurie concluded. "When you cut up, you on Ms. Laurie's name. You on Ms. Charles's name. You on your coach's name. You on your captain's name."

When Laurie finally released the students, they darted out as quickly as they could without breaking into a run.

"Both are very smart and very capable," Laurie told Coach Powell after the students had left. "This has been a learning experience for me. The expectations should be so ingrained by this point they should behave well even for a sub. The solution can't be, 'This isn't working so I'll take it over.'"

Teaching provided Laurie with a reality check. She learned more about Walker's shortcomings and challenges. Most of the school's students arrived behind grade level, but Walker's sophomores had been at the school for close to two years. Students like Anthony shouldn't still be so far behind. And they all should know better than to behave so poorly when they thought they could get away with it. Walker had not done a good enough job setting and enforcing consistent behavior standards across the school.

Laurie already had too much crammed into her daily schedule when she decided to take over the English class. But Walker's other English teachers had full loads, and at least Laurie had Ms. Charles to assist her with running the class. On the positive side, teaching a class helped her get to know the students on a different level. That winter she had told her top

administrators that between the four of them (the three assistant principals and herself), she hoped someone would learn each student's story,
including their schooling history, family life, current grades, extracurricular interests, and long-term aspirations.

In the classroom, Laurie saw up close how technology and the Internet had changed the way students spoke, behaved, and studied. She
chuckled when students conducted entire conversations using abbrevia-
tions like LOL and OMG, or when they noted that texting had replaced
talking as their primary mode of communication. But it troubled her
deeply. "I worry that as we get further with technology, we lose our formal language," she said. "Shorthand language creeps in and you almost
get to this point where we have a generation that has no idea what you are
talking about." The opposite also held true: Sometimes she could not understand the kids. Almost all of Walker's big fights that school year had
started with a slight or a threat—perceived or real—posted on Facebook.
When Laurie went on the site to try to understand the conflict's origins,
she couldn't decipher half of what she read there.

She struggled to convince the boys in her sophomore English class to
do schoolwork at home, much less read a book. So much of what they
reviewed at the last minute in preparation for the state tests—grammar,
parts of speech, how to write a short essay—would come naturally if they
read more.

Laurie had always liked reading, even during busy or stressful times
when cheesy romance novels were all she could handle. That winter, a
few of her murmured requests for an e-reader had registered with her
husband, and he gave her a Kindle as a gift. She debated whether to start
with *The Autobiography of Malcolm X* or *Gone with the Wind*, two long-
time favorites, even though they are "as opposite as you can be." At
Walker, she brought the Kindle outside with her during lunch sometimes so the students would see her reading. Since it was a Kindle, they
could not glimpse the cover and would never know if their principal
chose to devour a work of great literature or *When Beauty Tamed the
Beast*. The only drawback was that she had not yet figured out how to flip
to the last page of the book using the e-reader. She liked to make sure a
novel would not end too badly before diving in. Laurie had never read
Anna Karenina, for instance, because she knew the heroine killed herself
by jumping in front of a train. Real life had enough tragedy in it.

Starting in mid-March, Walker's students faced a seemingly endless series of tests. The state board of education voted in 2010 to phase out Louisiana's testing regimen for high schoolers. The old system included a "graduate exit exam" (GEE) that students started taking in tenth grade and had to pass by their senior year in order to graduate. Under the new system, in place of the GEE high schoolers had to complete a series of "end-of-course" exams each year (known as EOCs) starting in the spring of 2011. By senior year, they would need to pass three EOCs to graduate. The sophomores and juniors were caught between the new way and the old one: They still had to complete the GEE, but they also had to start taking the new EOCs.

Laurie's class of sophomores confronted the English portion of the graduate exit exam first. For part one, they had to write 250-to-300-word responses to prompts that might, for instance, ask them to nominate a teacher for an outstanding educator award. On the day before the exam, Charles handed out sheets with grammar and linguistic tips devised by an O. Perry Walker administrator: THAT is almost never necessary; *'cause* is NOT a word; *good* describes a noun and *well* describes a verb.

Charles read one of the first tips on subject-verb agreement. "*He write well* is wrong," she said. "*He writes well* is right."

"That for white people," a student murmured.

Charles continued, reminding the students to use "would have," not "would of."

"That the same thing!" a student cried out.

"No, it's not the same thing," she said. "It doesn't have a helping verb."

The student pushback grew more forceful as the class reviewed the next two tips:

6. Remember Your Audience
   Your reader may not know what it means to "feel played." They may not know who Freddy and Jason are. Stay away from slang.

7. Write Like a Newscaster Speaks
   CORRECT: For instance if my best friend and I are "play fighting" and a group of boys are around and make a comment, I would want to fight.
   INCORRECT: For instance, say me and my best friend be play fighting and a whole group of boys be standing around and she

punch me too hard then I'm not going to worry about but the boys like girl you scary I'm going to feel played and want to fight.

Some of the students complained they shouldn't have to change the way they talked. One said the tips misrepresented his speech. Others, including Anthony (the student Laurie had tutored after school), seemed genuinely confused.

"Even if we speak good, we still not speaking formal English?" Anthony asked.

"When I talked to you individually I said, 'Do not write how you talk. Do not write how you talk! *Do not write how you text,*'" Charles said. "You don't write how you talk to your associates, your friends, or even your parents. You don't write, 'I broke up with her 'cause she was trippin'.'"

She debated with them for a few minutes about whether *'cause* is a word before moving on to the importance of writing "going to" instead of "gonna" or "gone," and the appropriate use of contractions.

"If you are not sure of the correct contraction, just use both words," Charles said.

As the lesson continued, Anthony spoke again, this time in a more defiant tone. "We talk the way we talk," he said. "This ain't French class."

"This is how we talk, the majority of us, we talk like this," agreed Charles.

"Who do you mean by 'we'?" a student interrupted.

"I am saying 'we' as a universal," said Charles. "'We' as in our culture. 'We' as in from down South."

"They don't understand us, Ms. Charles," said one student in a wounded tone.

"I know they don't understand," she replied. "But they going to *have* to understand on this test, baby."

"Does your mama talk like that?" asked the student who took umbrage with the tip sheet.

"Does *yours* talk like that?" Charles replied. "All of us—I am not excluding myself—*I* talk like this. Because it's the culture of New Orleans, okay. So therefore when you are writing, you are writing in a formal manner. Look at these examples."

The students relaxed a bit as they reviewed the need to include commas after prepositional phrases and the importance of good handwriting.

Just before Ms. Laurie walked in to take over the class—her presence bringing an end to most rebuttals—Charles gave the students a pep talk. She insisted that despite the grammatical challenges, and despite the existence of a mysterious "they" who did not understand New Orleans speech patterns, the boys would do just fine.

"You guys all can do this," she said. "There is nothing to get freaked out about. You are all capable. You all can pass."

O. Perry Walker faced a common dilemma for urban schools: how to overcome the language barrier between their predominantly low-income, minority students and the predominantly middle-class, white creators of standardized tests. Experts have scrutinized the ways in which income affects school readiness: Children from lower-income households tend to learn far fewer words in their early years; they grow up in homes with fewer books than their wealthier peers; and they take fewer trips to libraries and museums. But only a small number of researchers have examined the ways in which regional linguistic and cultural norms might affect school performance. The limited research that exists suggests that students from low-income, African-American neighborhoods in the Deep South face unique and unfair challenges on the battery of standardized tests that determine their educational fate.

One such study showed that New Orleans schoolchildren use African-American (vernacular) English more frequently than their peers in northern cities. Higher rates of black vernacular, in turn, correlate to lower reading scores. The study compared groups of elementary schoolchildren in the poorest neighborhoods of Cleveland, Washington, D.C., and New Orleans. Veteran teachers asked dozens of children in each city to repeat sentences and then retell a story in their own words. For both tasks, the New Orleans schoolchildren incorporated far more African-American English features than youngsters in Cleveland and Washington, D.C. (Common features include modified tenses—"I be walking" as opposed to "I often walk"; the absence of the verb *is*; and absence of the *g* in the-*ing* sound, so *tripping* sounds like *trippin'*.) The results of the cross-city comparison were not surprising given that New Orleans was the southernmost city in the sample and many, although not all, traits of African-American English mirror speech patterns heard across racial groups in the South. The author, Anne H. Charity Hudley, also surmised that in some communities, including New Orleans, African-American

English may be more accepted by adults of different social classes and treated as a source of cultural identity and pride.

Educators need to ensure students understand their own speech patterns and how they differ from standard English, said Charity Hudley, an associate professor of English, education, and linguistics at the College of William and Mary. Adults and children alike are often unaware of these patterns and tend to be unreliable narrators of their own speech habits. In seminars with educators, Charity Hudley discourages them from presenting one way of speaking as right and another as wrong. "We hear a lot about respecting people's culture, but language is mysteriously left out of that," she said. Charity Hudley encourages teachers and students to think more consciously about speech and then establish the idea of a "school language" and a "home language." But it's unrealistic, she says, to expect students to "turn off" the way they have talked since childhood—and the way everyone around them has talked—at a moment's notice.

Not only do New Orleans schoolchildren speak in African-American vernacular at higher rates than their peers elsewhere, they also have their own rich vocabulary of words and expressions recent transplants to the area might fail to recognize. Throughout its history, New Orleans has been a melting pot for people of diverse racial, ethnic, and linguistic backgrounds. Most of the art forms and cuisines that make the city famous—gumbo, jazz, bounce music, Mardi Gras Indians, second lines— emerged from a fusion of cultural traditions. The speech of New Orleans schoolchildren is no exception. Along with the African-American vernacular and Southern colloquialisms, listeners can hear French influences, including heavy use of the word *beaucoup*, which means many or a lot. Students describe themselves as beaucoup hungry, in need of beaucoup money, or sick and tired of all the beaucoup rules. It's not uncommon to see a young teacher from the Northeast or Midwest respond with a puzzled look when the word is uttered. In one case, a teacher new to the city dismissively informed a third grader that *beaucoup* was not a word. The nine-year-old pulled out the dictionary and taught his teacher a lesson that day.

Between the graduate exit exam, the end-of-course tests, and the school's hundreds of students, Walker administered thousands of tests that spring. "It felt like we were going from test to test," said Laurie.

The five different EOCs taken by Walker students posed endless logistical challenges. All of the sophomores had to take the biology exam, but the girls had completed biology class in the fall and the boys in the spring. That meant teachers had to interrupt the girls' spring classes to conduct biology refresher lessons and the boys were tested on a course they had not finished. The tests were available only on the computer, and had to be taken on desktops, not laptops. Walker owned hundreds of laptops but had only one fully functioning technology lab with stationary computers. School officials purchased new routers, but the servers still crashed repeatedly in the middle of tests. State rules required schools to construct partitions between student workstations if students worked in close quarters. So at the last minute staff had to go out and purchase supplies that would allow them to create mini-cubicles in the testing rooms. Everything took longer than planned. One afternoon late in the school year, several juniors worked on a state exam through lunch, since computer glitches had slowed their progress in the morning. But the cafeteria would not release their lunches without student identification numbers, which no one had on hand. "They're talking to me about numbers," Laurie muttered. "I'm trying to get these kids fed."

Laurie supported testing as she always had. But she often reflected on everything the numbers failed to capture. She thought about Tyrone, a sophomore in her English class, for instance. Tyrone had accidentally shot himself in the arm near the beginning of the school year. Then, just days before he was supposed to take his first test, someone else shot Tyrone, wounding him again. He recovered in the hospital while his classmates tackled the writing exam. Laurie never learned the details surrounding the second shooting. But she knew Tyrone's mother had died and his father played no part in the teen's life. He lived with a grandmother who agreed to supply a bed, but nothing else. Walker's staff worried more about finding Tyrone a permanent home, and keeping him alive, than how he would do on the state's standardized tests that year.

"Imagine yourself in the world by yourself," Laurie said. "A place to lay your head at night doesn't make for a home."

Walker would take Tyrone back when he recovered from the second shooting, as it had done after the first. But if the school's leaders had applied the cold, clear calculus of maximized attendance rates and test scores, they could have found a way to use one of the two shootings as an excuse to expel him.

A trap confronted schools: If they took the students with the most intense needs, their numbers might suffer. But the state would shut them down if their numbers suffered too much and for too long. Then who would take the neediest?

"I believe in accountability and autonomy," said Laurie. "But the system doesn't measure all the work we call education."

One morning, Laurie sat in an office chair on the curb in front of Walker, chatting with math teacher Nolan Grady and several other school staff members. Laurie wore a gray sweatshirt with the hood pulled up over a black knit cap, even though the temperature topped 70 degrees. She was always cold. The group made for an odd sight, looking more like old acquaintances gathered for a barbecue than veteran educators on a busy school day. But today wasn't an ordinary day. Just as the first school buses began to arrive earlier that morning, a fire had broken out in the teachers' lounge adjacent to the front office. Someone spotted it right away and no one was hurt, although the smell of smoke would linger in the main building for several days. Administrators canceled school and sent the school buses back along their routes to drop off the kids at their homes.

What started as a near catastrophe turned into a party. While fire officials completed their investigation and maintenance crews carried smoke-damaged ceiling tiles from the building, the educators sat in the sunlight, bantering with the students and alumni who flocked to the gathering as the day progressed. A staff member had baked chicken, macaroni and cheese, and brownies for an honor society induction that had been scheduled for that morning. She unwrapped the aluminum-foil covered plates and everyone began to feast. By midday the dance troupe returned from a morning performance and the marching band from filming a scene in the television show *Treme*. The crowd of teenagers circulating in front of Walker was so large no one would ever guess school had been canceled.

Laurie appeared as relaxed as ever. She caught up with a 2010 Walker graduate who attended a nearby branch of Delgado Community College, quizzing the girl about her family, classes, and scholarship money. Rawlins, the band director, told Laurie how they played the same song a dozen times on the *Treme* set. The scene had been filmed outside of the former Douglass High School building, where KIPP Renaissance was located.

For the filming, the Walker students wore uniforms from the fictitious Homer A. Plessy school, named after the plaintiff in the *Plessy v. Ferguson* case that established the doctrine of separate but equal. Laurie joked that from now on any misbehaving students would be sent to Plessy. Spying two tall basketball players, she said, "Y'all can't lose tomorrow. There's a new high school called Plessy where we might send you."

Grady read the newspaper and contributed occasional wry remarks. A tall male student from the dance team sat down beside him as the day wore on. "Mr. Grady, I don't mean no harm," he said in a serious tone. "But you look like an old grandpa sitting there."

Grady was used to his students imparting such opinions. Sometimes they told him, "Mr. Grady, you should have been a preacher. *Oh, how you preach*." He did not think he had missed his calling, though. His calling was right there at Walker. Schools provided his arena and his pulpit. Like a congregation of earnest repentants, he knew the kids heard every word he uttered even when they pretended not to listen. "Your words are like an edged sword," one had said to him. He had to be careful not to cut too deep.

Grady turned to the young dancer, his eyes twinkling. "I don't mean no harm," he said. "But I'd rather be an old grandpa than a young fool. You got to get to where I am intact. No scars. No bruises. Then you can call me whatever you like."

The day ended on a light note. But every so often, a minor yet jarring event like the fire served as a reminder of the ways in which Katrina's trauma still affected the kids. When school officials had boarded the buses that morning to announce the news, the students sat in total silence for several minutes. Laurie and Grady could tell they were processing the information, wondering if this event, too, might morph into something that would change their lives forever. Grady likened the children's emotions to a river flowing beneath the ground: You couldn't see it, yet it was always there, affecting the behavior on the surface. "I don't think they ever got past the emotional part of Katrina," said Laurie. "When little things like [the fire] happen, we remember Katrina. We start thinking, 'What is this going to turn into? What does this mean? Oh, my God, what's next?'"

Walker survived another school year—not without bruises and scars, but relatively intact.

School officials would not learn the school's performance score for months to come, although early results from the spring tests looked promising. The passage rate on each of the end-of-course exams was at least 75 percent. More than 90 percent of tested students passed the math graduate exit exam. As usual, English proved to be the school's weakest area, with just over 60 percent of students scoring basic or above on the GEE. Walker scored below New Orleans high schools with selective admissions policies, but above most of those with open enrollment.

Laurie warded off a last-minute threat to Walker's on-site health clinic, which provided crucial medical and psychological services to the students. The school struggled to quantify its impact in a way that justified the expense to funders. The clinic's doctor, for instance, gave several seminars to the students on sex and their bodies each fall. But the seminars did not count as "encounters" like a medical checkup. And the number of "encounters" did not meet expectations. As usual, Walker struggled most when it came to numbers.

The health clinic stayed open partly because of Laurie's zealous support. She told the oversight committee in an impassioned plea, "We are talking about thousands of children in crisis because their families are still in crisis. Just tell me what we have to do to increase the numbers." Laurie had been one of the first principals in the city to lobby for a school-based health clinic before Katrina. "I don't want to lose something we were on the forefront of fighting for," she said.

SUNO, too, narrowly avoided closure. The state legislature never took a final vote on the bill to merge SUNO with the University of New Orleans after it became clear SUNO's opponents, including Governor Bobby Jindal, did not have enough votes to win. The end result pleased SUNO defenders who worried that hundreds of low-income New Orleans students, including dozens of Walker graduates, would have lost out on a chance at a university degree. But it did nothing to address the broader inequities in the state's higher education system or the long-term viability of SUNO. That so many in the black community cheered the survival of an institution they had decried as the continuation of Jim Crow fifty years earlier showed just how much skepticism existed about the prospect of equitable and meaningful integration.

Walker sent 73 percent of its graduating seniors off to college that summer, although that was not as many as Laurie would have liked. One student with solid academic credentials who suffered from a physical disability made no plans at all. Laurie feared he would continue to shy away from risks, missing out on life's richness. Mervin, the top student who had almost missed his college deadlines, decided to stay in town at Xavier. Laurie worried Mervin would be less likely to see college through, surrounded by family in his hometown. She wanted him to learn that "whole other worlds" existed outside New Orleans. "I so wanted him to go away," she said.

The new charter schools could overreach in their college boosterism. But sometimes Walker's leaders worried they had not done enough to grow their students wings; the teenagers lingered, clinging to home.

An unusual calm pervaded at Walker during the final weeks of the 2010–2011 school year. It almost felt like a grace period, a chance to rest up for the formidable challenges that lay ahead.

Laurie knew survival would grow more difficult in the coming years: Competition for students, money, and buildings would increase. Schools would have to meet an ever-rising standard, defined largely by test scores, to stay open. A new leader would take Vallas's place as Recovery School District superintendent that summer, bringing fresh uncertainty over the future. John White, twenty years Vallas's junior, boasted a résumé similar to many of New Orleans' young school leaders: After graduating from the University of Virginia, he spent several years with Teach For America as a corps member in Jersey City, teacher coach and mentor in New Jersey, and executive director in Chicago. His skills were further groomed working in New York City, another "reform-minded" district, for school chancellor Joel Klein.

White promised continued support for Vallas's policy priorities— particularly the rapid spread of charters and the speedy closure of schools that failed to meet state standards. He was, however, more technocratic and methodical than his predecessor. He had close ties to the nonprofits and foundations that wielded significant power in the New Orleans public schools, including Teach For America and the Broad Foundation.

The homegrown Algiers Charter Schools Association, which oversaw Walker and seven other schools, had few allies in those circles. Already the Algiers association had lost control of one of its schools because of weak test scores. The association suffered from mounting political and financial problems. It did not have deep-pocketed donors like other charter organizations, and individual school leaders privately complained they lacked sufficient autonomy because of micromanaging from association leaders.

While the chartering of the city's schools moved full speed ahead, some out-of-school support structures for the city's youth deteriorated—or disappeared. In 2009, for example, the city lost the New Orleans Adolescent Hospital, which catered to the mental health needs of children and supplied at least a limited number of in-patient beds. Governor Bobby Jindal had successfully lobbied to move many of its beds and programs across Lake Pontchartrain to the wealthier St. Tammany community.

Such losses were felt acutely throughout the city's schools. Between the instability wrought by Katrina and New Orleans' high rate of gun violence, arguably no city in America had a larger proportion of teenagers suffering from some form of post-traumatic stress disorder. As 2011 progressed, the city's homicide total was on pace to top the previous year's 175 victims, most of them in their teens or twenties. City leaders knew the tide of killings took a significant toll among the city's schoolchildren. In a speech, mayor Mitch Landrieu railed that a student attending New Orleans' John McDonogh High School between September 2010 and February 2011 was more likely to be killed than a soldier in Afghanistan. But he, and other city leaders, were powerless to stop the devastation.

Despite the packing up and carefree attitude, Wednesday, May 25, did not feel like a last day of school. No one seemed to be leaving, at least not for good. Even after dismissal, the cheerleading squad worked out under the breezeway located in the heart of campus. Students milled around wearing T-shirts that played off Walker's school colors with the slogans ORANGE CRUSH and I BLEED BLUE AND ORANGE. As students trickled out, new ones filtered in, including day-old graduates like Donnisha. With no assignments left and no classes to attend, Donnisha settled on a bench beside Laurie. Wearing a blouse and hoop earrings—a contrast to the school uniform of orange shirts and Dixie khakis—she looked dressed for a party or the first day of work.

"Oh girl, didn't you graduate yesterday?" Laurie asked her.

Laurie quizzed Donnisha about her college plans. Unlike some of her classmates, the teen had the grades and ACT scores she needed to get into many of Louisiana's public universities. A couple had already accepted her. But she had not made a final decision yet and was still trying to clarify her application status at two local colleges. Getting information out of SUNO, her top choice, had been a logistical nightmare.

Laurie asked Donnisha why she did not apply to Grambling, a historically black university about five hours' drive to the north of the city.

"Too far," Donnisha said.

"Not far, especially with the way you drive," Laurie joked. "I saw you come roaring out of the driveway . . ."

"I did that just because I knew you was watching," the girl grinned.

"August can't come without you in someone's school," Laurie said, refusing to let the subject drop. "I *wish* you would go."

"I don't want to leave."

"You've got to leave. You've got to grow."

"I just want to stay here."

Laurie didn't answer right away. She wore a bright orange T-shirt and perfectly circular glasses. With her hair pinned back in braids, she looked a bit like a schoolgirl herself, albeit an aging one.

"You should get a Facebook page!" Donnisha blurted out.

"Who . . . ?" When Laurie realized the student was talking about her, she said quietly, "I don't think so, baby."

A departing cheerleader passed by on her way out. Spotting Donnisha, she asked, "You don't ever get tired of Walker?"

"A true Charger doesn't ever get tired," Donnisha replied.

Laurie carefully picked pieces of dirt off the bench for a few minutes and wiped it clean with her hand.

"We were trying to get you wings to fly," she said.

"I can fly—back home."

A moment later, the assistant principal called Laurie off to an emergency meeting. Donnisha remained on the bench. She stayed at Walker well into the evening, waiting as long as she could to say good-bye.

Laurie, too, struggled to let go at times. As much as she wanted students like Donnisha to go forward into the world and lead good lives, she did not believe in abrupt change or self-reinvention. In Laurie's opinion, what people viewed as change often just meant traveling full circle. She thought of her own life. She had grown up listening to gospel music yet could not tolerate it—or church—after the deaths of her sons. In recent years, however, Laurie found herself drawn to the familiar strains and chords once again. "You change, but then you don't," she said. Despite the most radical of events, the past always retains its grip.

The same could be said of the city's schools. There had never been a clean slate. The destroyed institutions lived on through the people who persisted. Laurie knew that as well as anyone. She thought often about Woodson Middle School and her unfinished work there. She sometimes wished she had ignored those who said the building was unsalvageable. She could have reclaimed the space and reopened the school. It was too late now, with the building long gone and a new structure on its way. But Woodson—its people, the building, the way it smelled and sounded, the lessons she learned there, the emotions she felt there—would shape her work until the day she retired. And Laurie hoped that would not be anytime soon.

"People always say, 'Go home and rest.' I'm like, 'I am rested.' This doesn't wear me out," said Laurie. "I have no passion for cooking or for shopping or for keeping house. I don't want to go to another high school. I don't want to go to another middle or elementary school. I am Walker. I am Woodson. I am Guste."

Laurie had no plan to turn Walker into a franchise, no dream of becoming the CEO of anything, no desire to spend time outside New Orleans. She had no ambition to move up or move on. But since Katrina had prevented her from seeing Woodson through, she would finish what she had started at Walker. Many days that simply meant maintaining a place where kids could come and, as she put it, "just be"; a place where, if she set her mind and heart to the work, there would be more good days than bad ones, more happy stories than sad ones; a place where, over time, her heart might hurt a little less.

"In every child I see my children," she said. "I see every hope, every desire, every wish, every teacher who ever taught them, every kind person who ever crossed their path. I spent many nights wondering, Would I be as good at my work if that had not happened? I don't believe bad stuff happens to make you better, but it does define and shape what you do. Part of that energy that allows me to put in the hours and do the work well is trying to save for the two I could not save. If I could bring them back to life I would. But if the work I do means my reality might not be another family's reality, that I spare some parents pain, maybe that's the saving I get to do."

Yes. She could see a future for Walker and its children. She could see herself sitting in the courtyard on a sunny afternoon ten years later. She would be grayer, wearier, maybe on the verge of a reluctant retirement as her seventieth birthday approached. Perhaps the auditorium would remain locked and in disrepair, the classrooms would still alternately swelter and freeze, ceiling tiles would continue to come undone. But the foundations would hold. A flower or plant would be blossoming in the courtyard, since in New Orleans something was always in bloom. And the kids would remain kids: their futures wide open before them.

THE TEACHER

"Is it that our kids are able to see through some things their teachers blindly follow?"

Aidan's first-period class laughed nervously one morning when their teacher showed up wearing suspenders attached to his corduroy pants and carrying a stuffed teddy bear in his arms. They had grown accustomed to some odd clothing choices from Mr. Kelly—bright pink socks on Valentine's Day, the occasional bow tie—but this seemed bizarre even for him.

"As you may have surmised, my name is Theodore Roosevelt and I was president over one hundred years ago," Aidan began. He had considered shaving his beard into a mustache to complete the costume, but chickened out at the last minute.

The giggles and pointing continued until he declared, "I wear suspenders. Deal with it."

Aidan stayed in character as he fired off questions about imperialism and the Spanish-American War, including the meaning of yellow journalism and the significance of the slogan "Remember the *Maine!*"

He pulled a military camouflage shirt over his suspenders as he displayed a picture of Roosevelt with his Rough Riders, the volunteer cavalry the future president led in the Spanish-American War. "Me and my boys," he said to peals of laughter as he gestured at the photo. "That's Petey. That's Jeff. That's Joe. Joe was crazy."

Overnight Aidan had become not Teddy Roosevelt, but a social studies teacher. The Sunday evening before he donned the suspenders, the junior class teachers and advisors had held an emergency meeting in one of their homes, called just hours earlier. New interim testing data suggested not all the juniors would pass the graduate exit exams in science and social studies in April. So in one evening, the teachers upended all their plans for the next few weeks. To make absolutely sure all of the students would be prepared, they planned to triple-dose them in social studies and science review every day by cutting several English, math, and Spanish classes from the schedule. They called the effort Operation Dominate and borrowed the camouflage apparel from a student's father who had served in the marines.

Aidan reviewed trust-busting, big-stick diplomacy, the rise of progressivism, the Great Depression, the New Deal, World War II and internment camps, the Gulf of Tonkin incident and resolution, the Civil Rights Act of 1964, the assassinations of JFK, RFK, Malcolm X, and Martin Luther King Jr., different kinds of economic structures, and the Vietnam War among other subjects. He kept the tone light by telling plenty of jokes, sometimes at his own expense. The students laughed when he broke into the hip-hop classic "Ruff Ryders' Anthem"—*Stop, drop, shut 'em down, open up shop*—to help them remember Roosevelt's Rough Riders. Few cracked a smile, however, when he said that both Theodore and Franklin Delano Roosevelt attended "the greatest institution in the world." Pause. Harvard.

Aidan had just started to hit a groove in his junior English classes when the plans changed. The shift meant he had to postpone indefinitely the essay he planned to assign his two American Literature classes on *The Great Gatsby*. It meant copies of *A Raisin in the Sun* would sit untouched through the remainder of the school year. It meant that a winter devoted to getting students thinking and talking about literature would turn into a spring devoted more to lecturing and quizzing them on historical terms. It meant that the desks moved from a semicircle or U shape, intended to foster discussion, to traditional straight rows, intended partly to prepare students for the testing environment.

Students like Je'on Domingue felt the test preparation helped, "but takes away from other things. Especially since we are there until five P.M. I think they could do it another way so we wouldn't miss core classes we need for college."

But the teachers never questioned the decision as they embraced their new roles; they could not risk any student's failing the final component of the graduate exit exam. "It's a cost-benefit analysis," said Aidan. "I hate to take time away . . . but the alternative would be to play Russian roulette with their passing." He hoped every student would know enough to earn at least a "basic" in social studies on even their worst day. He thought of two juniors engaged in a tempestuous romantic relationship. If they broke up right before the test, he wanted them so prepared they would still pass. Aidan hesitated to assign the somewhat pejorative label of "test prep" to the weeks of review, noting that if the teachers planned and executed the lessons well they would enrich the students' learning well beyond the graduate exit exam. But everyone at Sci would be happy when the last round of students completed the GEE in 2012.

Aidan planned to return to Sci in the fall of 2011. His confidence had increased between October—when he told Ben Marcovitz he did not intend to teach for a second year—and March. He relaxed in the classroom when he started teaching the junior English classes midwinter, letting himself enjoy talking about books he loved. Students still rolled their eyes, talked out of turn, walked around, or slept during class. But such behavior was the exception. Aidan never felt as if he was going to lose control of the classroom anymore. Students like Marquisha appreciated that he went out of his way to help students in just about every subject, but "doesn't take himself too seriously."

Outside of school he had developed more confidence and control over his life as well. He religiously took Saturday nights off from work and had started to date a fellow Teach For America alum who taught at another charter school. He worked seventy to eighty hours a week, as opposed to the eighty-five to ninety he had sometimes clocked at the start of the school year. "There are some weeks when things click and I have no papers to grade and it's only seventy," he said.

Next year, he would take on expanded responsibilities at Sci as the dean of English. Most second-year teachers assumed some kind of administrative role. Like Ben Marcovitz, Aidan believed Sci had the opportunity to create templates other charter schools across the country could follow. He hoped his work building an Advanced Placement class for students who started high school behind grade level, for instance, would help guide those who followed. He did not mind the constant adjustments and readjustments—of teaching technique, class schedules, and course offerings—that defined life at Sci. In his view, good schools and teachers modified their approach every day in response to new data points, just as the junior-class teachers had done when they decided to prioritize science and social studies review in the early spring.

Sometimes the data points came in the form of "scores on the wall and sometimes from the students cursing in your face," he said.

His decision to stick with classroom teaching for a fourth year put him in a minority for Teach For America alums. Many of his peers from the 2008 Greater New Orleans corps had departed for law school, jobs at companies like Google and JP Morgan, or to work for Teach For America. In his circle of friends, Aidan knew more people who still taught in New Orleans than had left. But most of those who remained had, like him, left their original posting, often to move from a traditional school in the city or suburbs to a charter school in New Orleans.

Teach For America's own data shows that in Aidan's original group of 250 teachers, only 10 percent remained in their original classroom placements by the end of 2011.[1] Another fifty-six teachers, or 22 percent of the initial cohort, still taught in the Greater New Orleans area, just not in their original school. Twenty-four of Aidan's peers worked in education in the New Orleans area, but not teaching. They had gone on to leadership positions at charter schools, become involved in policy or advocacy, or worked directly for Teach For America. Increasingly, the organization's alums ran the show in the New Orleans education landscape. But they did not stay in the classroom—particularly in the same school—for long. A majority of Aidan's cohort, 59 percent, had left either New Orleans or education.

One national study published in 2011 found that just over 60 percent of Teach For America instructors remained public school teachers beyond their two-year commitment and 35.5 percent taught for more than four years (although many switched schools at least once). According to the study, Teach For America's retention rates were lower than the average for new teachers across all schools, but not far off from estimates in high-poverty schools. The data gave ammunition to both Teach For America's critics and supporters. More important, it suggested that if the organization focused more attention and resources on long-term retention and support, then it might become a positive force for teacher stability in low-income schools, not a neutral or a negative one.

As spring wore on, students tired of the endless exams and practice sessions. Those who struggled most on the tests acted out to vent their frustration. During one of the final days of social studies review, Aidan asked the name of the group of journalists who exposed bad governmental practices in the early twentieth century. A student sitting in the back row murmured "muckrakers" under his breadth. But when Aidan called on him five seconds later, the student shrugged his shoulders and said, "I forgot." In another class a week later, Aidan had the students quiz each other with their own questions until the exercise devolved into silliness:

Who was president when a bomb was developed? Who was president for four terms? Who was president during the New Deal? Who framed Roger Rabbit?

For many of the juniors, the graduate exit exams were only the beginning. They also faced the ACT in June—by mid-April, Sci had turned over two hours of the juniors' school day toward ACT preparation—not to mention the Advanced Placement language and U.S. history exams in May. Just over a third of the juniors took an AP class. They formed a distinct clique at Sci: In the cafeteria during junior lunch, one half of the room filled with mostly AP students, the other half with the rest of their classmates.

Aidan also found himself helping out with ACT preparation. Sci had hired a private tutor to teach a Princeton Review–style ACT prep course to half the juniors. Many of the tutor's regular customers were children who attended elite area private schools. Aidan and Sci's other teachers took responsibility for prepping the rest of the students. Some days, that meant reviewing English, math, science, or reading. Others, it meant serving as proctor while the students took practice tests over and over and over again.

"I am, as always, impressed by your perseverance, going at these with the same enthusiasm every day, knowing the better we do on these, the easier the test will be," Aidan told a group of juniors one morning before handing them reading passages followed by questions of the kind they would encounter on the ACT. For the first passage, the students had to read an excerpt from Joseph Conrad's *Heart of Darkness* and answer such questions as, *The narrator's point of view is that of: A) An omniscient observer B) A member of the ship's crew C) Another ship's captain D) A person watching from shore.*

The students grew restless toward the end of the practice session, so Aidan attempted a pep talk. "Okay, please track," he began. "Your future is not an endless succession of sitting taking practice tests in Sci Academy polo shirts. Your future is college, and the better you do on this, the more options you will have of what kind of life you want for yourself."

He told them everyone felt the urge to quit at times, but "feelings are just data your brain sends you about how it thinks you should be feeling. The choice you make to give up or keep going is what makes you who you are."

Preparing students for the Advanced Placement language exam consumed most of Aidan's time and energy. The class had had two other teachers before he took over in the middle of the school year. After the juniors took their graduate exit exams in April, he devoted himself to the AP class, continuing to learn everything he could about the test and holding after-school sessions for his students. He met one student for tutoring sessions at McDonald's (the teen was out on suspension for a drug-related incident). The students faced a daunting task preparing for a college-level exam while simultaneously worrying about the ACT and college visits—not to mention trying to squeeze in some time before the end of the school year for reading and discussing literature apropos of no particular test.

The AP exams were in a different league from the state's standardized tests, and even the ACT. Many of Sci's students would have passed the social studies and science assessments regardless of whether their teachers added the extra month of preparation time. But Aidan knew it was quite possible *none* of his students would pass the AP no matter how hard the class worked. The state exams measured whether students could do grade-level work. The AP exams, on the other hand, were designed to assess whether students could handle college-level work and thinking while still in high school (many colleges award credit to students with passing scores or let them skip introductory-level courses). On the one full practice test Aidan's class had taken in the winter, nine students earned 1s, seven earned 2s, and two students passed with 3s.

Most of the questions on the English portion of Louisiana's graduate exit exam test basic comprehension skills. A sample question might ask: *From the information in the poem, the reader knows that the speaker A) has a wealthy family B) is not concerned with tradition C) was born in Bohemia D) has a difficult time paying bills.* The AP questions, on the other hand, assume a baseline comprehension and test students on the use and meaning of advanced rhetorical devices. One sample question reads: *In the sentence beginning "There were times" (lines 58–63), the speaker employs all of the following except A) concrete diction B) parallel syntax C) simile D) understatement E) onomatopoeia.*

Nationally, the number of teenagers taking AP exams has expanded in recent years, as schools like Sci introduce the courses to less privileged students. In 1999, 1.1 million students took the exams, compared to 2.9 million ten years later. As the number of students taking AP tests has exploded, passage rates have dipped. During the same ten-year span, the percentage of students who passed the test fell from 63.5 to 58.5.

Since very few low-income minority students attempted the AP exams until recent years, comparatively few experts have studied the tests for possible racial, class, and geographic bias—at least not to the extent they have analyzed the SAT and ACT. In one infamous example of cultural bias on the (now defunct) SAT analogy section, students were asked to find a relationship comparable to "runner" and "marathon." The correct answer, "oarsman" and "regatta," prompted a small firestorm of bad publicity because of its bias toward those more familiar with the upper-class sport of sailing. The test makers have scrubbed the exams of such blatant prejudice in recent years, according to Jay Rosner, executive director of the Princeton Review Foundation. But his recent work has found that test makers include questions they know—based on advance vetting in unscored experimental sections—white and male students are statistically more likely to answer correctly than minority and female students. What's not clear, because the test makers refuse to release detailed demographic data on all but a few questions, is whether the testing companies have rejected significant numbers of questions that favor female and minority students.

To blame the gaps on the tests would be convenient—and not without some degree of truth—but the reasons white and wealthier students outperform their peers on national aptitude tests are complex. Low-income students are more likely to suffer from malnutrition and obesity, move often as young children, and experience hunger and other forms of literal want that can make it difficult to focus on schoolwork. They are less likely to grow up in homes with access to books and quiet spaces to study, travel outside their hometown, or meet adults from different professions. Low-income students are more likely to attend under-resourced schools with high teacher-turnover rates. They are less likely to attend schools with experienced educators and politically connected parents. Moreover, they learn fewer words as youngsters. One oft-cited study estimated that by the age of four, children of professional parents have heard an average of forty-eight million words addressed to them while children in poor families who receive government assistance have heard only thirteen million.[2]

The AP language test measures how well teenagers can understand and manipulate the English language based on a set of formal and sophisticated literary conventions. But when it comes to such skills, Sci's students have had the odds stacked against them since birth. They wield language in sophisticated and smart ways themselves—just not ones that typically score points on the AP's metrics. The students had only a few months to compensate for gaps formed over more than a dozen years.

The multiple-choice portion of the AP rhetoric exam includes stilted language most of Aidan's students had never encountered. When answering practice questions, students stumbled over phrases like "pseudo cynical," "wholly objective," "cautiously optimistic," and "incredibly pedantic." Aidan knew that if students did not know the meaning of most of the terms used on the test, their chance of passing would be remote. "If you don't know the words, you're screwed," he said.

His main strategy in the final month before the test was to have the students practice the types of questions they would face as much as possible. In addition to the multiple-choice sections, they would have to write several short essays. He marked up their practice essays with different-colored highlighters. Topic and thesis sentences he highlighted in blue, supporting details in green, and analysis and commentary in yellow. Most of the essays, he stressed repeatedly to the students, did not have enough yellow on the page when he handed them back.

One day not long after the students took their graduate exit exams, Aidan reviewed practice essays the students had written on the following prompt: *Adversity tends to elicit talents in men that would lie dormant otherwise. Do you agree or not?* The class discussed Marquisha's essay on rapper Lil Wayne, who had recently been released from Rikers Island after serving an eight-month sentence for illegal gun possession. Marquisha had summarized many of the events in Lil Wayne's life but made no argument about the role of adversity. Aidan told her she had skipped the all-important "commentary."

"Why you have to have so much yellow anyway?" a student asked.

Marquisha jumped in, noting that she had to give background on Lil Wayne in case the reader did not know much about him. "I'm trying to give you info so you know what we talking about because who knows if you know what we talking about," she said.

Aidan replied that instead of devoting paragraphs to the details of Lil Wayne's climb to fame, Marquisha should summarize—writing that he wrote several hit singles, for instance—and then move straight into her argument.

"Yellow gives you the most points," he said. "Get to that as quickly as possible."

"When you put 'AWK,' what that mean?" a student asked.

"What's 'adversity' mean?" asked another.

"I don't know how to relate my commentary to my points without repeating myself," said a third.

Aidan answered each question, explaining that it would be better to risk repetition than leave out commentary altogether.

When he announced they would transition into practicing multiple-choice questions, the classroom erupted with gasps and moans.

"Chill, chill, chill," said a male student.

"What do you guys remember about multiple choice?" Aidan asked.

"It was hard."

"It was boring."

"Remember when you read [passages] that seem dense and full of weird words, you are looking for two things: the meaning and the methods that created it." As Aidan passed out a practice round of questions, he reminded them the AP exam was equivalent to a college-level course and they should not feel badly if they didn't know everything.

"I'm scared, Mr. Kelly," said a student.

"I know. We're all scared. That's why we are doing this—to get less scared."

"Are you doing this to torture us?" said another student, half joking.

Despite their protests, the students bent their heads and worked intensely on the questions for the next several minutes. When the timer went off, they complained that the words *aesthetics, ornamentation, objective,* and *grotesque* had eluded them. They reviewed the meanings of the words, focusing on *aesthetics* and *objective* in particular. Both were words students bound for college should know, Aidan said. "The term *objective* is one that you will likely encounter—sorry, that you will definitely encounter—again and again in your college career."

During the course of the class, Ben Marcovitz observed for five minutes; he sent Aidan an e-mail applauding him for cold-calling the students. Jerel Bryant, the dean of humanities, also popped by. In his feedback, he asked Aidan if he had thought about creating a list of vocabulary words for the students to keep in their class binders.

Aidan concluded with words of encouragement before breaking some bad news. "I know these are hard. You guys are working so hard and doing so well. Every time you do one of these, the structure embeds itself in your mind. You are already making progress. You are going to do awesome." And just to make sure the essay structure became fully embedded, he added, they would be writing about fifteen more of them before exam day.

On open-ended essay questions like the one about adversity, Aidan's students often wrote from personal experience or about figures from popular culture like Lil Wayne. A few of the students focused on characters in books like *Lord of the Flies* or *The Great Gatsby*, but they were the exception. Essay graders were supposed to remain neutral on the topic and evaluate essays based on the quality of writing, structure, and analysis. Aidan worried total neutrality as to subject matter was impossible, however. If a student wrote a well-constructed essay about Tiger Woods overcoming adversity and going on to sleep with many women (as one student had), a judge might score that a point or two lower than an essay of similar quality analyzing the character of Tom Buchanan in *The Great Gatsby*, another womanizer. Or if they wrote about their own experiences with consumerism, that might rate more poorly than a piece focused on the national gross domestic product.

"I am worried my kids will write about things that are very germane to them and that whoever is grading this in Louisville, Kentucky, might not relate," he said, particularly if they wrote from personal experience. "But my bigger worry is making sure they can do the essays." Structure and writing skill would always matter more than content; of that Aidan was convinced. So he focused his efforts on teaching essay structure and encouraging more analysis, not trying to control the topics. If students left out analysis altogether, it would not matter whether they wrote about Tom Buchanan or bandied about terms like GDP: They would fail that section of the AP.

Aidan set his sights on boosting as many students as possible to passing scores of 3. He had a feeling many of them would hover on the line between a 2 and a 3. If students passed, they would not only receive credit at many universities, but $300 cash. Sci received support for its AP program from a local nonprofit called AdvanceNOLA, which committed the $300 payouts as a small incentive. The group also provided professional development and mentors to area public schools trying to build AP programs.

AdvanceNOLA had not sent out many midsummer, congratulatory checks in its short history. During the 2009–2010 school year, for instance, it supported AP programs at four local public schools—two traditional and two charter. Of the 162 AP exams taken in different subjects across the four schools, only three students had passed: Nineteen had earned 2s, and 140, or 86 percent, had scored 1. Still, many local educators felt the AP programs were worth the time and investment, even if

few students passed the exams. The classes exposed students to challenging, rigorous work of the type they would encounter in college. Proponents of the AP classes also argued they boosted student self-esteem. But
that was a highly debatable proposition, depending on the individual
student in question.

Aidan offered his own incentive to the students in the weeks before
the exam: If nine of them passed, he would shave his scalp, but not his
beard. And if *all* of them passed, he would shave every hair on his head,
including his eyebrows. His goal was a 50 percent passage rate. But he had
set that in January, before he knew so much of his time with the class
would be sucked away by preparing for other exams. If he had to shave
his head in July when the scores came out, he would consider himself
very lucky indeed.

Five days before their AP language exam, most of the students took the
AP U.S. history test. The ordeal left them feeling as if they had been
punched in the face. Yet they soldiered on through their last class session
with Aidan before exam day, not complaining when he passed out one
final round of practice multiple-choice questions. The end was in sight.
The mood was optimistic, even buoyant at moments. They quizzed their
teacher about how they would get their $300 checks in the middle of the
summer and when they would see him with no hair. Then they dove into
the final practice questions.

The students remained unfazed by jargon-laden questions about the
"rhetorical function of switching from second person to first person"
and which phrases "illustrate the notion of the abhorrence of loneliness."
They discussed the meanings of *paradox, abhorrence, effusive,* and *me-
tonymy,* the last of which Aidan promised them more than 99 percent of
people they met on the street would never know. They snapped exuber-
antly when a classmate guessed the correct answer on a hard question;
several shouted out, "I got beaucoup right!" as Aidan read the right answers; one even performed a little dance at his desk to celebrate a feat of
rhetorical prowess.

"The enthusiasm over this is warming my heart," said Aidan. "I'm
seeing improvement every time."

Everything went well until the last ten minutes of class when D'Rell,
one of the students, counted up his final tally of correct answers. "I failed,"

he said, realizing he had gotten more wrong than right. He put on his backpack, making it clear he was ready to go.

"Now we are going to go through pacing," Aidan announced.

D'Rell had had enough.

"I thought we were fucking through."

All the energy seemed to evaporate from the room with his words.

"D'Rell, would you step outside?" Aidan said.

D'Rell refused to budge for a few seconds, keeping his head buried in his arms. But when Aidan asked a second time, he stormed angrily from the room.

No one said a word as they crammed a last-minute primer on pacing into the final four minutes of class.

Late spring brought seasonably warm temperatures and encouraging news to Sci Academy. In April more than 350 students applied for 130 spots in next year's freshman class, a sign of the school's growing reputation and popularity. The school would accept no new upperclassmen for now—a bone of contention for charter school critics who point out traditional schools cannot so easily control how many new students they admit in older grades.[3]

The large number of applicants for freshman seats meant that Sci would hold a lottery to determine who got in. In practice, lotteries were bittersweet affairs: Some families inevitably left elated, others crushed. Lotteries had become a curiously iconic image of the charter school movement by the time Sci Academy held its first. Two pro–charter school documentaries, Waiting for Superman and The Lottery, put more narrative emphasis on lotteries than classrooms and the actual business of running a school. Many charter school leaders view lotteries as a sign of their arrival, a symbol that consumers (in this case, parents) covet their brand. They tell stories of the emotional events—describing devastated mothers who leave crying with confused children in tow—in their political lobbying efforts.

Indeed, those who attack charters as an assault on public schools would be wise to talk to parents who attend the lotteries. From them, they might learn that the despair and desire of some of the nation's most vulnerable families (and not just the ideology and dollars of billionaire philanthropists and hedge fund managers, as some skeptics claim) drive the charter school movement. But those who tout the lotteries as proof that the old system is broken and charters must be expanded should remember that only some of the nation's thousands of charter schools are so in demand they have to hold lotteries. There is no single iconic image that represents charter schools because their results and experiences are so varied, just like those of traditional public schools.

Charter schools originated in the early 1990s, partly with the goals of nurturing innovative practices that could then be spread to other public schools, and expanding choice for parents. The image of a lottery stands in stark contrast to these founding premises: Instead of forces for good throughout public education, the best charter schools become islands in a sea of "dysfunction." An acceptable public education becomes a coveted prize rather than a universal right. Schools grow commendable by virtue of their capacity to exclude rather than include. No one, regardless of how they feel about charter schools, should see much to brag about in such a scene.

About one hundred people crowded into Sci Academy's cafeteria for the lottery, most of them quiet and stone-faced. Marcovitz began his short speech by recalling the school's founding just three years earlier. He had been Sci's only employee at the time and promoted the school by posting signs with his cell phone number—since the school had no building to visit or office to call—on neutral grounds across the city. "This year, instead of having to do all of that, we ended up with three people for every spot," he told the assembled applicants. "That's a strange feeling. Imagine what it means to the scholars here. They have had to work very hard and invested in a place no one knew about. Now people want to be like them."

He touted the advisory system to prospective parents, telling them each student has an advisor whose "number goes into your cell phone so you have an adult you can call who can tell you everything." Then he addressed the students, saying, "If you work with us here, you will go to the college of your dreams. There is a belief here that anybody can work hard and achieve. The scholars right in this room have shattered the expectations for themselves." Marcovitz assured the families that a student's academic history did not matter at Sci. They could arrive with poor grades and a long history of discipline problems yet still thrive at Sci. Each freshman started with a clean slate.

"This is not a place where your past matters at all," he said.

Marcovitz wore a red Sci Academy T-shirt with THE FUTURE IS NOW written on it. A row of students stood in the back of the cafeteria, snapping whenever he said something positive about the school. Throughout the lottery, they provided a quiet chorus each time gleeful parents heard their child's name called out. The snaps ceased, however, after the first 130 names had been read; those who remained lingered to hear where their children fell on the long wait list. As the evening wore on, only the sound of names and numbers being read could be heard, followed every minute or so by a discouraged family quietly shuffling out.

In reality, Sci's staff knew they would probably be able to admit most, if not all, of the families on the wait list over the summer. New Orleans parents increasingly hedged their bets and applied to several different schools, since they knew they weren't guaranteed admission at any single one. Many of the families who won admission that night would ultimately choose other schools. Charters in New Orleans often begin the school year with half the number of expected students, since families commit to multiple places. The large number of spring applicants signaled that Sci, because of its high test scores, might be attracting more connected or well-prepared students and families than it had in its first three years—a suspicion that would be supported a few months later when the new freshmen tested modestly higher than the previous years' classes, Marcovitz said. In a school landscape like New Orleans', a reputation for academic success could become a kind of self-fulfilling prophecy as academically ambitious families and students—not to mention private funders—gravitated to the well-rated schools, bolstering their chances of continued success.

A second piece of good news arrived just a couple weeks later: For a second year in a row, Sci triumphed on the state standardized tests, posting the highest overall scores of any open-admission high school in the city. Eighty-seven percent of the juniors passed the social studies graduate exit exam and 91 percent passed in science. The sophomores also performed well, with 79 percent passing the state's English exam and 85 percent passing in math. Marcovitz called a school assembly to announce the scores. He even allowed the students to cheer.

Before showing students the slides with their results, Marcovitz reminded them the best was yet to come. High test scores would pale in comparison to the college acceptances that would begin pouring in for the juniors in just a few months.

"Next year around this time," he said, "all the juniors will be throwing T-shirts in the air saying what college they are going to. Talking about test scores will be like talking about the minors when you are in the major league."

Aidan and Sci's top six students—who all happened to be girls—took a trip to the major leagues of colleges and universities that June. Over the course of three days, they hit Columbia and New York University before traveling farther north to visit Boston University, Northeastern, and Aidan's beloved alma mater. Most of Sci's juniors took out-of-town college trips that week, sandwiched between final course exams and the ACT. The school divided them into groups based on grade point averages, sending the ones with the best academic records off to the more elite institutions and distant locales. It made sense for Aidan, a New York City native and Harvard alum, to lead the trip to the Northeast. A mother of two of the girls, twins who both hoped to become veterinarians, chaperoned the excursion.

During two days in New York, the group squeezed in sightseeing and shopping in Union Square, Chinatown, and Times Square along with tours at the two universities. They loved NYU, but Columbia left them cold. The NYU guide was easygoing and unpretentious. He made a point of telling them NYU students accepted everyone exactly as they came and welcomed those with diverse interests and values. He told stories about goofy traditions, like how students sought out the president for bear hugs before graduation. He made them laugh. The Columbia tour guide, on the other hand, emphasized the university's academic prowess and elite trappings. She repeated over and over again (just in case the students missed it the first time) that Columbia was a member of the Ivy League. She told them Columbia students enjoyed talking about dialectics in their free time (whatever that meant). She described in great detail the university's "core curriculum," which required all students to take several courses in common. They would read masterpieces like Dante's *Inferno* and Sophocles' *Oedipus the King* and discuss the meaning of individuality, community, and human existence. Some of the Sci students openly fidgeted.

The group arrived by bus in Boston on a sunny June morning, still revved with travel adrenaline and glad to be far, far away from the classrooms of Sci. Aidan took them for a brief hike on the Freedom Trail, and then they headed over to Boston University for an afternoon tour. At BU, the students showed off knowledge accrued on countless tours past with detailed questions about the maximum number of credits they could earn in a semester, whether they would have to be fluent in another language to study abroad, the minimum grade point average and ACT score required for admission, if BU accepted weighted or unweighted grade point averages, and whether they could major in premed.

The BU tour was particularly slick. Lee Anne, a guide in training, and her mentor guide both wore dark sunglasses and ear microphones. They walked backwards without tripping as if they had been doing it their whole lives.

BU did not bore the high schoolers like Columbia, but it failed to inspire as much as NYU. They listened with curiosity, if not excitement, as Lee Anne described the university students' love for ice hockey and "broomball," an intramural sport that involved hitting a ball with brooms on ice while sliding around in tennis shoes. Other popular BU activities—including rugby, cribbage, and singing in a cappella groups—sounded just as foreign as broomball, yet more entertaining than four years of dialectics and the common core. In the end, most of the Sci students dismissed BU as a nice enough place, but not their dream school.

Like most teenagers, they seemed more interested in the Harvard Square pizza place where they would eat dinner, Pinocchio's, than they had been in BU. As they approached Cambridge on the T subway system, they peppered Aidan with questions about the size of the pies and whether they could pick their own toppings. Aidan had eaten at Pinocchio's two or three times a week as an undergraduate during some periods; he gave up the treasured pizza one year for Lent.

They regarded the thick, square slices a little suspiciously at first, but dug in quickly. With everyone worn out from the day's walking, they focused more on eating than talking; the whole meal took less than thirty minutes. Satiated and tired, some of the girls clearly wished the Pinnochio's visit was the final event of the day.

After dinner, Aidan asked the students to pose with him for a photo in front of Pinocchio's, and then the group headed over to Harvard for an evening tour with Aidan as guide. As they wound their way through Cambridge's streets and alleys, Aidan put on his Harvard cap, literally bounding with excitement. The girls, less enthusiastic and full of pizza, struggled to keep up.

Arriving at campus, Aidan told the students, "As soon as I got off that T stop I felt happy in my heart. This is what I want most for you guys: a place where three years later you can return and feel happy in your heart." He switched into tour-guide character, saying, "My name is Aidan and I'm a member of the class of 2008 with a History and Literature concentration living in Cabot House."

"Your name is Matthew," a student corrected him. (He had gone by his middle name, Aidan, since he started at Harvard so he would not be mixed up with other Matthews. But Matthew was, in fact, his given first name.)

"And it's not 2008," a second student pointed out.

This would be a tough tour—tougher, in some ways, than the ones he had conducted as an undergraduate as part of his effort to get over stuttering.

"Yes, it is 2008. Let's go," he said, striding off across campus.

"How come you don't have a microphone?" a student asked.

"They were walking backward at BU . . ." pointed out another.

Aidan ignored them. "There is old and important stuff underground wherever you step, so step really carefully." He tiptoed in an exaggerated fashion.

"Is this really how he gave his tour?" a student mused.

"It sounds like Mr. Kelly," replied another.

Over the course of the next hour, Aidan showed them the residence halls where notable alums like Natalie Portman and JFK had lived. He told the story of all John Harvard's books burning in a 1764 fire and described how the library's rare books today are protected by a special system that can suck all the oxygen out of the room "so the books live, but the people die." He pointed out the freshman cafeteria in Memorial Hall, which to the students looked more like a grand church. He told them about the housing system and course distribution requirements (a piece of cake compared to Columbia's common core). He said annual tuition and costs were expensive at about $50,000 a year, but Harvard had "the most generous financial aid in the country," covering tuition for students whose families earn less than $80,000.

The Sci Academy students took in all of this information. They were perturbed that Harvard, like BU, did not have many pre-professional majors.

"Do you have music business?" one girl asked.

"No pre-professional majors," said Aidan. "We teach you how to think. Our graduates get internships and jobs because our graduates learn how to think."

"Y'all have premed?" asked one of the twins.

"We don't have that either," he said. "We have it as a track. There are English majors who follow the premed track. Harvard is about teaching you how to think critically."

The students looked surprised when Aidan told them more than 94 percent of Harvard's graduates found employment, despite the university having so few courses or majors that sounded like job positions. They looked even more shocked when he said he learned more as a Harvard student through conversations than anything else. This ran counter to everything that had been drilled into them about college providing the path to income and books to knowledge. They sought universities with specific majors that would prepare them for specific jobs. Despite Sci's relentless focus on higher education, even many of the school's best students did not view college as a place to network or, more important, learn to think deeply and critically.

After the tour, Aidan bought the students Pinkberry frozen yogurt and fruit. He chose frozen yogurt because it seemed like "the college thing to do," although one girl referred to it as "wannabe ice cream." They had thirty minutes that evening to comb through Cambridge's sights and shops on their own before heading back to the hotel. He wanted them to experience a university neighborhood independent of a structured tour or information session.

With their first graduation ceremony less than a year away, Sci's teachers realized they had not talked in enough depth with their students about the purpose of college. Some of the juniors viewed higher education as a "paycheck enhancer." Others saw it as a way to ensure they could live and work where they wanted. Almost without exception, however, the students thought of college as a means to an end. The school's leaders knew they bore some of the blame for this. At Sci everything was presented that way: You studied hard to get good grades. You behaved well so you would not get in trouble. You ate your breakfast to have more energy. You endured Sci's rules so you could someday be a college graduate. That was where the story stopped.

Sci called its students "scholars" from the moment they arrived. But few of the teenagers thought of themselves that way. The notion of college as a place to immerse yourself in a particular passion—or redefine yourself—largely eluded them. It would help in future years when Sci's alums returned to talk about college life. But for the time being, the teachers scrambled late in the game to convince students that college could be as much about the experience of going as the status of having gone.

The students on Aidan's trip found the elitism of some of the institutions offensive in a way he had not anticipated. At their age he would have left Columbia enthused by the idea of the common core because he had been brought up to revere certain institutions. If something worked for Columbia, Harvard, Princeton, Stanford, or Georgetown, he would not have questioned it. He had aspired to become a "Boston College man" or a "Georgetown man" throughout high school. If it meant changing who he was, he would have seen it as growth. Sci's students, on the other hand, loved NYU for its come-as-you-are message.

"Our kids are like, 'I don't want to change who I am,'" Aidan said. "They are not seeing it as growth; they are seeing it as an imposition."

On one hand, he felt tempted to do what Sci always did when a glitch arose: reevaluate and change course. Next fall, the teachers could communicate from the very beginning of freshman year that "there are certain institutions which, if you get into, you should just go." He did not want Sci Academy graduates to miss out on a Columbia or Harvard education if they could get in.

But part of him felt ambivalent. The girls' attitudes toward college had been shaped for years by their families and communities, just as his had been. He thought back to parents who had asked him during Harvard tours whether the university's graduates do well in business, or whether you can become a doctor without a premed major. At the time he had been slightly condescending; now he thought he understood where they were coming from. Maybe they were right to question whether you should accept Harvard just because it's Harvard. Maybe his students, too, understood something he had failed to grasp.

"Is it that if you go to Columbia you should be able to recognize how great that is, and our girls are missing out on that?" he said. Or "is it just because I grew up in Westchester County that I would kiss the ground that Columbia walked on—and my girls are able to see through that? . . . Is it that our kids are able to see through some things their teachers blindly follow?"

There was no easy answer to these questions. And the truth, Aidan decided, probably lay somewhere in the middle. He would keep pushing many of his students to aspire toward prestigious colleges: institutions, he believed, that had earned the right to rest on their laurels. But moving forward he would talk—and think—about college somewhat differently.

THE FAMILY
"They say they love us already, but they don't really know us."

Snaps had turned into derisive sounds of mockery by KIPP Renaissance's first spring. Shout-outs turned cruel. The good wolf faded into the background. The students had managed to subvert KIPP's very language.

The Friday-morning school-wide assemblies, which featured the highest concentration of KIPPisms, became torturous affairs. A few students had always talked or caused disruptions during the assemblies, but the majority took the meetings seriously in the school's opening months. As the end of the year approached, the weekly events became parodies of their former, more earnest, selves.

At the meetings, Principal Brian Dassler asked students to volunteer "shout-outs" for classmates and teachers who had done something well, and "apologies," or public confessions of contrition. When he asked students if they had any of the latter during one April assembly, only the usual suspects raised their hands. Dassler said he wanted to hear some new voices.

Stillness and silence greeted the request.

"No one is ready to make the maturity leap just yet," he said, calling on Mario, a frequent contributor who often raised his hand.

"I want to apologize to Ms. Luzader because our class wasn't taking duck duck goose seriously," Mario said, eliciting snickers from those who sensed his sarcasm.

Floyd, the next student to speak, offered "a shout-out to Mounina for seventh period when she told Ms. Luzader that she was cheating [off] my test."

"Floyd's not quite ready for mature comments," Dassler said. "That's okay. You will be. We will get you there."

Floyd shot his roundtable advisor an annoyed, you-see-I-*tried* look, then turned his back on his classmates.

After a few more painful attempts—including one in which a chubby student could not utter her apology because of loud laughter—the teachers took over.

Ms. Alpert gave a shout-out to the lacrosse teams "for their dedication and commitment to trying a new sport."

Mr. Dassler praised Rogers, a student, for knowing "to stand up when you meet someone new and they are standing and you are not. That's social intelligence."

Mr. Benz bestowed snaps on his reading group for the "mature, adult discussion" they had had the other day.

Geraldlynn snapped very occasionally when she heard something she liked, although that rarely occurred during school-wide assemblies; she seldom raised her hand to volunteer a shout-out or apology. She spent this one resting her head on her arms, drifting in and out of sleep. Geraldlynn had been falling asleep in classes often lately, particularly algebra, geometry, and Spanish. Sometimes she tried to doze in physics as well, but it never worked because the teacher is "all in your ear." She had started wearing her bangs long just so teachers would be less likely to see her eyelids shut and forehead droop. Geraldlynn knew she had only herself to blame for the nights she stayed up late talking and texting on her cell phone. But it did not help that she often had to rise at five A.M. so the whole family could drive into the city and drop Raquel off at work more than two hours before the girls were due at school; nor that so many of Renaissance's classes bored her.

After that morning's assembly, Jason Saltmarsh asked his advisees why so few people participated anymore. They told him morning assembly had become a joke since the same students raised their hands each time. It had become difficult to tell whether many of the shout-outs and apologies were sincere or cruelly intended. Even when everyone spoke the same language, their words and gestures carried very different meanings.

Despite all the struggles, KIPP Renaissance celebrated a few triumphs its first year. Some students, particularly those who came from the worst middle schools, welcomed Renaissance's structured enthusiasm and excelled. The hardworking teachers maintained a strong camaraderie. The school fielded cross-country, basketball, and lacrosse teams, hosted dances, held monthly PTA meetings, and sent its fledgling marching band and dance troupe to perform in four Mardi Gras parades.

Yet by the final weeks, the school year felt defined by soured ambition, optimism, and hope. Several teachers put out feelers for jobs at other schools. Students grumbled about finding new high schools.

Between fifteen and twenty of Renaissance's 140 freshmen had left over the course of the school year, about 12 percent of the student body. The group included a few of the school's strongest students, whose parents grew frustrated with the chaos, and some of its biggest challenges, like Brice. At least a few of the students were forced or cajoled into voluntarily "withdrawing," staff said. Another fifteen students from Renaissance's inaugural class would transfer to new schools over the summer, and an additional fifteen would leave in the first half of their sophomore year. All told, about a third of the school's initial cohort would be gone a year and a half into Renaissance's existence.

Some experts have criticized KIPP schools for their high attrition rates, although the research on the subject is widely disputed. One study by researchers at Western Michigan University found that students left KIPP at significantly higher rates than other public schools, but another study by Mathematica concluded that the attrition rates were comparable to those at nearby schools. In New Orleans the lack of a centralized student-level tracking system made it difficult to gauge how Renaissance compared to other schools. But the midyear and summer exodus disturbed even the teachers. Students did not leave because of the high expectations or the rigorous demands. Some left because they (or their parents) thought the school was poorly run; others because they were forced, or encouraged, to do so. Despite the allegations of coerced withdrawals, KIPP Renaissance had no formal expulsions on the books at the end of the school year.

Dassler put much of the blame for Renaissance's shortcomings on the teachers he had hired and, occasionally, on his own inability "to manage their expectations" surrounding the behavior they would encounter in classrooms. He spoke of the challenges faced by the school as "brutal facts" to be acknowledged and controlled for through good teaching and "cultural competency."

Dassler said he didn't realize "how hard it is to improve teaching. It's really hard. It just takes time. I thought the example I set around relationships and cultural competency was enough for the teachers to do those things, too."

He remembered a recent time when a fight broke out in a classroom and the teacher said she felt less than 50 percent responsible. "I said, 'You can't work here and believe that. You just have to believe that everything that happens in your classroom you created, that it's all yours.'"

A few teachers grew frustrated with the notion they were always to blame, however. One of them sarcastically recited the school credo, "We Believe," in the teacher's room during lunch one afternoon. The credo went: "We believe students want to do the right thing; students will do the right thing when they know what it is, believe they can, and believe it will get them something they want; when students don't do the right thing it's because of something I did or didn't do." Some things, a few teachers felt, were out of their control.

Dassler also laid some of the blame on the intense, incentive-based structure of the KIPP middle schools. Many of Renaissance's most persistent troublemakers were boys who graduated from KIPP Believe. Once outside the familiar confines of middle school, they rebelled. "I'm pretty frustrated with the old-school KIPP middle school model—all these carrots and sticks and paychecks," he said. "The more I see the way it plays out . . . We're not training kids to run mazes in a laboratory, and that's all carrots and sticks do."

Geraldlynn still preferred her middle school (carrots and sticks included) to her high school, although she admitted the reasons were complex. A few days after Dassler criticized the approach at the middle schools, she wondered if Renaissance actually needed *more* structure. She wasn't sure. The school's problems defied simple explanations or easy solutions.

"Either the principal is too weak or the students don't meet what the school needs," she said.

"He need like a little help, more manpower," Raquel volunteered. "I don't know if he needs more males—"

"He needs more strength," said Geraldlynn.

"He too nice, for one."

"There's like this war. And he's not winning."

Even though Brice returned to school after his suspension ended, his thoughts remained elsewhere. Whenever administrators were too distracted or overwhelmed to stop him, Brice roamed the hallways with his friend Broderick and other boys: their expressions angry, words edgy, almost willing someone to take them on. One afternoon, he nearly came to blows with Trey, a popular student who had grown into one of the school's leaders and biggest success stories. Months earlier, Brice had comforted Trey when he tripped on the cord at the school dance, telling him, "You straight. You straight." This time it was Trey who took the high road, stopping the fight and lecturing Brice: "This isn't who you are, this tough nigger who is always frontin'. You're scared like everybody else. This is not how you have to do it. I'm tired of brothers pretending, thinking the only way to do things is to get rough and tough—like they can intimidate people."

A few days later, Brice paced the hallway before his seventh-period English class, cursing and muttering, refusing to catch anyone's eye, his skinny frame and dreadlock-rimmed face looked so tense it seemed like the touch of a feather might cause him to explode. Arriving for class, Ms. Childs, six months pregnant, took one glance in his direction and said, "Brice, chill out." He ignored her, and continued to curse.

A male student on the outs with Brice walked past, making a point of jostling him ever so slightly. Brice looked ready to jump. All of a sudden, his friend Broderick appeared by his side. Another of their enemies approached. The pair walked toward the rival menacingly. Within seconds, everyone knew, a fight would break out—a fight born of small, petty grudges and gaping unmet needs.

Ms. Childs intervened when Brice and Broderick stood within a few feet of their target. Exerting the power she had as their favorite teacher, she draped an arm gently around each boy, whose grandmothers she had made a point of befriending (she went to the same church as Broderick's grandma), and walked them away from their enemy. Mr. Dassler showed up a few seconds later. When he shouted, "Stop it!" his cry carried a desperate tone.

Brice never made it to English, where Geraldlynn and the rest of her classmates, rattled by the near fight, tried to finish short essays on *Their Eyes Were Watching God*. He and Broderick spent the remainder of the afternoon under the supervision of Mr. Lang, the school disciplinarian, who left them in the library while he went off to take care of something else. During eighth period, when Brice should have been in college-readiness class, the two friends could be heard imitating the sound of guns exploding: "Pop! Pop! Pop!"

Brice's mother, Tamika, had a bad feeling on the evening of April 11—just a few hours after Brice's near fight at Renaissance. Some teens in the neighborhood had recently threatened Brice, so she prohibited him from leaving the porch in the evenings. Every so often, Tamika poked her head out the door to make sure Brice was still there. Months later she would berate herself over and over again for not requiring Brice to stay inside, or at least joining him on the porch. Sometime after seven P.M., an older man in his thirties pulled up in a black Crown Victoria and called out to Brice, inviting him to get a daiquiri. The next time Tamika checked on her son, he was gone. The man, named Daniel, had befriended Brice over the winter. He made beats when Brice went to a neighborhood studio to record rap songs.

Over the next several hours, Tamika tried Brice's cell phone repeatedly. He never answered or called back. Brice always responded, even when doing stuff he knew his mother would frown upon. All through that night, Tamika tortured herself with thoughts of Brice's neighborhood rivals killing him and dumping the body somewhere. She did not hear any news until five A.M. the next morning, when police called. They had arrested Brice just before midnight. They said he had been inside a black Crown Victoria in Hollygrove when one of the passengers fired rifle shots at a passing car with a twenty-one-year-old man, a twenty-five-year-old woman, and her two young children inside. Reportedly, Daniel had an ongoing feud with the man. Bullets struck the car, although none hit anyone. A witness to the shootings called police, who pursued the Crown Victoria down Claiborne Avenue into Jefferson Parish, watching as the front passenger hurled the gun from the window.

The driver lost control a few minutes later, slamming into a curb. All three of the car's occupants fled on foot. Police caught Brice first, after he tripped. While the officer handcuffed him, police said he exclaimed, "Looka man, I'll give you names, the guy in the backseat gave me the gun and told me to throw it out so I did." The officer cut him off and asked his age. "Man, I'm fifteen," Brice said. Police said Brice injured himself when he tripped, scraping the left side of his face so badly they took him to University Hospital before bringing him to jail. His mother, however, said police held Brice facedown to the ground as they handcuffed him, and then stepped down hard on the back of his leg and face, grinding them into the hot concrete.

Another officer caught the backseat passenger, an eighteen-year-old who went by the nickname D-Nice. Daniel escaped on foot. Brice insisted someone else had fired the gun. But authorities booked both of the teens for attempted murder.[4]

Brice's name disappeared from the KIPP Renaissance rolls almost immediately. No one at the school talked about what had happened in a public forum. But everyone knew. Some of the kids started a "Save Brice" Facebook page and a couple of his teachers tried, without success, to visit him. Lionel Williams, the music teacher, thought the school should have used Brice's arrest as a teachable moment, a reminder to the school's more troubled boys that the path they were walking did not have a glamorous ending. Brice himself sent word to his friend Broderick that he needed to straighten up because living behind bars was nothing to envy. For the most part, however, the school tried to brush the incident under the rug.

Initially, police held Brice in the Youth Studies Center, the city's detention facility for juveniles. But after authorities charged him as an adult, Brice moved to the notorious juvenile wing of the Orleans Parish Prison where, at 105 pounds, he became the smallest prisoner. His mother worried constantly about his safety. On the street, you could bluff your way out of a fight and move on. In jail, Brice had no escape. Guards often told the fifteen- and sixteen-year-olds who arrived there they would have to fight. Teenagers slept four to a cell by choice as a means of protection from the juvenile wing's most hardened, predatory inmates.

Tamika berated herself for moving Brice to their old neighborhood, the violence and bad role models of which she blamed in part for his troubles. She planned to keep the rest of her children as far away from that corner of town as she could. She had always been close to Brice, her oldest son. He had inherited her charisma, fierce intelligence, and unstoppable mouth. When Tamika heard of Brice's arrest, she resumed old drinking and drugging habits in an attempt to escape the pain. "I went back to hell again," she said.

But after a couple weeks of bingeing, she stopped cold turkey. Her sister came by the house to pray. She insisted on giving Tamika a bath. "God won't answer your prayers if you're like this," her sister said, rinsing Tamika with water and ammonia. The words hit home.

Tamika managed to avoid a relapse partly because she knew the jail only allowed visitors between seven and seven forty-five A.M. on Sunday mornings, and Brice called at odd, unpredictable hours. It would break Brice's heart if—hungover or high—she missed a Sunday visit or telephone call; right now her son needed her strength and support more than ever.

Brice's lawyer promised the family he would try to get the teen released in exchange for testifying against the shooter. If that happened, Tamika planned to move the family to another city where Brice would be out of harm's reach. But the case, as with so many others in Orleans Parish courts, languished for months with little news or progress. Brice briefly attended school while he stayed at the Youth Studies Center, but the classes ended once he arrived at the adult jail. When his mother visited, he talked about KIPP and his desire to return to Renaissance someday.

"Brice loved that school, although he didn't always show it," said his grandmother, Frances McShane.

One day Brice called one of his old classmates from jail. The student told Brice the school would never take him back even if the jail released him: KIPP didn't educate criminals.

Tamika saw the hurt in her son's face when he recounted the story during one of their Sunday morning visits. She insisted it was only a rumor.

"Brice, please don't believe that," she said. "Don't worry about it. We're not going to live here in New Orleans anymore when you get out."

Tamika and her mother worried Brice's forty-five day suspension from the school might have led indirectly to his arrest. Everyone knew Brice lived dangerously before the suspension: The school could not take all the blame for what befell him. A few of his teachers and his mother were convinced, however, that Brice dug himself a deeper hole during the month he was banned from school. One of his teachers said, "It's our fault. We send a kid home for [forty-five] days for being about to get into a fight. What do you think he's going to get into? . . . We had a chance to reform him and we slipped. He came here humble. When he came back he was talking a certain way and wearing his pants a certain way."

His grandmother never understood why school administrators had suspended him so often and for so long. "When we were going to school, we didn't have all these suspensions," she said. "Now, pretty much anything you do, they say, 'You are suspended.' That's not helping—the kids aren't learning anything at home."

If it hadn't been for those weeks out of school, the teen might have felt more optimistic about his future. He might not have started spending so much time with a troubled man twenty years his senior. He might never have stepped inside the Crown Victoria that night.

No one would ever know.

Brice, too, felt the forty-five-day suspension for fighting had been unjust. In his view, administrators used the fight as a pretext to punish him for smaller acts of insubordination he'd committed all year long. He told Mr. Dassler, "Y'all didn't suspend me for the one lick I passed. You suspended me for every day I been here."

KIPP Renaissance stopped handing out monthlong suspensions in the spring, relying more on in-school suspensions with Mr. Lang. But its leaders remained unsure how to handle their most troublesome students. At times they grew desperate, as during a brief period when administrators indirectly encouraged families to employ corporal punishment (not a KIPP-sanctioned or encouraged practice) as a means of scaring the school's wayward teens into obedience.

Much of the optimism that had defined the school's planning and opening had evaporated by the spring. Dassler had hoped to create a school that combined the ambitious structure of a Sci Academy with the familiar warmth of an O. Perry Walker. But as Renaissance floundered, the school introduced more structure, curtailed student freedoms, and cut activities the kids enjoyed.

In the summer of 2010, when several students had failed to show up for a required weeklong orientation for KIPP Renaissance, the teachers drove around the city looking for them. They picked up every student they could find, including a small boy whose mother dragged him to their van kicking and screaming. But by the final parent meeting of the year nine months later, Dassler told the mothers in attendance: Next year "if you don't come to stuff we're doing, you're done. Last year, we basically went around looking for you."

In the school's opening weeks, Dassler had also insisted that Renaissance balance structure with freedom so its students would not arrive at college unprepared for all the independence. He encouraged teachers to be creative and not feel too constrained by state standards as they developed curricula for their classes. But at that last parent meeting, he made it clear that moving forward, KIPP Renaissance would put greater emphasis on rules, particularly when it came to uniforms. A parent said she worried some families might not be able to afford the expensive oxford shoes Renaissance planned to require as part of the uniform the next school year. Dassler responded: "It's going to be oxford; if you can't buy oxford, you can go someplace else or talk to Mr. Dassler and he'll buy them for you." When one of the mothers asked if Renaissance helped prepare students for standardized tests, he replied: "Not enough, we learned . . . We need to focus more on test strategies."

The parents—at least the ten who attended the meeting—supported Dassler's sterner approach. One mother fondly recalled a KIPP middle school principal who would not let children enter the building unless their shoes were completely black. Other mothers asked to see copies of the Explore, or pre-ACT, test so they could see exactly what their children were up against. They spoke dismissively of parents who could not find the time to attend school meetings or even inquire as to how their children were doing in school. "Some parents will just come when there's a problem and bring the ghetto out," said one mother. A second added: "Some kids are good; some are not."

Dassler tried to stay focused on the school's overarching goal of college preparation and success. To achieve that, he felt Renaissance needed to grow more rigid about testing, behavior, uniforms, and rules. "I don't think I've ever let us lose sight of the big picture, the big goal, even when it would have been easy to say, 'All right, this isn't working. Let's start over,'" he said that spring. "I never acted or said that the sky was falling even though eight out of ten people in the room thought it was."

Dassler's heart remained in the right place much of the time. He calmly countered the mother at the meeting who had belittled some of her peers, noting that in his experience most parents are just trying to do right by their kids. He agonized constantly over what else, more, and better he could do to help Renaissance thrive. He grew so obsessed, however, with the school's main goal that he lost sight of just about everything else, including helping some of the neediest students. Unlike Brice's, Dassler's future did not fall victim to the failings of a school and city. But much of his idealism did.

As her final days of ninth grade approached, Geraldlynn's thoughts turned to the end-of-school trip—the part of the KIPP program she had most cherished since the day her middle school principal Adam Meinig recruited her on the family's front stoop. Unlike middle school, where the whole grade visited the same city, each roundtable at KIPP Renaissance picked their destination. Geraldlynn's group planned to rent cabins near the beach on the Florida Panhandle and take day trips to visit colleges. The fourteen-year-old talked more in the weeks leading up the trip about the cabins and beach than her classes and end-of-year tests.

Geraldlynn's grades dipped slightly as the school year progressed, although she maintained her honor roll standing at the end. She made a point of finishing her final assignments on time so she wouldn't miss the Florida excursion. Dozens of her classmates had to finish makeup work during the trips because they still had grades of incomplete, or I, in some of their classes. KIPP Renaissance did not give Fs to freshmen during the school year—a bone of contention for some of the teachers who argued that a failing grade would send a message to kids in a way an I never could. Dassler remained obstinate on the point, however. He did not want a low GPA from the first year of high school to sabotage a student's chance of getting into college or qualifying for TOPS. "In a knowledge era, no one has to fail," he said. "There's every reason to say 'incomplete' or 'not yet.' In an industrial era, if you failed there was still a job for you."

But passing grades did not guarantee passing scores on standardized tests and the kids, as always, had to soldier their way through plenty of those. Geraldlynn did not have to endure another year of the iLEAP and LEAP, the state standardized exams she had taken annually since fifth grade. She did, however, have to take two of the state's new end-of-course exams in geometry and algebra. Despite her trepidation over the geometry one, she scored in the "good" category on both (the tests were graded excellent, good, fair, or needs improvement). "I was just one down from excellent," she said.

She also took the Explore pre-ACT test, performing slightly below KIPP Renaissance's average. (No one told her how she scored, prompting Geraldlynn to wonder if their silence signaled she had "failed.") She had in fact earned a 13, meaning she was on pace to earn between a 16 and a 19 on the ACT by the end of high school, just out of range of qualifying for TOPS. Students could make above-average growth and rise from a 13 to the low 20s over the course of high school if they practiced the test and had strong teachers, however. Geraldlynn would need both.

She increasingly tangled with teachers over minor issues as the school year drew to a close, receiving a few detentions as a result. One stemmed from a dispute with Ms. Bard in Spanish class over whether Geraldlynn was copying down vocabulary words per the instructions. In another case, Mr. Williams said she was stomping her feet loudly when he asked her to move to a seat in the front of the room. (Geraldlynn insisted she just walks heavily.) She could not remember the reasons for a couple others.

She wavered all year as to whether the school needed more rules or fewer. One evening in early May she came down against rules, saying, "Every time you turn your head there's a rule added on. The stricter you get, the more you running people away." She also complained that by making families sign contracts committing to their regimen, "KIPP is, like, kidnapping me." But she saw more keenly than most adults that the never-ending back and forth over uniforms and rules masked deeper issues. She would accept just about any rule the school threw at her (with maybe a little grousing; she was a teenager, after all) if she trusted her teachers and found the classes interesting.

Her middle school, KIPP Believe, had had more rules than she could count. Moreover, Ms. Drake, her favorite teacher there, had always been up in her ear about something or other she should be doing better. But at KIPP Believe, "They gave us chances and tried to help us do right," said Geraldlynn. "At [Renaissance] they say they love us already, but they don't really know us. They probably just saying it." One Renaissance teacher hung signs in her room that stated: "EVERY STUDENT WHO IS 1ST IN HIS OR HER FAMILY TO GO TO COLLEGE ENDS POVERTY IN HIS OR HER FAMILY LINE FOREVER," and "I CARE ABOUT ALL OF YOU. I WANT YOU TO SUCCEED."

"I think she was just trying to decorate her room," Geraldlynn said of the signs.

She thought it would help if Renaissance allowed students to pick classes that interested them and move around more throughout the school day. Geraldlynn hated spending several hours a day sitting still at a desk. Toward the end of the year, she participated in class mainly to make the minutes pass faster. "I might as well make use of my time," she said. "It's not going to go well if I just there waiting for the bell to ring."

Raquel agreed with her daughter that Renaissance's staff should introduce classes and programs that appealed to the kids. She wished the schools had not abandoned trades and technical training so completely. Geraldlynn, she knew, would love a class or seminar on hairdressing. But she reminded her daughter that high school had been just as boring in her day. Raquel arrived at many Cohen High School classes in the late 1980s and early 1990s to find the work written down on the chalkboard. The students spent the whole period copying it on their own. Some of the teachers spent the classes talking to each other outside in the hallway; others slept. "There were only two classes where I did not sleep at the end," said Raquel. In those "the teachers were very talkative so you had no other choice but to stay up."

When you compared Renaissance to the schools Raquel attended, it looked all right with its big ambitions and intense focus on college preparation. But when you compared it to the school Geraldlynn wanted, and deserved, Renaissance still had a long way to go.

Geraldlynn typically came off as more cynical than her parents: joking that KIPP had kidnapped her, rolling her eyes at all the rules. But underneath her skeptical teenage shell, she remained fiercely idealistic—more idealistic even than her parents and teachers. Geraldlynn wanted to attend a high school where she could trust the teachers with her deepest fears; where the classes were interesting and motivated her to want to learn for the sake of learning; where the adults called her out when she did something *really* wrong, not just for petty transgressions. "If I show up with everything on but my tie, they are like, 'Better go back home,' " she said.

She wanted a high school where she developed the confidence in her academic abilities she would need to make it through college. Pledges of one thousand college graduates by 2020 meant little to her. The everyday realities of her life over the next three years meant a lot. The teachers could say how much they cared and wanted every student to graduate from college until they were blue in the face. But unless the students believed them, the words carried little meaning.

"In my opinion, half of that school will not make it to college," Geraldlynn told her mother in May.

"They are not college ready?" Raquel asked.

"They are not college bound," said Geraldlynn.

As the 2010–2011 school year ended, Geraldlynn's cousin, Maurice, suffered a relapse. After a long stretch of good behavior (by KIPP's standards) and the relative freedom that accompanied it, he found himself sitting on the Bench once again. He called his mother first thing on his way home from school one May evening to break the bad news. By Maurice's account, a teacher benched him for being loud and disruptive in class even though he had only been trying to ask if he could go get a Band-Aid. By his teacher's account, he had been loud and disruptive, period.

Geraldlynn's older sister, Jasmine, and Maurice's older brother, Lionel, both finished junior year with little idea which colleges they planned to pursue in the fall. Jasmine distressed her stepfather, Langdon, when she talked about joining the military. He wanted her at least to make an attempt at college. She had yet to take the ACT. Lionel was more excited about college, but at a loss as to how to get there. He alone of all the cousins attended Raquel and Roxanne's alma mater, Cohen High School. Cohen did not have the best track record when it came to college attendance and graduation, either pre- or post-Katrina. In 2009, for instance, fourteen of forty-four graduating seniors had continued on to Louisiana's colleges and universities (no one tracked how many students went on to out-of-state institutions, but the number was very small). Of those fourteen, ten needed to take remedial courses in college and the average ACT score was 13.9. Whenever Lionel thought about college, he felt overwhelmed by all the unknowns: how to pick a school where he would be comfortable, whether he would like it, how he would physically get to campus. His mother struggled just to retrieve Maurice after detention at KIPP Believe across town. He wished the Recovery School District high schools he attended after Katrina had done a better job preparing him.

"Booker T. [high school] and Cohen took three years out of my life," Lionel said.

Geraldlynn's stepsister Mary had the opposite dilemma: too much help and too many choices. That spring, the exclusive—and expensive— Country Day school accepted her into its high school program. Mary hesitated before committing because she knew no one else bound for Country Day. The teachers and approach at KIPP had struck her as foreign at first, but at least there she was among students who looked like her and came from similar backgrounds. At Country Day, she would be one of only a small number of low-income African-American students amid a sea of white middle- and upper-class teens, many of whom had attended school together for years. In the end, she heeded the advice of Ms. Feingerts, KIPP Believe's college counselor, and the wishes of her mother and grandmother, who did not want her to pass up the opportunity. The Jack Kent Cooke scholarship would provide $15,000 toward the annual $22,000 cost and fees, as well as Internet access, summer travel, and Mary's transportation to and from school. Country Day would pick up most of the remainder. Mary's mother would be responsible for about $600, since the school wanted all parents to contribute some amount.

Country Day's college-acceptance profile stood in stark contrast to that of Cohen High School. Whereas the number of Cohen graduates continuing on to college could only be found buried in a state report, Country Day touted the destinations of its recent graduates on its website: Princeton, Brown, Dartmouth, Cornell, Stanford, Johns Hopkins, Vassar—the list went on and on. The middle half of Country Day's most recent graduating class scored between 25 and 29 on the ACT. More than 80 percent of students who took Advanced Placement exams scored 3 or higher. Mary dreamed of attending Yale because she liked the idea of a large university and one of her favorite sixth-grade teachers from KIPP Believe graduated from there.

Mary could tell from her first visit to Country Day the students lived in a different world. Many of them paid the full tuition up front. For her mother, who worked in a restaurant, $600 was a significant expense. Mary would have to think about what she wore to school every morning—a frightening prospect—since Country Day had no uniform. She had always assumed all students ate breakfast once they arrived at school, but Country Day did not serve breakfast. Mary had found KIPP Believe's classes entertaining and challenging ever since she transferred there in the middle of fifth grade. But one of Country Day's deans told her KIPP emphasized basic remediation. "KIPP is more about urgency with a focus on getting you to a certain level," he said. "Country Day is focused on getting you to work at your own pace."

"I never really knew that," said Mary. "I didn't think we were about urgency, but I guess we were." She steeled herself for more surprises.

Geraldlynn wore blue eye shadow that matched the blue streaks in her hair on the first full day of her end-of-year-trip. The temperature hit 90 degrees by midmorning when the students began their visit to Florida State University in Tallahassee, a three-hour drive from their cabins on the Gulf Coast. The information session left most of the KIPP Renaissance students, including Geraldlynn, more than a little intimidated.

Almost all of them sat in the back of the room, watching as an amiable middle-aged white man flipped through a slick PowerPoint presentation. Geraldlynn munched on a Snickers bar in the last row. The opening slides touted Tallahassee's low crime rate and youthful feel. Gradually, the man worked into a raft of ominous statistics: The annual tuition and fees of $31,097 for out-of-state students, which the man described as "pretty cheap compared to places like Tulane"; an ACT range of 25 to 29 for the middle half of the freshman class and a GPA range of 3.4 to 4.1; even *higher* ranges for honors students—29 to 32 on the ACT and 4.1 to 4.4 GPAs. The KIPP Renaissance students shook their heads, wondering how that was even possible. "This school is beaucoup hard to get into," one muttered.

The admissions officer said he had a daughter just two years older than them. He taped data about GPA and ACT ranges on the refrigerator to inspire her to keep her grades up. He also made sure she took both the ACT and the SAT, since some students perform much better on one. The students shuffled impatiently in their seats. Geraldlynn could not imagine her mother knowing Florida State University's admissions data, much less seeing fit to display it on their refrigerator door. And she felt scared enough about the ACT. Why would she want to take another test anything like it?

The man stressed that some students fell outside the GPA and ACT ranges. More than anything, the university wanted to see growth in students over time. "Florida State wants to see you climbing the ladder," he said. "So you guys are the first class then? That's cool. You are carrying a torch. It's a big responsibility for the rest of the program. Ninth grade is a crucial year."

The presentation wrapped up with a description of some of Florida State's more unusual draws, including hide-and-seek and pie-eating clubs, as well as a man-made beach beside the campus lake. The obscure clubs meant little to the KIPP Renaissance students. They would have settled for a football team, fully functioning air-conditioning, and classrooms free of mice. During the Q&A, only the teachers asked questions.

A couple of KIPP Renaissance students lingered, awed and impressed by the presentation. One even scrambled to copy down contact information for the admissions office before the campus tour began. But most, including Geraldlynn, quickly channeled their fear and intimidation into teenage nonchalance.

Geraldlynn spent most of the campus tour texting on her pink cell phone and complaining about the heat. She asked only one question—a plant from Mr. Saltmarsh—about whether the university had a museum honoring its Seminole Indian mascots. The guide, a sophomore with light brown skin named Lisa, delivered her spiel and answered questions with a quiet reserve. She said little that piqued the younger students' interest as they walked amid brick buildings, Spanish moss trees, and omnipresent recycling bins. The temperature continued to rise, and with it the students' impatience. They whined and said they wanted to lie on the beach.

"We still got to go to Florida A&M this afternoon," muttered a student named Daniel.

"Why don't we go there tomorrow?" ventured Geraldlynn.

"Let's do FAMU tomorrow," Daniel agreed.

"It's hot," said Geraldlynn. "I hate drinking water."

"I'm tired," said Daniel.

A few minutes later, Geraldlynn said she had reached the conclusion that Florida State was "too big. It's pretty, but I need a place that's"—she paused—"closer." Geraldlynn said the last word in a way that suggested she wasn't exactly sure what she meant by it.

Mr. Saltmarsh looked more animated than anyone. He grew obsessed by Florida State's Seminole Indian symbols, which appeared on banners and lined campus walkways. He had been thinking a lot lately about issues surrounding ownership and cultural heritage. He wondered what right the university had to control the land they walked on and appropriate the Indian symbol. Next year he would be teaching civics at Renaissance instead of college readiness. Most of Renaissance's teachers planned to return, despite the challenges of the first year and applications sent off elsewhere.

Saltmarsh wanted to teach civics in a more "culturally relevant" way than he had taught past classes. He had started to read Gloria Ladson-Billings's *The Dreamkeepers: Successful Teachers of African American Children* in search of advice. Based on the book, he planned to incorporate more from his students' backgrounds in his lesson plans, comparing the bylaws of the Constitution to the bylaws of African-American civics organizations, for instance.

Increasingly, Mr. Saltmarsh felt Renaissance's problems that year stemmed at least partly from inattention to the culture, socioeconomics, and specific needs of its students. If the teenagers could not see themselves in the history their teachers taught or at the universities they were told to aspire to, then all their work would be for naught.

"No wonder there are behavior problems from these really smart, high-intensity kids," Mr. Saltmarsh said. "We have a lot of work to do at Renaissance."

The kids' campaign to postpone the second college visit and hit the beach failed. The group, weary from touring Florida State in the heat, climbed back into their vans and headed across town to Florida A&M, the nation's largest historically black university. Given the general crankiness and lackluster response to Florida State, no one had high hopes for the next few hours.

But a funny thing happened at Florida A&M.

The campus wasn't as picturesque as Florida State, the presentations not as polished. Worst of all, the tour began with everyone having to hike up a steep hill in 93-degree heat to reach the center of campus. Geraldlynn took one look and declared, "I don't do hills."

But in spite of the hill, the heat, and the campus tour fatigue, Florida A&M captivated many of the students, particularly Geraldlynn. Their tour guide, Daphne, was a senior from Tampa, majoring in broadcast journalism. She handled the KIPP Renaissance students' questions with a deft ease; she spoke their language.

"You all got a lot of white people here?" one of them asked after spying a few pale-skinned university students wandering around campus.

Daphne explained that Florida A&M had a more diverse population than most historically black universities, enrolling a few hundred white students. That said, Florida A&M embraced black culture: Daphne touted the school's famous marching band, its gospel choir, the shuttle buses Baptist Community Ministries ran every Sunday from campus to nearby churches, and the presence of a hair salon and beauty supply store on campus that catered to the needs of the university's predominantly African-American population.

"We are like a family here," said Daphne, adding that she liked going to a school where everyone said hello as they passed and someone was always on hand to give her a ride home to Tampa if she grew homesick. From an objective standpoint, Florida A&M was a fairly large university—thirteen thousand students. But the KIPP Renaissance students referred to it as "small" after listening to Daphne's description of the close-knit environment.

One KIPP Renaissance student peeked nervously into the beauty supply store, reporting back in a reassured tone, "It's like a real beauty mart in there, like in New Orleans." The kids descended, scouring the contents and prices. Geraldlynn bought new hair tracks.

From that point on, she sprang to life in a way she rarely did when surrounded by her classmates in a school-related setting. She saw "more of my culture" at Florida A&M than at Florida State. Much of what Geraldlynn encountered there, including the salon and Daphne herself, felt like affirmation that you could grow, change, and move on without leaving all of your old self and interests behind.

Geraldlynn fired off questions as fast as Daphne could answer them.

"Do y'all accept disabled students?"

"Do y'all have it like where you can go to another state for a foreign language?"

"Like in Spain?" a classmate chimed in.

"Do y'all university presidents stay on campus?"

"Do y'all have something where you check in on people to see what they're doing? What kind of grades they are earning and stuff?"

As Daphne described a new mentoring program Florida A&M hoped to start, the group walked up to a flame burning on top of a tall, thin tower right in the center of campus. Daphne explained that the fire symbolized the resilience and spirit of the Florida A&M campus. Thousands of students had stood around it two and a half years earlier, watching results come in on a gigantic screen the night of Barack Obama's election, she said. The KIPP Renaissance students could relate to the image she described. Geraldlynn's mother rarely voted because of her busy schedule. But Raquel had made sure to find the time to cast a ballot for the country's first black president.

"Does anyone know what the fire's called?" Daphne asked.

"The eternal flame!" Geraldlynn shouted. Daphne looked a little surprised she knew.

Geraldlynn's questions resumed, each one challenging the tour guide more than the last.

"What happens to the flame when it rains?"

"If you get deep in something can it be hard to switch majors?"

"How this college compare to Howard?"

"What are the admissions criteria?"

Daphne told her that students needed a minimum high school GPA of 2.5.

"Why so low?"

"It gives people a chance," said Daphne. "We're the underdog, but once you leave here it's like you are transformed. They really mold your mind. College is great. I wish I could stay here a lot longer."

As Daphne continued talking about how much the university meant to her, the younger girl crept in closer and closer. Their shoulders almost grazed as Geraldlynn bent in to listen, taking in every word.

Epilogue

(July 2012)

As I write this, nearly seven years after Katrina, the schools in New Orleans continue to improve. Across the board, state standardized test scores have risen substantially since the flood; for the first time in generations, black students in New Orleans have started to outperform their peers in the rest of the state; ACT scores inch up each year; more students than ever take Advanced Placement classes; the schools have benefited from federal disaster relief money and private grants; dozens of nonprofits have opened to support the schools; and hundreds of energetic educators have come to work in them. Most important, the changes have brought renewed hope to thousands of poor families, many of whom felt underserved by the schools for decades.

Much work remains, and a comprehensive accounting of the changes will only be possible years from now, when the country learns not only how many New Orleans public school students graduate from college, but whether they can find sustainable jobs and safe neighborhoods in their hometown. Moving forward, the community should compare the schools not to their pre-Katrina iterations, but to what they can—and must—become. With that in mind, policymakers should reimagine contemporary school reform in a few key respects.

First, the approach must be more holistic. The schools will be hamstrung in their progress by a lack of attention to the breadth and depth of the challenges facing poor children growing up in New Orleans and all of America, challenges that extend far outside the schoolhouse door. For too long, some have used poverty as an excuse for not improving the schools. Our leaders should not now make the opposite mistake and use the success of a relatively small number of schools serving low-income children as an excuse for not addressing poverty's many dimensions.

Improving the quality of education in low-income communities is a crucial part of reducing inequality. But unaccompanied by broader changes throughout American life, the wide gaps in opportunity, educational attainment, and income that have come to define our society will persist.

Moreover, the New Orleans schools must evolve in a way that honors the culture, values, and history of the students and families they serve. That's not to say the city should return to the pre-Katrina model, when a mere fraction of public school parents voted in school board elections and a similarly small percentage of their children received an adequate education. Nor should American cities return to the rigidly, de jure segregated, but community-based schools of the first half of the twentieth century. A new way must be found that honors both a community's right to self-determination and its right to quality schools.

Describing his mixed feelings about Booker T. Washington's ascendancy, W. E. B. Du Bois wrote: "If the best of the American Negroes receive by outer pressure a leader whom they had not recognized before, manifestly there is here a certain palpable gain. Yet there is also irreparable loss,—a loss of that peculiarly valuable education which a group receives when by search and criticism it finds and commissions its own leaders. The way in which this is done is at once the most elementary and the nicest problem of social growth." If the schools want to succeed in the long run, the education they offer must become an extension of the will of a community—not a result of its submission.

Finally, Americans must take a more bottom-up approach to understanding education policy and assessing its impact. While I reported and wrote this book, the debate about education was mired in a set of abstractions that bore little resemblance to what I saw happening inside homes and schools. Yet those abstractions were all that hundreds of millions of Americans knew about urban public schools. According to one narrative, wealthy hedge fund millionaires and foundation leaders had hijacked the schools in pursuit of their own interests and would stop at nothing short of destroying public education as we know it. According to the opposing narrative, teachers' unions had hijacked the schools in pursuit of their own interests and would stop at nothing short of destroying public education as we know it.

Very little about the stories and experiences of the schools and families I followed fit within either narrative. However well intended, top-down accounts of school change too often fail to capture the complex realities of children and educators. They shatter under the weight of true narratives: the stories of people.

Aidan did not have to shave the top of his head when his students' Advanced Placement scores arrived in the middle of the summer. He had promised to take a razor to his hair if nine of them passed. But, although several rose from scores of 1 on the practice test to 2s on the actual exam, only two of his students passed with 3s. Of the 168 students from open-enrollment public high schools who took the AP language test in New Orleans that spring, more than half, or ninety-one, scored 1s. Ten students earned 3s and two students posted 4s. (At O. Perry Walker, thirty-six students scored 1 on the test; nine students, 2; two students, 3; and one student, 4.) The scores represented a significant improvement over the previous year.

Aidan took the blame for the lackluster showing. "Their poor performance was on me," he said. "It was my job to get them to pass . . . The kids are absolutely capable of passing the test in droves." His students fared better on the state tests: Eighty percent of Sci's students passed the Louisiana graduate exit exam in English that spring.

The results motivated him even more for the upcoming school year, when he would be teaching many of the same students Advanced Placement literature (the course that usually follows language in the AP sequence). This time, Aidan hoped he would have most of the school year to prepare the students—not just a few weeks in the second semester sandwiched around ACT coaching and social studies review. He dove in that fall, teaching *Huckleberry Finn*, *Heart of Darkness*, and several other works of literature. Aidan felt more content than he had in any of his three previous years in the classroom; he no longer thought about what he could be doing if he had not become a teacher. "At no point so far this year have I been depressed about my choices," he said. "It's been my busiest but most centered year."

Sci graduated its first class in the spring. The ACT results and college acceptances were more encouraging than the AP returns. By February, 60 percent of Sci's students scored at or above the state average of 20 on the ACT. By April, 94 percent of seniors had been accepted by at least one four-year college. Of those, more than 90 percent would be first-generation college attendees.

Staff members at Sci were proud as the admissions letters poured in—to Dillard University, Amherst College, Bard College, Louisiana State University, and several others. Some of the boys who had once hoped to play in the NFL had formed more realistic ambitions. But many of the students' academic goals stayed constant. Twins bound for LSU to study veterinary medicine had always planned to study veterinary medicine at LSU. A star student who hoped to learn Japanese in college had long wanted to learn Japanese. The teenagers had given over much of their lives to Sci's demanding regimen for four years, and now they were reaping the benefits. As they ventured out into the world, however, their dreams remained their own.

Aidan committed to Sci for a third year—but not as a classroom teacher. When Sci opened for the 2012–2013 school year, he would be director of curriculum and instruction (DCI). Conversations with colleagues convinced him he would be "doing the most good" for Sci's students in the new position. As DCI, Aidan hoped to explore how the school could "teach our kids to deeper understandings" even if that meant sacrificing on breadth at times. In English classes, for instance, they might read fewer books but write longer papers on them. At the end of the day, however, Aidan planned to follow one guiding philosophy in his new role: "What works is awesome, what doesn't is unacceptable."

It would be a year of transitions at Sci Academy. In the summer of 2012, two spin-off schools would open. Three of Sci's teachers—two in their twenties and one in her thirties—would become principals of the sister schools, and Ben Marcovitz would take over as CEO of the network, called Collegiate Academies. The two new schools were slated to open at the site of Carver High School in the 9th Ward. While the new programs would start with just freshmen, Sci teacher Isaac Pollack would take over the reins of the existing Carver as it phased out grade by grade.

The move prompted an immediate pushback from Carver alumni leaders and other community members, who said they wanted broader input in the campus's future. The group tried to recruit an African-American-led and staffed charter operator to take over, and protested with signs that read, HANDS OFF CARVER. Collegiate Academies' leaders scrambled to ward off more protests when the new schools opened, engaging in a series of talks with the community leaders that brought about at least some rapprochement. They planned to forge ahead with the expansion regardless. "I've always had to prove myself," said Marcovitz. "I did it with

Sci Academy, and I'll have to do it with the new school[s]." He remained optimistic that strong results would convince skeptics in the end.

The 2011–2012 school year was a rough one for Mary Laurie and the O. Perry Walker staff. Gun violence continued to claim the lives of too many New Orleans schoolchildren. A few weeks before the start of the school year, the Walker community lost Jacberio Griffin, a nineteen-year-old with special needs. Jacberio spent so much time at Walker he managed to convince a few of his teachers he had no home. He always seemed to be around, joking with Ms. Laurie or pleading with Coach T, his mentor, to borrow a few dollars. No one ever found out why Jacberio and another man were shot dead on a July evening at the site of the former Lafitte public housing complex. But it convinced Laurie that Walker should stay open even longer hours to keep its students safe.

During the summer, O. Perry Walker's name appeared on a list of school buildings RSD officials described as "opportunity campuses." It was a euphemistic way of saying the RSD would no longer put any money into building repairs or renovations. Walker's staff and students tried to sway district officials, but they made little traction.

In the fall, Walker received a new lease on life. The high school's enrollment was booming, presenting a stark contrast to L. B. Landry High School, which had reopened a mile away in a gleaming new building a year earlier. Landry struggled to attract enough students; its first-year test results put it in the state's failure zone. Keeping a thriving school in a decrepit building and a floundering school in a palatial one made little sense. In December, RSD officials floated a proposal to merge the two schools at the Landry site in 2013, with Mary Laurie as principal. The decision angered community groups whose applications to run Landry had been rejected. They threatened fierce resistance to a combined school and, worse, potential violence if the two student bodies clashed. By the end of the school year the long-term situation remained unresolved, although Walker would stay put for at least another year.

Political turmoil rocked the Algiers Charter Schools Association throughout the school year, starting in the fall when association leaders tried to end their participation in the state's teacher retirement system. In May, the association's CEO announced her departure. The future of the eight charter schools appeared increasingly uncertain. Test scores dipped at many of the schools that spring, including at Walker. Around the same time, Laurie learned Walker would lose the on-site health clinic she had fought so hard to keep.

The charter association's board of directors brought in a New York–based turnaround consultant at the end of the 2011–2012 school year in a bid to improve academic performance across its schools. The consultant, Aamir Raza, upended the leadership ranks: He fired two of Walker's assistant principals. He then reassigned Laurie to head the struggling Algiers Technology Academy as part of an effort to put stronger principals at the helm of weaker schools. Laurie declined. She would stand her ground at Walker. During an energetic protest in June, one community leader railed that Raza has "fired people, and he doesn't know them from the label on a can of paint." The board of directors relented after the protest, saying there would be no principal changes at Walker for now.

It had been six and a half years since Laurie told the assembled teenagers in Walker's courtyard, "We're a family now." She would have to fight as hard as ever to keep that family whole.

Brice remained in Orleans Parish Prison well over a year after his arrest for second-degree attempted murder. Initially, his grandmother and mother remained optimistic Brice might get released quickly. But as the months wore on, his mother's faith faltered and Brice lost interest in school. He complained that the teacher assigned to the jail came infrequently and mistakenly assumed all the inmates were slow.

"He doesn't talk about KIPP at all, not no more," said his mother, Tamika.

One of Brice's friends from the neighborhood eventually joined him in jail on an unrelated charge. With someone he trusted and liked nearby, the teenager grew less anxious behind bars. He no longer talked with his mother so much about going back to school, or what his life would be like outside of prison. He expressed reluctance to testify against others who had been in the car that night.

Tamika and Frances McShane, Brice's grandmother, had seen other boys like Brice arrested when they were fifteen, sixteen, or seventeen, and then exonerated years later. The overburdened criminal justice system almost always moved slowly. In certain cases, public defenders deliberately dragged out proceedings, hoping the prosecutor's case dried up. And young men like Brice sometimes hesitated to testify against co-defendants they considered friends, further delaying the process.

By the time the teens finally arrived home, they felt too old and jaded for school. With no high school diploma, they could not find jobs. With no jobs, they returned to the friends and habits that had gotten them into jail the first time. Tamika brainstormed constantly about how to keep Brice off the streets after his release. She tucked away video games and posters so there would be a room full of things her son liked ready. "I don't want him to feel like *this is it*," Tamika said. "And that's the feeling I'm starting to get from him. I don't want him to get comfortable. And it sounds to me like he's starting to get very comfortable . . . They are institutionalizing him."

Fifteen months after his arrest, Brice finally returned home to his mother. His lawyer negotiated a plea deal in July that dropped the charge to a misdemeanor. Brice, sixteen, had grown taller and heavier in jail; he now looked more like a man than a child. He scarcely resembled the young teenager who had enthusiastically signed himself up for KIPP Renaissance two years earlier. Within a year, Tamika hoped to send Brice to Italy to live with his older sister, who served in the air force. In the meantime, she needed to find her son a new high school. Brice's faith in the power of education had faded, and he resisted many of her suggestions. He wanted a break from the past, a place where no one knew him and he knew no one. But for a young black male with a troubled history and a criminal record, New Orleans wasn't an easy place to start over.

Geraldlynn returned to KIPP Renaissance for her sophomore year. More than fifteen of her classmates had transferred to different schools over the summer, most because they felt dissatisfied at Renaissance. Geraldlynn liked having a new crop of freshmen around; they made her feel old and experienced. But she found the state of affairs at Renaissance much as she had left it: rebellious, unruly students coupled with too many inexperienced teachers and a principal who seemed at a loss as to how to run a high school. Renaissance brought in new security officers in an attempt to keep order.

Geraldlynn was returning from the grocery store with her parents one bright Sunday afternoon in September when they all heard gunshots coming from the park just a few feet away from their apartment building. Two teenage girls lay on the ground, felled just moments earlier by a spray of eighteen gunshots fired into an area crowded with children and families. Geraldlynn and Jasmine rushed to the side of one of the girls, a sixteen-year-old they both knew. Geraldlynn feared that her friend, shot in the abdomen, would not survive. But she tried her best to be brave, forcing back tears as she comforted the injured girl. If she let the tears come, she reasoned, the wounded girl might assume they signaled death was near and give up hope.

Within a few minutes, paramedics brought the two girls to the hospital, where doctors listed both in critical condition. Raquel and her daughters spent hours at the police station while officers interviewed Jasmine about what she had seen. The playground's Booster Club president said the shooting appeared to have been retaliation for a recent robbery at a card game. The two girls had allegedly tipped someone off to snatch cash at the game. They nearly lost their lives over a few dollars.

The next day at school, Geraldlynn could fight back her tears no longer. She went to the office of a guidance counselor, hoping to talk. The woman gave Geraldlynn a Kleenex, told her everything would be all right, and sent her back to class. Weeks later, it still bothered Geraldlynn that the counselor had brushed her off.

Over the fall semester, Geraldlynn's grades dipped and she received a string of demerits and detentions, mostly for small infractions like arriving tardy to class. She skipped a detention and narrowly escaped a suspension as a result. She ended the first semester of her sophomore year with a 2.78 GPA, brought down by Cs in English and Algebra 2. Geraldlynn acknowledged in a January meeting with her mother and advisor, Mr. Saltmarsh, that she was not putting enough effort into her classes. That same month, Dassler announced he would be stepping down as principal at the end of the school year.

Renaissance dropped many of its extracurricular activities, scaled back on roundtable, struggled with ceaseless fights, and scheduled fewer college trips. "I think the school is falling apart," Geraldlynn said in April. "Every blue moon, they talk about college. I wish they did talk about it more because I'm losing hope."

Dassler said he made the changes so Renaissance could refocus on teaching and learning after a tumultuous autumn. "We were a really unstable school in the fall," he said. "There were weeks I had to wonder if I could do the job we had promised students and families we could do."

By the end of the school year, he had accepted a new position as chief academic officer at the New Orleans Center for Creative Arts, which offers training to students in musical theater, drama, visual arts, jazz, and

Geraldlynn Stewart stands near Touro Street in New Orleans' 7th Ward, the neighborhood where she grew up. After living in an apartment complex in the suburb of River Ridge for a couple years, Geraldynn's family returned to the 7th Ward in the fall of 2011. Photo by Susan Poag.

other areas. "It's really not the story I would have written," he said. "But for me, on a few different levels, it's the right story."

As his principalship came to an end, Dassler criticized other charter schools that pushed out challenging students, yet he remained reluctant to apply that same critique to his own actions. He stared wordlessly when asked about a specific student he had allegedly convinced to withdraw. He described Brice's fate as one of his "great sadnesses . . . I'm still personally looking for strategies that meet the needs of our most scared young men."

KIPP New Orleans hired new co-principals from the Noble Network of Charter Schools in Chicago that spring. Not long after, KIPP Renaissance's remaining families learned nearly all of the school's founding staff and teachers would be gone by the summer of 2012. Some left voluntarily over the course of the school year; others were told by the school's new leaders that they no longer had a position at Renaissance, or would have to reapply. Families already had little reason to trust the school. Now they were being asked to place their faith in new leaders and an almost entirely new staff. "Those [teachers] we are closest with are the ones who are leaving," lamented Geraldlynn. The new principals did, however, hire some well-regarded teachers from KIPP Believe, Geraldlynn's middle school. "Kids and parents really wanted change, which is why we ended up where we did," said Rhonda Kalifey-Aluise, the network's executive director in New Orleans.

Mr. Saltmarsh started tutoring Geraldlynn some Saturdays. Her grades rebounded modestly; she ended her sophomore year with three As, four Bs, and one C. Geraldlynn's pre-ACT score shot up that spring to a 17, putting her on track to earn a 20 by her senior year. She also became involved her sophomore year with an after-school program in the Lower 9th Ward called Our School at Blair Grocery, which taught students about urban farming, the environment, and sustainable food production. She hoped to work for the group throughout the summer of 2012, but it went on a temporary hiatus in June. That month, Geraldlynn turned sixteen.

Most teenagers want something to hold on to—a place, activity, sport, school, or mentor that is safe and stable and makes them feel good about themselves. As her junior year approached, Geraldlynn struggled to find her niche.

That summer she lobbied her mother for permission to transfer to McDonogh 35, her sister's alma mater. (Among other motivations, Geraldlynn worried KIPP Renaissance would not have a real prom like McDonogh 35.) Raquel had long resisted such entreaties. But KIPP Renaissance's struggles and upcoming move across town to eastern New Orleans—while its 9th Ward building was renovated—made Raquel nervous. She contemplated buying uniforms for both McDonogh 35 and KIPP Renaissance to keep the family's options open. But despite some last-minute scrambling, they missed the deadline for submitting application materials to 35. Geraldlynn would return to Renaissance for her junior year. Meanwhile, Jasmine planned to enroll at Southern University at New Orleans (SUNO) in the fall.

Not long after the shooting near their River Ridge apartment, Raquel and Langdon had found a rental across the street from Roxanne's house and moved back to the 7th Ward. New Orleans wasn't always an easy place to live, but Raquel could not imagine moving anywhere else. During one of the family's last car trips between River Ridge and the 7th Ward, her nephew, Lionel, rode along. When Lionel spoke, which was rare, he often asked philosophical questions. On this car trip he quizzed every-one in turn as to how they would spend the money if they won the lot-tery. All of the children agreed they would leave New Orleans as fast as possible and travel the world. Beyond that, their plans were vague.

Much of what Raquel desired she already possessed, including a lov-ing family. But she knew precisely what she would do with an unexpected windfall. She would stay in New Orleans and use the money to buy a house, a more reliable car, and a college education for her daughters. That was all she had ever really wanted. For the time being, however, she would content herself with the rental in the 7th Ward, the bike she shared with her sister, and a hope for her daughters that never faltered.

Acknowledgments

Meaningful education journalism is not possible without access to schools and homes. While reporting this book, I was fortunate to meet countless New Orleans educators and families who invited me into their classrooms and living rooms, submitted to my endless questions, and discussed their work and lives with openness and passion. Geraldlynn, Raquel, Aidan, and Mary Laurie were particularly gracious with their time and trust. I would also like to thank Brian Dassler, Jason Saltmarsh, Brice, Tamika, Ben Marcovitz, Michael Ricks (Big Mike), Catina Massey, Mary Dillon, Langdon Dillon, Jasmine Stewart, and the family of Roxanne Glasper for their faith and insights. In addition, conversations with Robyn Gulley and Vanessa Douyon provided crucial context that shaped my thinking and writing.

Many, many individuals and organizations responded to my neverending requests for information and other queries. Here are just a few: Teresa Falgoust, Damekia Morgan, Brandon Armant, Rene Greer, Willie Zanders, Jim Randels, Leslie Jacobs, Morgan Carter Ripski, and the staffs at the Greater New Orleans Community Data Center and the Cowen Institute for Public Education Initiatives.

Several friends and colleagues read all or part of this manuscript, each with generosity and good humor. Thanks especially to Katy Reckdahl, Mary and Edward Ducharme, Greg Toppo, Llerena Searle, Lolis Eric Elie, Catherine Michna, Rashida Govan, Michael Schwam-Baird, Lauren Bierbaum, and Elizabeth Rainey. They bear no responsibility for any flaws or errors in this book, but much of the credit for its strengths.

Journalist Kari Dequine helped me hunt down elusive facts. Photographer Susan Poag and graphic artist Ryan Smith greatly enhanced the book with their beautiful photos and map. Columnist Stephanie Grace graciously helped proofread pages.

Farley Chase, my agent, believed in this project when it was only a kernel of an idea and helped shape it from the start. Pete Beatty, my editor, improved the final product immeasurably through his smart critiques. Thanks also to Brian Thevenot, the gifted wordsmith and editor who co-authored the first draft of the proposal, and to Linda Perlstein, who offered much-needed support and expertise in the project's early stages.

Columbia Journalism School professor LynNell Hancock inspired me to start writing about schools more than a decade ago and has served as a mentor since, particularly when I returned to Columbia for a Spencer Education Journalism Fellowship in 2010. Along with the entire Spencer crew, LynNell enlightened, sharpened, and challenged my understanding of the issues this book explores.

My colleagues at the *Milwaukee Journal Sentinel* and New Orleans *Times-Picayune* made newspapers fun and stimulating places to write and work for many years. I hope such newsrooms continue, against increasingly long odds, to nurture and sustain future generations of young reporters. I have been especially lucky to share the education beat with Alan J. Borsuk and Darran Simon: class acts, great journalists, and dear friends. I am fortunate now to work with a group of rock stars at the Hechinger Report, a nonprofit dedicated to high-quality education journalism.

Several journalists and writers—some famous, others who should be— inspired and informed my work. Donald E. DeVore and Joseph Logsdon provided crucial context and history (from which I have drawn extensively) in their painstakingly researched *Crescent City Schools*. And J. Anthony Lukas provided an inimitable model of reporting on a city and its schools in his epic *Common Ground*.

My friends and family have borne with me gracefully—probably too gracefully at times—while I immersed myself in this project. I am sorry for all that I have missed. A special thanks to my big sister, Priscilla Carr, who accomplishes more in a day than many do in a year. I look forward to turning whatever expertise I gained reporting this book to the scrutiny of each of my one-year-old nephew's future schools. And a big hug to my parents, the only people with the patience and fortitude to read just about every word I have ever written. Someday I hope to live up to the example of community devotion, fundamental decency, and passion for living they have so lovingly set.

Notes

I gathered material for this book through three primary means: firsthand observation, interviews, and reading. The notes that follow all refer to places in the text where I felt it was important to provide additional context or cite interviews that helped me re-create specific scenes and events. A selected bibliography of books, articles, and websites that informed my writing follows.

Part II: Rebirth

1 "School reform" and "reformers" are fraught terms in the education debate. When using the terms, I refer to politicians, educators, and others seeking changes of the kind outlined here. It would be erroneous and simplistic to suggest these changes always improve the education system, however, given the mixed success of charter schools, state takeovers, mayoral control, and the elimination of teacher-tenure laws and collective bargaining. Sometimes the "school reform movement" is synonymous with the "charter school movement," particularly in New Orleans, where most "reformer-led" schools are charters. But hundreds of charter school leaders and educators across the country support collective bargaining, tenure, and locally elected school boards. So the terms are not always synonymous.

2 I have heard variations on this idea of "two opposing narratives" from multiple people, including Lance Hill, executive director of the Southern Institute for Education and Research at Tulane University.

3 Test scores improved during Vallas's tenure across all school types: charter and non-charter. But the charters significantly outperformed the schools under Vallas's direct control. Vallas struggled to lift the Recovery School District's high schools, in particular, out of the academic failure zone. It's not entirely fair to compare the Recovery School District's charter schools to the non-charters, however. The charters served fewer students with disabilities,

on average. They could also close off enrollment over the course of the school year, whereas the non-charter schools often had to continue accepting new students. For additional context, see "Recovery School District High Schools Have Much to Do to Reach Goals," New Orleans *Times-Picayune*, March 12, 2010; and "LEAP Scores Improve in New Orleans for Third Straight Year," New Orleans *Times-Picayune*, October 15, 2009.

4 Free and reduced lunch rates are an imprecise measure of the relative poverty of student bodies in New Orleans since the vast majority of the city's public schoolchildren qualify for free and reduced lunch. So far, there has been no systemic way to gauge the percentage of students at a given campus who live in extreme poverty, which in New Orleans would provide a more telling look at the relative challenges faced by different schools. Similarly, overall special education rates can be misleading since they do not capture the percentage of students with moderate to severe disabilities (which can vary significantly between campuses with similar overall rates). Some have questioned how Sci's students passed the eighth-grade LEAP test to advance to high school if so many arrived at such a low reading level. School officials say they used a Fountas and Pinnell reading assessment in their early years, a very different kind of test than the LEAP. They dropped Fountas and Pinnell after two years, however, because they did not believe it was the most reliable test, and switched to the GSRT (Gray Silent Reading Test).

5 For college graduation rates, I relied on census data which showed that 7 percent of black men in New Orleans have a bachelors degree. For incarceration rates, I relied on data compiled for the New Orleans *Times-Picayune* series "Louisiana Incarcerated" (Cindy Chang, May 2012). Chang reported that in recent years one in seven black men (14 percent) in New Orleans are under correctional control at any given time (correctional control figures encompass those on probation and parole). The percent of black men who have been under correctional control at some point in their lives is far higher.

6 For my description of Mary Laurie's years at Woodson and Guste, I relied on interviews with her. I also pulled several quotes and details from a profile published during her final year at Woodson (Brian Thevenot, "Woodson Reborn: A Campus Shooting Four Years Ago Marked a Turning Point," New Orleans *Times-Picayune*, January 9, 2005).

7 The employees were not technically fired until several months later, but on September 15 the school board put them on disaster leave without pay, which amounted to firing in many eyes. The school board did not send out a letter, but announcements were posted online telling employees they had been placed on leave and could pick up their last paychecks at Western Union. Various media outlets also covered the news. When the full firing took effect

in March 2006, Laurie had already been reinstated through her work at the Algiers Charter Schools Association.

8 I relied on interviews with lawyers at the U.S. Attorney's Office, Eastern District of Louisiana, to verify that all of the cases ultimately resulted in convictions—either through plea deals or trial proceedings.

9 In June 2012, a Louisiana judge ruled the employees had been wrongfully fired. Ethel Simms Julien, the judge, awarded more than $1 million to the seven people who sued the Orleans Parish School Board and the state. She said they had been deprived of "the vested property interest held in their tenured or permanent employment positions." The ruling opened the door for more fired employees to claim damages. The defendants appeared likely to appeal.

10 As the columnist Eugene Robinson pointed out in his book *Disintegration: The Splintering of Black America* (Doubleday, 2010), over the last several decades four distinct groups of black Americans have emerged: a small transcendent elite that includes the likes of Barack Obama and Oprah Winfrey; emergent groups, including individuals of mixed race and recent immigrants; a large abandoned class with little hope of rising out of poverty; and a mainstream middle class with professional jobs and mortgages. Robinson writes that by the time Katrina hit New Orleans, "the racially segregated but economically integrated model for African American neighborhoods until the 1960s had given way to a new model—still racially segregated, as far as the Abandoned were concerned, but now economically segregated as well. In New Orleans as elsewhere, concentrated black poverty was accompanied by concentrated black dysfunction."

11 This estimated passage rate on the teacher screening test came from Brian Riedlinger, former chief executive officer of the Algiers Charter Schools Association. Journalist Amy Waldman reported in 2007 that one fourth of teachers who took a similar skills test required by the Recovery School District did not pass (Waldman, "Reading, Writing, Resurrection," *Atlantic*, January 2007).

Part III: High Hopes

1 Rhetoric surrounding "teacher quality" has dominated recent efforts to overhaul the nation's schools while the subject of "principal quality" has gone relatively undiscussed. The rhetoric surrounding principals takes almost the opposite slant at times: Whereas "bad teachers" must be fired, "good principals" must be empowered; whereas teachers should be held more "accountable," principals should be given more "autonomy."

2 John Merrow, founder of Learning Matters, has pointed out that teachers are already members of an elite group in American society: college graduates. See "Where Do Teachers Come From?" posted on the Taking Note blog (www .takingnote.learningmatters.tv) on December 13, 2011.

3 Some scholars argue that when white people ignore race or say they are "color-blind" and "don't see race," it allows them to ignore or deny existing racial inequities, whether consciously or not. See Janet E. Helms's *A Race Is a Nice Thing to Have: A Guide to Being a White Person or Understanding the White Persons in Your Life* (Content Communications, 1992).

4 Organized gangs are not nearly as common in New Orleans as they are in many other cities. See Campbell Robertson's "New Orleans Struggles to Stem Homicides," *New York Times*, December 7, 2011; and "Crime in New Orleans: Analyzing Crime Trends and New Orleans' Responses to Crime," U.S. Department of Justice, March 15, 2011.

5 Some critics have even likened the Bench to a modern-day form of plantation-era discipline, arguing both forms of punishment are inflicted by whites on blacks in spaces over which whites want to assert control. For an example, see Catherine Michna's Ph.D. dissertation, "Hearing the Hurricane Coming: Storytelling, Second-Line Knowledges, and the Struggle for Democracy in New Orleans (Boston College, August 2011), p. 220.

Not all KIPP schools use the Bench as a discipline strategy. It evolved from a similarly named "Porch" adopted by KIPP's founders, Mike Feinberg and Dave Levin. Jay Mathews writes in *Work Hard. Be Nice: How Two Inspired Teachers Created the Most Promising Schools in America* (Algonquin Books, 2009): "Feinberg and Levin knew one of the most powerful forces in their class was peer pressure. Students wanted to be with, and be like, their friends. To cut them off from their friends was a useful motivator. At least that was what Feinberg and Levin thought. They began an endless series of experiments with the Porch and other forms of passive discipline."

6 By 2011, several new charter schools had started marching bands. For additional context, see Cindy Chang's "Charter Schools Join the Beat of New Orleans Marching Band Tradition," New Orleans *Times-Picayune*, March 6, 2011.

Part IV: Trouble

1 Many charter schools in New Orleans and elsewhere serve children with severe special needs. But I interviewed approximately a dozen parents who felt their children had been unlawfully turned away from public schools, both charter and non-charter, when I covered schools for the New Orleans *Times-Picayune* between 2007 and 2010. In one case, I witnessed firsthand as

a charter school administrator told a parent, "We only serve students with certain special needs." For additional context, see "Charter Schools Face Unique Challenges Educating Children with Special Needs," New Orleans *Times-Picayune*, April 18, 2010; and "Equal Treatment for Special-Needs Students in Short Supply at New Orleans Public Schools," New Orleans *Times-Picayune*, February 1, 2010.

2 This version of events is based on interviews with Brian Dassler and several other teachers at the school. Multiple attempts to reach the fired teacher were unsuccessful.

3 Rhonda Kalifey-Aluise, executive director of KIPP New Orleans, said KIPP Renaissance's early problems stemmed partly from the fact that it started without enough structure for both teachers and students. She said it's important to balance freedom with rules at the high school level so students won't arrive at college unprepared, but that Renaissance began "way too far on the side of freedom." Teachers also would have benefited from more consistent discipline policies, she said.

But Kalifey-Aluise pointed out that even some of KIPP's highest-performing schools, including KIPP Believe, took time to grow into their strengths. "KIPP Believe did not look in year one the way it looks today," she said. Kalifey-Aluise added, "High school is just harder whether it's KIPP or not."

Part V: Higher Education

1 The Explore test is scored on a different point range than the ACT, so Sci students' Explore scores would not necessarily translate into what they would have received on the ACT (if they had taken it on the same date).

2 The analysis of estimated college graduation rates was done by Soraya Verjee, the director of human capital at Collegiate Academies and a former Sci teacher.

3 Dr. King Charter School was approved as the charter operator for Craig school a year later.

4 H. Paul Friesema first put forth the "hollow prize" theory in a 1969 study titled "Black Control of Central Cities: The Hollow Prize." The theory has since been applied to the election of numerous black politicians, including President Barack Obama and Detroit mayor Dave Bing.

5 My description of the failure of the unionization effort was based on interviews with Wade Rathke and Bill Covington, both of whom worked on the campaign, as well as press coverage of the effort.

Part VI: Translations

1 The number of teachers who essentially stayed in their original placement may be somewhat higher since the operational control—and name—of schools changed frequently after Katrina.

2 Author Lisa Delpit (*"Multiplication Is for White People": Raising Expectations for Other People's Children*, New Press, 2012) has pointed out that researchers who conduct language studies are often unfamiliar with the terms and expressions used by African-American children and may underestimate the size and sophistication of their vocabularies as a result.

3 Sci officials say they created wait lists for the upper grades the night of the lottery and eventually offered admission to most of the students on the wait list.

4 My description of the events leading to Brice's arrest is based on police records and interviews with his mother. Brice ultimately reviewed my version of the account as well.

Selected Bibliography

Books

Brooks-Gunn, Jeanne, and Greg J. Duncan. *Consequences of Growing Up Poor.* New York: Russell Sage Foundation, 1997.

Brown, Eurnestine, and Norma J. Burgess. *African-American Women: An Ecological Perspective.* New York: Falmer Press, 2000.

Bulkley, Katrina E., Jeffrey R. Henig, and Henry M. Levin. *Between Public and Private: Politics, Governance, and the New Portfolio Models for Urban School Reform.* Cambridge, MA: Harvard Education Press, 2010.

Collins, Jim. *Good to Great.* New York: HarperCollins, 2001.

Delpit, Lisa D. *Other People's Children: Cultural Conflict in the Classroom.* New York: New Press, 1995.

DeVore, Donald E., and Joseph Logsdon. *Crescent City Schools: Public Education in New Orleans, 1841–1991.* Lafayette, LA: The Center for Louisiana Studies at the University of Southwestern Louisiana, 1991.

Du Bois, W. E. B. *The Souls of Black Folk.* New York: Simon & Schuster, 2009.

Gordon, Linda. *Pitied But Not Entitled: Single Mothers and the History of Welfare, 1890–1935.* New York: Free Press, 1994.

Hart, Betty, and Todd R. Risley. *Meaningful Differences in the Everyday Experience of Young American Children.* Baltimore: Paul H. Brookes, 1995.

Henig, Jeffrey R., Richard C. Hula, Marion Orr, and Desiree S. Pedescleaux. *The Color of School Reform: Race, Politics, and the Challenge of Urban Education.* Princeton, NJ: Princeton University Press, 1999.

Jensen, Eric. *Teaching with Poverty in Mind.* Alexandria, VA: Association for Supervision & Curriculum Development, 2009.

Klein, Naomi. *The Shock Doctrine: The Rise of Disaster Capitalism.* New York: Metropolitan Books/Henry Holt, 2007.

Ladson-Billings, Gloria. *The Dreamkeepers: Successful Teachers of African American Children.* San Francisco: Jossey-Bass, 1994.

Lareau, Annette. *Unequal Childhoods: Class, Race, and Family Life.* Berkeley: University of California Press, 2003.

Lemov, Doug. *Teach Like a Champion: 49 Techniques That Put Students on the Path to College.* San Francisco: Jossey-Bass, 2010.

Lukas, J. Anthony. *Common Ground: A Turbulent Decade in the Lives of Three American Families.* New York: Knopf, 1985.

Mathews, Jay. *Work Hard. Be Nice.: How Two Inspired Teachers Created the Most Promising Schools in America.* Chapel Hill, NC: Algonquin Books, 2009.

Perry, Andre. *The Garden Path: The Miseducation of a City.* New Orleans: University of New Orleans Press, 2011.

Ravitch, Diane. *The Death and Life of the Great American School System.* New York: Basic Books, 2010.

Robinson, Eugene. *Disintegration: The Splintering of Black America.* New York: Doubleday, 2010.

Skocpol, Theda. *Protecting Soldiers and Mothers: The Political Origins of Social Policy in the United States.* Cambridge, MA: Harvard University Press, 1992.

Tough, Paul. *Whatever It Takes: Geoffrey Canada's Quest to Change Harlem and America.* Boston: Houghton Mifflin, 2008.

Waldfogel, Jane. *Britain's War on Poverty.* New York: Russell Sage Foundation, 2010.

Washington, Booker T. *Up From Slavery: An Autobiography.* Garden City, NY: Doubleday, 1963.

Whitman, David. *Sweating the Small Stuff: Inner-City Schools and the New Paternalism.* Washington, D.C.: Thomas B. Fordham Institute, 2008.

Woodson, Carter G. *The Mis-Education of the Negro.* Trenton, NJ: Africa World Press, 1990.

Periodicals

Anderson, Nick. "Education Secretary Duncan Calls Hurricane Katrina Good for New Orleans Schools," *Washington Post,* January 30, 2010.

Brill, Steven. "The Teachers' Unions' Last Stand," *New York Times Magazine,* May 17, 2010.

Campanile, Carl. "NAACP's 'Slave' Shock," *New York Post,* June 7, 2011.

Carr, Sarah. "Charter Schools Face Unique Challenges Educating Children with Special Needs," New Orleans *Times-Picayune*, April 18, 2010.

——. "Debate over Charter Operator Raises Questions About Neighborhood's Role in Remaking Local Schools," New Orleans *Times-Picayune*, March 8, 2010.

——. "Learning Curve: Their Enthusiasm Makes New Teachers Attractive Hires, but Many Say They Could Use Some Guidance from Classroom Veterans," New Orleans *Times-Picayune*, February 15, 2009.

——. "Long-Troubled Douglass High Could Lose Its Identity," New Orleans *Times-Picayune*, September 20, 2008.

——. "Louisiana Educators to Be Tested in Race to the Top," New Orleans *Times-Picayune*, February 14, 2010.

——. "Marching Bands Unite in Tribute to Brandon Franklin, Slain at 22," New Orleans *Times-Picayune*, May 22, 2010.

——. "Meaning of LEAP Scores a Mystery to Most Parents," New Orleans *Times-Picayune*, July 6, 2010.

——. "New Orleans Teachers Earning Bigger Paychecks," New Orleans *Times-Picayune*, April 13, 2008.

——. "Recovering District: Can the High-Powered School Superintendent Achieve Lasting Change?" New Orleans *Times-Picayune*, June 9, 2008.

——. "Recovery School District Closures and Changes Can Leave Families with Whiplash," New Orleans *Times-Picayune*, July 4, 2011.

——. "Recovery School District Increases Per-pupil Spending," New Orleans *Times-Picayune*, March 2, 2008.

Chang, Cindy. "BESE Rejects Bid by MLK Charter—9th Ward School Had Record of Success," New Orleans *Times-Picayune*, December 10, 2010.

——. "Sci Academy a Bright Spot in New Orleans School Landscape," New Orleans *Times-Picayune*, November 7, 2010.

Clark, Laura. "Half of Teachers Quit the Classroom Because of Violent Pupils and Red Tape," *Daily Mail*, January 1, 2010.

Dillon, Sam. "Schools Chief from Chicago Is Cabinet Pick," *New York Times*, December 15, 2008.

Eggler, Bruce, and John Pope, "SUNO's Very First Chancellor Dead at 93: Bashful Served from 1959 to 1987," New Orleans *Times-Picayune*, February 28, 2011.

Finch, Susan, and Coleman Warner. "Feds Raise Pressure on Schools," New Orleans *Times-Picayune*, February 16, 2005.

Foster, Kelsey. "Board Taking Steps to Open Two New Schools on Carver Campus," *The Lens*, June 22, 2012.

Gillum, Jack, and Greg Toppo. "Failure Rate for AP Tests Climbing," *USA Today*, February 3, 2010.

Goldstein, Dana. "Obama Loses a Mayor," *Daily Beast*, September 15, 2010.

Green, Elizabeth. "A Great Debate—Make That, Wiki-War—Over an Obama Adviser," GothamSchools, November 14, 2008.

Hechinger, John. "Oprah-Backed Charter School Denying Disabled Collides With Law," Bloomberg, September 20, 2011.

Hess, Frederick. "Our Achievement-Gap Mania," *National Affairs*, Fall 2011.

"Human Resources," *This American Life*, WBEZ, February 3, 2008.

Lemann, Nicholas. "The Kids in the Conference Room," *New Yorker*, October 18, 1999.

Lewin, Tamar. "Student Loan Default Rates Rise Sharply in Past Year," *New York Times*, September 12, 2011.

Maggi, Laura. "Murder Rate in 2010 Remains Little Changed in New Orleans," New Orleans *Times-Picayune*, January 2, 2011.

Maggi, Laura, Brendan McCarthy, and Brian Thevenot. "New Orleans Is Breeding Bold Killers—About Half of Murders Happen in Daylight," New Orleans *Times-Picayune*, January 25, 2009.

Moller, Jan. "Gov. Bobby Jindal Urges Consideration of UNO-SUNO Merger," New Orleans *Times-Picayune*, January 18, 2011.

———. "UNO-SUNO Merger Suggestion Is Expected to Touch Off Heated Debate," New Orleans *Times-Picayune*, January 18, 2011.

Noah, Timothy. "The United States of Inequality," *Slate*, September 3, 2010.

Nossiter, Adam. "Crises Multiply at Schools in New Orleans," *Seattle Times*, April 19, 2005.

Pope, John. "Jackson Takes a Stand on School Merger 'Battle Line': He Urges Students, Staff to Fight to Keep SUNO Separate," New Orleans *Times-Picayune*, March 15, 2011.

———. "Merger Talk Is Nearly as Old as SUNO and UNO: Southern's Status Stirs Controversy," New Orleans *Times-Picayune*, January 23, 2011.

———. "SUNO's Graduation Rate, 8%, 2nd-Lowest of Urban Schools: It Fares Worst Among Public La. Colleges," New Orleans *Times-Picayune*, February 12, 2011.

Rasheed, Aesha. "Falling Short: The Graduate Exit Exam Stopped Bridget Green from Being Valedictorian. Some Say the N.O. Schools Robbed Her of an Education," New Orleans *Times-Picayune*, August 10, 2003.

Ravitch, Diane. "School 'Reform': A Failing Grade," *New York Review of Books*, September 29, 2011.

Reckdahl, Katy. "Fifty Years Later, Students Recall Integrating New Orleans Public Schools," New Orleans *Times-Picayune*, November 14, 2010.

Ritea, Steve. "Charter Schools Urged for N.O. District: La. Education Chief Cites System's Woes," New Orleans *Times-Picayune*, October 25, 2005.

———. "Schools Use Federal Dollars as Teacher Bait: Anticipating a Need to Hire 425, District Casts Its Net Out of State," New Orleans *Times-Picayune*, April 20, 2007.

———. "Standoff over School Delay Is Resolved: With St. Claude Site Still Unready, MLK Will Open at Another Campus," New Orleans *Times-Picayune*, September 7, 2006.

Shaw, Andrea. "Algiers Charter Schools to Celebrate Third Year of Student Gains," New Orleans *Times-Picayune*, December 2, 2010.

———. "Gretna Magnet School Principal Suspended Amid Testing and Admissions Irregularities," New Orleans *Times-Picayune*, October 16, 2010.

Simon, Darran, and Sarah Carr. "Contractors Helped RSD Hit Ground Running: Records Show Superintendent's Early Reliance on Crisis Squad," New Orleans *Times-Picayune*, March 25, 2008.

Thevenot, Brian. "Deeper Cuts in Line for New Orleans Schools: Mass Layoffs Likely to Fill $48 Million Hole," New Orleans *Times-Picayune*, August 9, 2005.

———. "Hatchet Men: The Company Hired to Solve New Orleans Public Schools' Financial Woes Is Proud of Its Rock-Ribbed Reputation. It Slashes Jobs. Closes Schools. And Saves Money," New Orleans *Times-Picayune*, June 26, 2005.

———. "New Orleans School Employees Plead Guilty in Fraud: Teachers, Clerks, Broker Admit Paycheck Kickbacks, Shakedown," New Orleans *Times-Picayune*, July 3, 2004.

———. "Woodson Principal's Painful Past Has Shaped Her: Mean Streets Created Reserve of Empathy," New Orleans *Times-Picayune*, January 9, 2005.

Tough, Paul. "What If the Secret to Success Is Failure?" *New York Times Magazine*, September 14, 2011.

Turque, Bill. "Poll: Polarizing D.C. Schools Chief Rhee Helps, Hurts Fenty Among Democrats," *Washington Post*, September 1, 2010.

Vanacore, Andrew. "New Orleans Public School Achievement Gap Is Narrowing," New Orleans *Times-Picayune*, August 7, 2011.

Winerip, Michael. "A Chosen Few Are Teaching for America," *New York Times*, July 11, 2010.

Yerton, Stewart. "Choosing Sides in Living Wage Issue Not Easy," New Orleans *Times-Picayune*, January 6, 2002.

————. "Labor Pains: A Drive to Unionize New Orleans Hotels Has Workers Caught in the Middle," New Orleans *Times-Picayune*, March 19, 2000.

————. "New Orleans Voters Approve Minimum Wage Increase," New Orleans *Times-Picayune*, February 3, 2002.

Reports, Studies, and Legal Judgments

Allensworth, Elaine, and John Q. Easton. "What Matters for Staying On-Track and Graduating in Chicago Public High Schools," Consortium on Chicago School Research at the University of Chicago, August 17, 2007.

Almy, Sarah, and Christina Theokas. "Not Prepared for Class: High Poverty Schools Continue to Have Fewer In-Field Teachers," Education Trust, November 2010.

Biggs, Andrew G., and Jason Richwine. "Assessing the Compensation of Public-School Teachers," Heritage Foundation, November 1, 2011.

Bradley, Robert H., and Robert F. Corwyn. "Socioeconomic Status and Child Development," Center for Applied Studies in Education at the University of Arkansas at Little Rock, 2002.

Chait, Robin, and Raegen Miller. "Teacher Turnover, Tenure Policies, and the Distribution of Teacher Quality: Can High-Poverty Schools Catch a Break?" Center for American Progress, December 2008.

Charity, Anne H. "Regional Differences in Low SES African-American Children's Speech in the School Setting," *Language Variation and Change*, 2007.

"Comparison of Graduation Exit Examination (GEE 21) with ACT," Louisiana Department of Education, December 2004.

"Crime in New Orleans: Analyzing Crime Trends and New Orleans' Responses to Crime," U.S. Department of Justice, March 15, 2011.

Cross, Freddie, and Ashley Keigher. "Teacher Attrition and Mobility: Results from the 2008-09 Teacher Follow-up Survey," National Center for Education Statistics, August 2010.

Donaldson, Morgaen L. "Teach For America Teachers' Careers: Whether, When, and Why They Leave Low-Income Schools and the Teaching Profession," Project on the Next Generation of Teachers, Harvard Graduate School of Education, 2008.

"Education Pays 2010," College Board Advocacy and Policy Center, September 2010.

"Elementary School Children: Many Change Schools Frequently, Harming their Education," United States General Accounting Office report, February 1994.

Epstein, Diana. "Measuring Inequality in School Funding," Center for American Progress, August 2011.

"Evaluation of New Texas Charter Schools," Texas Center for Educational Research, July 2007.

Flexner, Abraham. "Medical Education in the United States and Canada," Carnegie Foundation for the Advancement of Teaching, 1910.

Gill, Brian P., Ira Nichols-Barrer, Christina Clark Tuttle, and Philip Gleason. "Student Selection, Attrition, and Replacement in KIPP Middle Schools," Mathematica Policy Research, April 2011.

Grier, Sonya, and Shiriki Kumanyika. "Targeting Interventions for Ethnic Minority and Low-Income Populations," *Future of Children*, Spring 2006.

"Help Wanted: Projections on Jobs and Education Requirements through 2018," Georgetown University's Center on Education and the Workforce, June 2010.

"It's About Respect: The Case for Fairness in New Orleans' Hospitality Industry," American Federation of Labor and Congress of Industrial Organizations, 1997.

Julien, Hon. Ethel Simms. Civil District Court for the Parish of New Orleans Judgment in the case *Eddy Oliver, et al. v. Orleans Parish School Board, et al.*, June 20, 2012.

Mathis, Tim. "TOPS and Go Grants: Louisiana's Financial Aid Programs Reward Too Much Mediocrity and Provide Too Little for Those in Need," Louisiana Budget Project, February 2011.

Miron, Gary, Jessica L. Urschel, and Nicholas Saxton. "What Makes KIPP Work? A Study of Student Characteristics, Attrition, and School Finance," co-released by the Study Group on Educational Management Organizations at Western Michigan University and the National Center for the Study of Privatization in Education at Teachers College, Columbia University, March 2011.

"Pathways to Prosperity: Meeting the Challenge of Preparing Young Americans for the 21st Century," Harvard Graduate School of Education, February 2011.

Perry, Andre, and Michael Schwam-Baird. "School by School: The Transformation of New Orleans Public Education," Brookings Institution, August 2010.

"The Promise of College Completion: KIPP's Early Successes and Challenges," KIPP Foundation, April 2011.

"The State of Public Education in New Orleans Five Years after Hurricane Katrina," Cowen Institute for Public Education Initiatives, July 2010.

"State of the World's Cities Report 2008/9: Harmonious Cities," UN-HABITAT, October 2008.

"Teacher Stability and Turnover in Los Angeles: The Influence of Teacher and School Characteristics," Policy Analysis for California Education, University of California, Berkeley, July 13, 2011.

"Transforming Public Education in New Orleans: The Recovery School District (2003–2011)," Cowen Institute for Public Education Initiatives, 2011.

"Urban School Superintendents: Characteristics, Tenure, and Salary," Council of the Great City Schools, Fall 2010.

Speeches

Obama, Barack. Remarks by the President on Education, July 24, 2009.

Washington, Booker T. "Democracy and Education," speech to the Institute of Arts and Sciences, September 30, 1896.

Websites and Blogs

Agenda for Children, www.agendaforchildren.org

Bridging Differences, *Education Week*, www.blogs.edweek.org/Bridging-Differences

Cowen Institute for Public Education Initiatives, www.coweninstitute.com

Deborah Meier on Education, www.deborahmeier.com

Greater New Orleans Community Data Center, www.gnocdc.org

The Lens, www.thelensnola.org/charterschools

Louisiana Department of Education, www.doe.state.la.us

The Simple Dollar blog, www.simpledollar.com

United States Census, www.census.gov

Index

A Note on the Author

Sarah Carr has written about education for the last twelve years, reporting on the growth in online learning in higher education, the battle over vouchers and charter schools in urban districts, and the struggle to educate China's massive population of migrant children. Her work has been honored with numerous national awards and fellowships, most recently a Spencer Education Journalism Fellowship at Columbia University. She lives in New Orleans, where she covered schools for the *Times-Picayune*. *Hope Against Hope* is her first book.